PRAISE FOR
Seeking Truth in a Country of Lies

"*Seeking Truth in a Country of Lies* is a dazzling journey into the heart of many issues—political, philosophical, and personal—that should concern us all. Ed Curtin has the touch of the poet and the eye of an eagle."
—Robert F. Kennedy, Jr.

"A powerful exposé of the CIA and our secret state . . . Curtin is a passionate long-time reform advocate; his stories will rouse your heart."
—Oliver Stone, filmmaker, writer, and director

"Grappling with the truth requires a very sensitive intelligence, the moral courage to explore forbidden territory, and learning of the sort that's now passé, and even actively discouraged, in "higher education." Ed Curtin has those gifts, or virtues, in abundance, as these exquisite essays clearly demonstrate. With extraordinary erudition, mordant wit, and an all-too-rare commitment to the affirmation of humanity, he helps us see through the U.S. government's "vast tapestry of lies," see over the hypnotic prison-walls of cyberspace, and see our way toward rediscovering not just the awful truths of our own history, but those far deeper truths, expressed in poetry and music, philosophy and art, that finally make our lives worth living."
—Mark Crispin Miller, Professor of Media Studies, NYU

"Edward Curtin puts our propaganda-stuffed heads in a guillotine, then in a flash takes us on a redemptive walk in the woods—from inferno to paradiso. Walk with Ed and his friends—Daniel Berrigan, Albert Camus, George Orwell, and many others—through the darkest, most-firefly-filled woods on this earth."
—James W. Douglass, author, *JFK and the Unspeakable*

"Ed Curtin is a subversive writer in the classic literary sense. Unlike other writers in his field, Curtin brings a liberating poetic sensibility to history and politics. Deeply personal and vast in scope, his work challenges the false assumptions upon which so many treasured beliefs are based. Curtin offers readers a chance to examine how they think about themselves, and thus a path to positive political and social change."

—DOUGLAS VALENTINE, author, *TDY* and *The CIA as Organized Crime*

"Ed Curtin invites us to go deep sea diving—beyond the shallows of U.S. political and spiritual life where most researchers and writers paddle, into the dark realms of intelligence operatives, paid killers, and institutions of deception. It is a disturbing journey but a necessary one, and he is a brilliant guide."

—GRAEME MACQUEEN, author, *The 2001 Anthrax Deception*

"The world is a terrible and terrifying place. There are few who possess both the artistry and political understanding to see and describe the depths of the deceptions practiced upon us. Ed Curtin is one of these few. His powerful and beautiful essays will give us reasons to look the truth in the eye, and to have hope."

—EMANUEL E. GARCIA, author, *Manhattan Stardust* and *Venetian Rogues*

"This is an amazingly good book. Curtin seeks to unearth the present era's "massive fraud"—he agrees with Harold Pinter that America has "exercised a quite clinical manipulation of power worldwide while masquerading as a force for universal good"—while Curtin's book is also "celebrating the beauty of life.""

—DAVID RAY GRIFFIN, author, *The Christian Gospel for Americans*

"Edward Curtin is one of the few people on the planet today who sees the intersectionalism of his own experience, the broader culture, politics, and the world of intelligence operations. These essays, constructed over a broad swath of time that encompasses some of the most significant events in world history, give insights guaranteed to expand your mind."

—LISA PEASE, author, *A Lie Too Big to Fail: The Real History of the Assassination of Robert F. Kennedy*

Seeking Truth in a Country of Lies

Edward Curtin

Clarity Press, Inc.

© 2020 Edward Curtin
ISBN: 978-1-949762-26-6
EBOOK ISBN: 978-1-949762-27-3

In-house editor: Diana G. Collier
Cover design: R. Jordan Santos

ALL RIGHTS RESERVED: Except for purposes of review, this book may not be copied, or stored in any information retrieval system, in whole or in part, without permission in writing from the publishers.

Library of Congress Control Number: 2020942666

Clarity Press, Inc.
2625 Piedmont Rd. NE, Ste. 56
Atlanta, GA 30324, USA
https://www.claritypress.com

*To Jeanne, my wife, and to my father,
who gave me far more than his name.
Deep gratitude to both.*

Acknowledgments

Thanks to Jeanne for urging me to do this book, and for her editorial and computer skills along the way. I would have been lost without her. Thanks to friends, Gary Corseri, Emanuel Garcia, and Graeme MacQueen for their encouragement. And to a wonderful editor, Diana Collier, thank you. For those who took the time to read the book and comment publicly on its merits, I will always be grateful. Lastly, to the invisible and unnamed ones who have inspired me – Bless you.

Table of Contents

Acknowledgments. vi
Introduction. 1
Inside America's Doll House: A Vast Tapestry of Lies. 6
What Are We Working for "At Eternity's Gate"?. 23
Walking with Fr. Daniel Berrigan, S.J., a Criminal for Peace . 30
The Disappearance of Silence. 39
The Message from Dallas: JFK and the Unspeakable 44
Why I Don't Speak of 9/11 Anymore. 54
The Sexual Passion of Winston Smith 61
Gina Haspel and Pinocchio from Rome 69
Without Poetry We are Dead: With It We Die Living. 73
American Values: Lessons I Learned from My Family 82
Will NPR Now Officially Change Its Name to National
    Propaganda Radio?. 90
The Art of Doublespeak: Bellingcat and Mind Control 94
Lost in the Theatre of Data, Dada, and Emotional
    Manipulation. 103
Albert Camus and Our Haunted World. 110
Denying the Obvious: Leftists and Crimestop 118
A Do-Nothing Anti-Labor Day: A Modest Proposal. 124
Looking Through the Screen at the World's Suffering 128
The Lies of 9/11 Miracle Workers 133
A Genuine Actor: Francesco Serpico 143
The Satanic Nature of the Atomic Bombings of Hiroshima
    and Nagasaki. 153
The Spirit of Existential Rebellion 158
Hovering in Cyberspace 162

Snow, Death, and the Bewildered Herd 168
Playing on The Devil's Chessboard: Allen Dulles and
    the CIA 177
Love is Lovelier the Third Time Around, Isn't It? 187
Ghostly Voices Dancing in the Rain 194
The Silent Cries of Hiding Children: Half a Century after
    MLK's Riverside Church Speech 198
The Cell Phone and the Virgin: A Montreal Odyssey 204
Slow Suicide and the Abandonment of the World 219
When Warriors Become Saints 227
Bob Dylan: A Masked Man in Search of Redemption? 232
Sometimes A Pair of Pants Can Give You Vertigo 243
Kevin Love: Making a Hole in Denial 246
Hillary Clinton: The Heartless Queen.................... 252
Answering the Mysterious Call of An Artist's Spiritual
    Vocation 255
A Conspiracy Theorist Confesses to his Petty Crimes 263
Painting a True Christ................................. 267
The Government that Killed Him Honors MLK Jr. with a
    National Holiday................................... 273
Between Heaven and Earth on a Spring Morning 277
Try Learning How Not to Ride A Bicycle So We Can
    Save the World 284
Speeding into the Void of Cyberspace as Designed 292
The CIA Then and Now: Old Wine in New Bottles 298
The Canaries That Sang "Things Suck".................. 308
The Assassination of RFK: A Lie Too Big to Fail 314
Happenings in the Land of the Free and the Home of
    the Brave.. 323
When Time Stands Still 330
Epilogue: The Messenger 336

"In a dark time, the eye begins to see."
—**Theodore Roethke, "In A Dark Time"**

Introduction

In putting together this selection of essays, I was reminded of what Albert Camus once wrote: "A man's work is nothing but this slow trek to rediscover, through the detours of art, those two or three great and simple images in whose presence his heart first opened."

While I do not claim that all these essays are art, they are my efforts to say in the most eloquent way I can what really has mattered to me in recent years, not just politically but personally, since they are entwined. Upon reflection, I see that what matters to me now is what mattered to me when I was young. Although the issues have changed in certain ways as they must, I have not—unless, or because, my wanderings through life with all its changes have paradoxically meant, in Nietzsche's words, that I have been becoming who I am.

This seems true to me, and the essaying of the words that follow are part of that becoming. Ortega y Gassett once said that "whether he be an original or a plagiarist, man is the novelist of himself." I agree. While a book of essays is not a novel, if read in its entirety, it does tell a story that reveals the times and the man who tells them; it expresses two stories simultaneously. And each story, if told well, always has a double dimension, the old and the new. Every life and every event is disclosed in an historical context, now and then and all the time in between.

While hoping I am an original, I know that I have learned and borrowed from many others. My greater hope is that what I say here is said in a way no other could, that it bears my original stamp. That it is novel. For I am convinced that we cannot grasp the unique nature of our current era simply by repeating straightforward political analyses. That approach is necessary but not enough. For it leaves out the hidden heart of a world that seems to be spinning madly toward some kind of denouement. It omits all the little thoughts, secrets, fears, and desires of so many people who wish to speak but can't find the words to express their thoughts.

From a young age, I have been obsessed with truth, death, and freedom. As I recall, those words have been synonymous for God for many thinkers. So I suppose you could say that I have always been intoxicated with God or for God, or maybe God has been intoxicated with me. I don't know, nor do I care to: knowledge is overrated. I know what I feel. My concerns have been those of many writers throughout the ages—poets, rebels, journalists, philosophers, passionate writers of every stripe, desperados for truth and a peaceful world of love and kindness. Those I have admired the most, believers or unbelievers—it is often hard to tell the difference, nor does it matter—were those who dismissed categories, distinctions, or labels, but who wrote freely because for them to write freely was to live freely and not to be caged by anyone's restrictions as to what they should be saying or how they were saying it. For them truth was their God, and through the weaving of words down a page they were always seeking to disclose what was hidden from common sight. They used language to open up cracks in the consensus reality that the great poet and writer Kenneth Rexroth called the "social lie": "Since all society is organized in the interest of exploiting classes and since if men knew this they would cease to work and society would fall apart, it has always been necessary, at least since the urban revolutions, for societies to be governed ideologically by a system of fraud."

Indeed, we live in the era of massive fraud where the transnational wealthy elites, led by the American war and propaganda machine, continue to try to convince the gullible that they are saviors of humanity even as they lie and cheat and murder by the millions.

So what follows are my efforts to unearth the fraud, while celebrating the beauty of life and telling little stories here and there that I hope exemplify its comedy and tragedy. I am always experimenting every time I sit down to write. Not consciously, since I let inspiration guide me. Often, as I think is evident in many pieces, thoughts come to me when walking, and from those initial thoughts comes the path I follow, not knowing exactly where I am headed. Some of these essays are highly intellectual and structured; some, straightforwardly political; others are meanderings that seek to express essential truths I sense in the telling. The process feels physical to me. It has a feel and smell. A rhythm. Like a song. Like a dawdling walk in the woods or by a flowing river.

If I call them all essays, it is to indicate that they are my attempts, my experiments, my experience (Latin: *exigere*: trial, attempt, try) to disclose to myself and anyone who might read them what is going on in the world that I find important and worth investigating. To use my artistic and sociological imagination to connect the dots between the personal and the social and in so doing to say something worth sharing with others.

Whatever my ostensible starting point—a major event, a book, an experience—you can usually be sure that by the time you have read to the end of the piece, I will have branched off down by-ways that lead to other trails that eventually reconnect to the main path. Or so I hope. While I usually see how the roads all lead back to one, sometimes I only intuit it and the reader is left to do the reconnoitering alone. I think this is good. For while these essays are set in ink within the covers of a book, verbal tenses and ink can be misleading. They suggest that the author's quest is over, that what motivated the initial words is past, that the case is closed and the reader and writer are dead-heads satisfied with their knowingness. For me, that is far from true. The paradox of having written these essays is that I have tried to do so in language that evokes in the reader the exhilaration I felt in writing them, and that such aliveness will be carried into the world as rebellion against war and injustice.

I have arranged the essays in no particular order, except to begin and end with a few that tell you something about me. I think it is always good to have some deeper sense of who the author is whose words you are reading, beyond the brief notices on the back of books. These essays cover a wide variety of topics:

propaganda, wars, government assassinations, work, nature, time, the CIA, silence, poetry, digital dementia, etc.

They range far and wide, as I try to connect the scattered dots to draw a coherent picture of our world today. Since I write with no particular goal in mind except truth as I see it, perhaps readers would be best served by randomly choosing a piece and seeing where it might lead them. As with living, I suspect that reading is best done somewhat randomly in the hope that one experiences a sense of liberation in the process. I have scattered some satirical pieces throughout to add a bit of levity to serious matters and hope the reader will not mistake their "authors" for the real me. But if so, that would add to the humor, something we need to survive.

Three authors whom I hold in high esteem and whose names I mention numerous times in this book are John Berger, Albert Camus, and James W. Douglass.

Berger is often described as a Marxist art critic, but such an appellation is misleading, for he was much more than that. While always situating his analyses in historical and cultural contexts, and never forgetting the class structure that underlies the cruel capitalistic order, he was acutely aware that consumerism and therefore global capitalism as well as philosophical materialism rested upon a "materialist fantasy" that denied the spiritual power of evil and the spiritual power of good to respond. As a counterweight, Berger always made sure to cling close to human reality and include what he called "enclaves of the beyond" in his writing. These were often the marginalized hiding places of hope where the spiritual faith in human love and solidarity was nourished and sustained despite the world's evil.

Albert Camus was very similar in many ways. An avowed atheist with a spiritual core, he was an artistic anarchist with a passionate spiritual hunger and an austere and moral Don Juan. He could not be pigeonholed. This drove many crazy. His allegiance was to truth, not ideologies. He tried to fight injustice while extolling life's beauty and the human search for happiness. He grasped the essence of the ever-recurring plague that evil doers inflict upon the world. He was preoccupied with death, freedom, and an absent God, but never gave up hope and insisted that rebellion was the only honorable course. Yet the fight against the plague must go on; that was Camus' message. If not, you will be destroyed by your own complicity in evil.

James W. Douglass, although a writer of a more overt spiritual sensibility, continues to write brilliantly about "the unspeakable" that has been used to cover-up the U.S. government's assassinations of its greatest anti-war leaders: JFK, Malcom X, MLK, and RFK. The unspeakable is a term coined by the Trappist monk Thomas Merton in the mid-1960s. He meant it to point to a systemic evil that permeates American society that defies speech: "It is the void that contradicts everything that is spoken even before the words are said; the void that gets into the language of public and official declarations at the very moment when they are pronounced, and makes them ring dead with the hollowness of the abyss. It is the void out of which Eichmann drew the punctilious exactitude of his obedience . . . ." It is, in other words, the plague that is us when we live in the nest of the unspeakable as obedient servants of the American Empire. Douglass makes the plague manifest in order to give us hope, and in speaking the unspeakable, he shows us both the radical evil and the redemptive courage that we are all capable of.

I mention these three brilliant writers here to say how grateful I am for their work. There are many others, of course, whom you will encounter in the course of reading these essays. For even when we write alone, even when we think we walk alone, we are always following in others' footsteps.

As Camus says in one of his short stories, it is hard to distinguish between solitary and solidary.

INSIDE AMERICA'S DOLL HOUSE: A VAST TAPESTRY OF LIES

"It never happened. Nothing ever happened. Even while it was happening it wasn't happening. It didn't matter. It was of no interest. The crimes of the United States have been systematic, constant, vicious, remorseless, but very few people have actually talked about them. You have to hand it to America. It has exercised a quite clinical manipulation of power worldwide while masquerading as a force for universal good. It's a brilliant, even witty, highly successful act of hypnosis."
—**Harold Pinter's Nobel Prize Acceptance Speech, 2005**

While truth-teller Julian Assange sits inside a jail cell, Chelsea Manning was imprisoned for more than eight years, and Edward Snowden lives in exile in Russia, the American people hole up in an illusionary dwelling constructed to reduce them to children afraid of the truth. Or is it afraid of the dark side? This is not new; it has been so for a very long time, but this house of illusions has become more sophisticated, a haunted doll's house, an electronic one with many bells and whistles and images that move faster than the eye can see. The old wooden ones, where you needed small fingers to rearrange the furniture, now only need thumbs that can click you into your cell's fantasy world. So many dwell in there.

In a 1969 interview, Jim Garrison, the District Attorney of New Orleans and the only person to ever bring to trial a case involving the Kennedy assassination, said that as a result of the CIA's murderous coup d'état on behalf of the military-industrial-financial-media-intelligence complex that rules the country to this day, the American people have been subjected to a fabricated reality that has rendered them a nation of passive Eichmanns, who sit in their living rooms, popping pills and watching television as their country's military machine mows down people by the millions and the announcers tell them all the things they should be afraid of, such as bacteria on cutting boards and Russian spies infiltrating their hair salons. Garrison said:

> The creation of such inanities as acceptable reality and unacceptable reality is necessary for the self-preservation of the super-state against its greatest danger: understanding on the part of the people as to what is really happening. All factors which contribute to its burgeoning power are exaggerated. All factors which might reveal its corrosive effect on the nation are concealed. The result is to place the populace in the position of persons living in a house whose windows no longer reveal the outside but on which murals have been painted. Some of the murals are frightening and have the effect of reminding the occupants of the outside menaces against which the paternal war machine is protecting them. Other murals are pleasant to remind them how nice things are inside the house.
>
> But to live like this is to live in a doll's house. If life has one lesson to teach us, it is that to live in illusion is ultimately disastrous.

In the doll's house into which America gradually has been converted, a great many of our basic assumptions are totally illusory.[1]

It is stunning to take a cue from Garrison's comment regarding the JFK assassination, when he suggested that, to test

---

[1] Interview with Jim Garrison, District Attorney of Parish of Orleans, Louisiana, May 27, 1969 at https://kennedysandking.com/images/pdf/garrison-interview-05-27-1969-trans.pdf

its plausibility, one transpose the official lone assassin scenario into the U.S.S.R. Could any American possibly believe that a former Russian soldier, trained in English and having served at a top Soviet secret military base, had defected to the U.S. and then returned home with the help of the K.G.B., then killed the Russian Premier with a defective and shoddy rifle and then was shot to death in police headquarters in Moscow by a K.G.B.-connected hit man? And that there would then be no trial, and that not even a mention of the K.G.B. connection would ever surface in official investigative reports? That would be a howler! So too, of course, are the Warren Commission's fictions about Oswald.

Fifty years have flowed into mist since the eloquent and courageous Garrison (read *On the Trail of the Assassins*) metaphorically voiced the truth, despite the CIA's persistent efforts to paint him as an unhinged lunatic through its media mouthpieces. These days they would probably just lock him up or send him fleeing across borders, as with Manning, Assange, and Snowden.

Snowden, Assange, and Manning

So following Garrison, let's transpose a more contemporary scenario. Picture this: that Snowden, Assange, and Manning were all Russian, and that they released information about Russian war crimes, political corruption, and Russia's system of total electronic surveillance of the Russian population, and were then jailed or sent fleeing into exile as a result. Who in the U.S., liberal or conservative, would possibly believe the Russian government's accusations that these three were criminals?

Nevertheless, Barack Obama, the transparency president, has treated Manning, Assange and Snowden as such, all the while parading as a "liberal" concerned for freedom of speech and the First Amendment. He made sure that Snowden and Manning were charged under the Espionage Act of 1917, and that Assange was corralled via false Swedish sex charges forcing him to seek asylum and effectively remain imprisoned in the Ecuadorian Embassy in London. He brought Espionage Act prosecutions against eight whistleblowers—Thomas Drake, Shamai Leibowitz, Stephen

Kim, Chelsea Manning, Donald Sachtleben, Jeffrey Sterling, John Kiriakou and Edward Snowden—more than all former presidents combined. He hypocritically pardoned Manning on his way out the door as if this would polish his deluded liberal legacy after making her suffer terribly through seven years of imprisonment. He set the stage for Trump to re-jail Manning to try to get this most courageous woman to testify against Assange, which she would not do, and for the collaborationist British government to jail Assange in preparation for his extradition to the United States and a show trial. As for Snowden, he has been relegated to invisibility, good for news headlines once and for a movie, but now gone and forgotten.

Obama and Trump, arch political "enemies," have made sure that those who reveal the sordid acts of the American murderous state are punished terribly. This is how the system works, and for most Americans, it is not happening. It doesn't matter. They don't care, just as they don't care that Obama backed the 2009 coup d'état in Honduras that has resulted in so many deaths at the hands of U.S trained killers, and now the Trump goons are ranting about all these "non-white" people fleeing to the U.S. to escape a hell created by the U.S.—as it has been doing throughout Latin America for so long. Who does care about the truth?

The Sleepwalkers

But even though a majority of Americans have never believed the government's explanation for JFK's murder, they nevertheless have gone to sleep for half a century in the doll's house of illusions as the killing and the lies of their own government have increased over the years and any semblance of a democratic and peaceful America has been extinguished. The fate of courageous whistleblowers Assange, Manning, and Snowden do not concern them. The fate of Hondurans don't concern them. The fate of all America's victims don't concern these insouciant Americans. Obviously, if you are reading this, you are not one of the sleepwalkers and are awake to the parade of endless lies and illusions and do care. But you are in a minority.

That is not the case for most Americans. When approximately 129 million people cast their votes, whether for Donald Trump or Hillary Clinton, in 2016's presidential election, you know idiocy reigns and nothing has been learned. Ditto for the votes for Obama, Bush, Clinton, et al. You can keep counting back. It is an ugly fact and sad to say. Such a repetition compulsion is a sign of a deep sickness, and it will no doubt be repeated in the 2020 election.

It is true that average Americans have not built the doll's house; that is the handiwork of the vast interconnected and far-reaching propaganda arms of the U.S. government and their media accomplices. But that does not render them innocent for accepting decades of fabricated reality for so-called peace of mind by believing that a totally corrupt system works. The will to believe is very powerful, as is the propaganda. The lesson that Garrison spoke of has been lost on far too many people, even those who occasionally leave the doll house for a walk, but who only go slightly down the path for fear of seeing too much reality and connecting too many dots. There is plain ignorance, then there is culpable ignorance, to which I shall return.

Denying Existential Freedom

One of the first things an authoritarian governing elite must do is to convince people that they are not free. This process has been ongoing for at least forty years. After the Church Committee's revelations about the CIA in the mid-seventies, including its mind-control programs that left everyone appalled at the epiphany, a different tactic was added. Now we have "experts," social, psychological, and biological "scientists," who repeat ad infinitum that there is no longer any mind control since we now know there is no mind; it is an illusion, and the residence of all intellect is the brain. Who aver biology is destiny, except in culturally diversionary ways in which freedom to choose is extolled—e.g. the latest fashions, the best hair style, gender identity, etc. We have lavishly funded programs for the study of the brain, while supporting and promoting a vast expansion of pharmaceutical drugs to control people, done in the name of helping them with their emotional and behavioral problems that are said to be rooted in their biology and beyond their control. Additional criteria are laid on to convince people that they are sick and that their distress has nothing to do with the truth coup d'état that has rendered them denizens of an anti-social police state.

We have been interminably told that our lives revolve around our brains (our bodies) and that the answers to our problems lie in more brain research, drugs, genetic testing, etc. It is not coincidental that the U. S. government declared the 1990s the decade of brain research, followed up with 2000-2010 as the decade of the behavior project, and our present decade being devoted to mapping the brain and artificial intelligence, organized by the Office of Science and Technology Project and more significantly, the Defense Advanced Research Projects Agency (DARPA). George H. W. Bush, Clinton, George W. Bush, Obama, Trump —the beat goes on! But this is the orientation of today's science and how it has decided to address the welfare of the world.

Drip by drip, here and there, in the pattern of the best propaganda, as the French sociologist Jacques Ellul says—"for propaganda is not the touch of the magic wand. It is based on slow, constant impregnation. It creates conviction and compliance through imperceptible influences that are effective only by continuous repetition"[2]—articles, books, media reports have reiterated that people are "determined," enmeshed in biological, genetic, social, and psychological forces over which they have no control. To assert that people are free in the Sartrean sense (être *en soi*, condemned to freedom), or free will as maintained by the Abrahamic religions, has come to be seen as the belief of a delusional fool living in the past, a bad philosopher, an anti-scientist, a poorly informed religionist, one nostalgic for existential cafes, Gauloises, and black berets. One who doesn't grasp the truth since he doesn't read *The New York Times* or watch CBS television. One who believes in nutty conspiracy theories.

---

2 Jacques Ellul, *Propaganda: The Formation of Men's Attitudes* (Vintage Books, 1973), pp. 17–18

The ultimate message of this conventional propaganda—I almost said wisdom—created through decades-long media and academic repetition, is that we are not free.

Let me repeat: we are not free. We are not free.

Investigator reporter John Rappoport has consistently exposed the propaganda involved in the creation and expansion of the Diagnostic and Statistical Manual (DSM), the bible used by psychiatrists and therapists to diagnose people's mental and emotional problems, with its pseudo-scientific falsehoods and collusion between psychiatrists and the pharmaceutical industry. As he correctly notes, the CIA's MKULTRA mind-control program has morphed into modern psychiatry, both with the same objectives of disabling and controlling people by convincing them that they are not free and are in need of a chemical brain bath.[3]

Can anyone with an awareness of this history doubt there is a hidden agenda behind this development? Once you have convinced people that they are not free in the most profound sense, the rest is child's play. Convinced that they are already puppets, they do indeed become puppets, submitting willingly to be jerked around. But the paradox here is exquisite, for Americans must simultaneously be told that they are free while being told they are not. So their acceptance of being jerked around by multiple strings must be seen as their free choice. Forget Alexander's solution to the Gordian Knot.

"He played with me just as I used to play with dolls," says Nora in Ibsen's *A Doll's House*.

Now what is the point of getting people to believe they are not existentially free but are determined by biological and social forces? The answer is obvious given a minute of thought. It is not just Nora's husband Torvald who sees the merit in that.

Even as I write these words, a perfect example of the persistence of the long-term, repetitive, constantly re-impregnating propaganda appears in news headlines everywhere. On Friday,

---

3 Jon Rappoport, "CIA mind control morphed into psychiatry?" July 11, 2017, republished on *Steemit,* https://steemit.com/news/@zen12/cia-mind-control-morphed-into-psychiatry.

August 30, 2019, Sirhan Sirhan, who has been in prison for fifty-two years for the murder of RFK that he did not commit, was stabbed by another prisoner. A quick click through the headlines reporting this will result in seeing that the same words are being repeated by all the corporate media as they fulfill their function as CIA stenographers. One example from CBS News will suffice: "Robert Kennedy assassin hospitalized after prison stabbing."[4] RFK assassin, RFK assassin, RFK assassin . . . all the media say the same thing, which they have been doing for fifty-two years. Their persistency endures despite all the facts that refute their disinformation. Lisa Pease, among others, has marshalled these in her comprehensive book, *A Lie Too Big To Fail: The Real History of the Assassination of Robert F. Kennedy.*

Sartre and Bad Faith

Lying and dissembling are ubiquitous. Being deceived by the media liars is then reflected in people's personal lives. People lie and even want to be deceived. They choose to play dumb, to avoid a confrontation with truth. They want to be nice (Latin, *nescire*, not to know, to be ignorant) and to be liked. They want to tuck themselves into an anodyne social and cultural framework where they imagine they will be safe. They *like* the doll's house. They choose to live in what Jean Paul Sartre called *mauvaise foi* (bad faith). He put it thus:

> In bad faith it is from myself that I am hiding the truth. But with this "lie" to myself, the one to whom the lie is told and the one who lies are one and the same person, which means that I must know in my capacity as deceiver the truth which is hidden from me in my capacity as the one deceived.

---

[4] Caroline Linton, "Robert Kennedy assassin Sirhan Sirhan hospitalized after prison stabbing," *CBS News,* August 31, 2019, https://www.cbsnews.com/news/sirhan-sirhan-stabbed-robert-f-kennedy-assassin-hospitalized-after-prison-stabbing-2019-08-31/

Such bad faith allows people to fabricate a second act of bad faith: that they are not responsible for their ignorance of the truths shielded from them by the government and corporate media's lies and propaganda, even as the shades of the prison house ominously close around us and the world edges toward global death that could arrive in an instant with nuclear war or limp along for years of increasing suffering.

Those of us who write about the U.S.-led demented wars and provocations around the world and the complementary death of democracy at home are constantly flabbergasted and discouraged by the willful ignorance of so many Americans. For while the mainstream media does the bidding of the power elite, now there is ample alternative news and analyses available on the internet from fine journalists and writers committed to truth, not propaganda. It doesn't take a genius to learn how to research important issues and how to distinguish between bogus and genuine information. It takes a bit of effort, but, more importantly, the desire to compare multiple, opposing viewpoints and untangle the webs the Web weaves. We are awash in information (and disinformation) and both good and bad reporting, but much truth is still available to the caring inquirer.

The problem is the will to know. But why? Why the refusal to investigate and question; why the indifference? Stupidity? Okay, there is that. Ignorance? That too. Willful ignorance, ditto. Laziness, indeed. Careerism and ideology? For certain. Upton Sinclair put it mildly when he said, "It is difficult to get a man to understand something, when his salary depends on not understanding it." Difficult? No, it's almost impossible.

But then, there are many very intelligent people who have nothing to lose and yet adamantly refuse to entertain alternative possibilities to the reigning orthodoxies that have them in their grip.

As do many others, I know many such people who will yes me to death and then never fully research issues. They seem afraid of the knowledge that would engender the responsibility that would require them to act. They remain in limbo or else wink to themselves that what may be true really couldn't be true. They close down. This is the great dilemma and frustration faced by those who seek to convince people to take an active part in addressing what is really going on in the world today, especially as the United States wages war across the globe, threatens Russia and China, among others, and expands and modernizes its nuclear weapons capabilities. As for Assange, Manning, and Snowden, to such, their plight matters not a whit. In fact, they have been rendered invisible inside the doll's house, except as the murals on the windows flash back their images as threats to the occupants, *Russian* monsters out to eat them up.

The Two-Headed Monster

On the one hand, there is the massive propaganda apparatus operated by American intelligence agencies in conjunction with their media partners.

On the other, there is the human predilection for untruth and illusions, the sad need to be comforted and to submit to greater "authority," gratefully to accept the myths proffered by one's masters. This tendency applies not just to the common people, but even more so to the intellectual classes, who act as though they are immune. Erich Fromm, writing about Germans and Hitler, but by extension about people everywhere,[5] termed this the need to "escape from freedom," since freedom conjures up fears of vertiginous solitude and the need to decide, which in turn evokes the fear of death. There are many kinds of little deaths that precede the final one: social, career, money, familial, etc., that are used to keep people in the doll's house.

Fifty years ago, the CIA used the term "conspiracy theory" as a weapon to dismiss the truths expressed by critics of its murder of President Kennedy, and those of Malcom X, MLK, and RFK. All the media echoed the CIA line. While the term is still used to dismiss and denounce, control of the mainstream media is so complete today that every evil government action is immediately seconded, whether it be the lies about the attacks of

---

5 Erich Fromm, *Escape from Freedom*, (Rinehart & Company, Inc., 1941).

September 11, 2001, the wars against Afghanistan, Iraq, Syria, Libya, Yemen, etc., the coups disguised as color revolutions in Ukraine, Venezuela, Hong Kong, the downing of the Malaysian jetliner, drone murders, the Iranian "threat," the looting of the American people by the elites, the alleged sarin gas attacks in Syria, the Putin bashing and the Russia-gate farce, the "criminals" Assange, Manning, Snowden—everything. *The New York Times*, *Wall Street Journal*, *The Guardian*, Fox News, the *Washington Post*, CNN, NPR, etc.—all are stenographers for the deep state.

So much of the ongoing propaganda travels under the banner of "the war on terror," which is, of course, the expeditionary opportunity unlocked by the attacks of September 11, 2001. Unforgettably named and constantly reinforced by 9/11 use for emergency calls, this appellation is an exemplary sleight of linguistic mind-control. It serves as a constant reminder to engender anxiety, depression, panic, and confusion, four symptoms that the DSM "experts" and their followers use to diagnose and drug those so suffering. The term 9/11 was first used in *The New York Times* on September 12, 2001 by Bill Keller, the future T*imes'* editor. Just a fortuitous coincidence, of course.

Jacques Ellul on Propaganda

Jacques Ellul has argued convincingly that modern propaganda in a technological mass society is more complicated than the state and media simply lying and deceiving the population. He argues that propaganda meets certain needs of modern people and therefore the process of deceit is reciprocal. The modern person feels lost, powerless, and empty. Ellul says, "He realizes that he depends on decisions over which he has no control, and that realization drives him to despair." But he can't live in despair, desires that life be meaningful, and wants to feel he lives in a world that makes sense. He wants to participate and have opinions that suggest he grasps the flow of events. He doesn't so much want information, but rather value judgments and preconceived positions that provide him with a framework for living. Ellul wrote the following in 1965 in his classic book *Propaganda*:

The majority prefers expressing stupidities to not expressing any opinion: this gives them the feeling of participation. For they need simple thoughts, elementary explanations, a "key" that will permit them to take a position, and even readymade opinions. . . . The man who keeps himself informed needs a framework. . . . the more complicated the problems are, the more simple the explanations must be; the more fragmented the canvas, the simpler the pattern; the more difficult the question, the more all-embracing the solution; the more menacing the reduction of his own worth, the greater the need for boosting his ego. All this propaganda—and only propaganda—can give him.[6]

Another way of saying this is that people want to be provided with myths to direct them to the "truth," but that such so-called truth has been preconceived within the overarching myth provided by propaganda. While it satisfies people's emotional need for coherence, it also allows them to think of themselves as free individuals arriving at their own conclusions, which is a basic function of good propaganda. In today's mass technological society, it is essential that people be convinced that they are free-thinking individuals acting in good faith. Then they can feel good about themselves as they lie and act in bad faith.

Culpable Ignorance

It is widely accepted that political leaders and the mass media lie and dissemble regularly, which, of course, they do. That is their job, and necessary in an oligarchy. Today we are subjected to almost total, unrelenting media and government propaganda. Depending on their political leanings, people direct their anger toward politicians of parties they oppose and those media that they believe slant their coverage to favor the opposition. Trump is a liar. No, Obama is a liar. And Hillary Clinton. No, Fox News.

---

6 Jacques Ellul, p. 140.

Ridiculous!—it's CNN or NBC. And so on and so forth in this theatre of the absurd that plays out within a megaplex of mainstream media propaganda, where there are many shows but one producer, whose overall aim is to engineer the consent of all who enter, while setting the different audiences against each other to keep their interest up. It is a very successful charade that evokes name-calling from all quarters.

In other words, for many people their opponents lie, as do other people, but not them. This is as true in personal as in public life. Here the personal and the political converge, despite protestations to the contrary.

But there is another issue with propaganda that complicates the picture further. Many people of varying political persuasions can agree that propaganda is widespread. Most people on the left, and some on the right, would agree with Lisa Pease's statement in her book on the RFK assassination that "the way the CIA took over America in the 1960s is *the* story of our time."[7] That is also what Garrison thought when he spoke of the doll's house.

If that is so, then today's propaganda is anchored in the events of the 1960s, specifically the infamous government assassinations of JFK, Malcolm X, MLK, and RFK, the truth of which the CIA has worked so hard to conceal. In the fifty or so years since, a vast amount of new information has made it explicitly clear that these murders were carried out by elements within the U.S. government, and were done to silence the voices of four charismatic leaders who were opposed to the American war machine and the continuation of the Cold War. To turn away from this truth and to ignore its implications can only be described as an act of bad faith and culpable ignorance, or worse. But that is exactly what even some on the left have done. Then to compound the problem, they have done the same with the attacks of September 11, 2001 and Russian influence on the 2016 elections.

One cannot help thinking of what CIA official Cord Meyer called these people in the 1950s: "the compatible left." He felt that effective CIA propaganda, beside the need for fascist-minded

---

7 Lisa Pease, *A Lie Too Big To Fail*, (Feral House, 2018), pp. 500–501

schemers such as Allen Dulles and James Jesus Angleton, depended on drawing leftists and liberals into its orbit. For so many of the compatible left, those making a lot of money posing as opponents of the ruling elites but often taking the money of the super-rich, the JFK assassination and the truth of September 11, 2001 are inconsequential, topics never to be broached, as if they never happened except as the authorities say they did. By ignoring these foremost in-your-face events with their eyes wide shut, a coterie of influential leftists has done the work of Orwell's crime-stop, effectively succeeding in situating current events in an ahistorical and therefore misleading context that abets overall U.S. propaganda.

Without drawing a bold line connecting the dots from the November 22, 1963 assassination of JFK up to the present, a critique of the murderous forces ruling the United States is impossible.

Among the most notable of such failures were Alexander Cockburn, Howard Zinn, and still Noam Chomsky, men idolized by many liberals and leftists. And there are many others. Their motivations remain a mystery, but there is no doubt their refusals have contributed to the increased power of those who control the doll's house. To know better and do as they have is surely culpable ignorance.

From Bad to Worse

Ask yourself: Has the power of the oligarchic, permanent warfare state with its propaganda and spy networks, increased or decreased in the past half century? Who is winning the battle, the people or the ruling elites? The answer is obvious. It matters not at all whether the president has been Trump or Bill Clinton, Ronald Reagan or George W. Bush, Barack Obama or George H. W. Bush, Richard Nixon or Jimmy Carter. The power of the national security state has grown under them all and everyone is left to moan and groan and wonder why. All the while the doll's house has become more and more sophisticated and powerful.

The new Cold War now being waged against Russia and China is a bi-partisan affair, as is the confidence game played by the secret government intended to create a fractured consciousness in the population. Trump and his followers on one side of the coin; liberal Democrats on the other. The latter, whose bibles are *The New York Times, NPR,* the *Washington Post, Democracy Now,* etc.—can only see propaganda when they can attribute it to Trump or the Russians. The former see everything as a liberal conspiracy to take down Trump. The liberals have embraced a new McCarthyism and allied themselves with the deep-state forces that they were once allegedly appalled by, as have the Republicans. For liberals, it surely isn't the bloodthirsty policies of the Trump administration or his bloviating personality that they reject, for they also allied themselves with Obama's anti-Russian rhetoric, his support for the U.S. orchestrated neo-fascist Ukrainian coup, his destruction of Libya, his wars of aggression across the Middle East, his war on terror, his trillion dollar nuclear weapons modernization, his enjoyment of drone killing, his support for the coup in Honduras, his embrace of the CIA and his CIA Director John Brennan, his prosecution of whistle-blowers, etc. The same media that served the CIA so admirably over the decades has become the liberals' paragons of truth. It's enough to make your head spin, which is the point. Spin left, spin right, spin all around, because we have possessed your mind in this spectacular image game where seeming antinomies are constant even through difference, where all the presidents are coined by the same process, where coin flipping serves to transfix an audience eager for hope and change in their actual real-life situation—that which they do recognize.

This is how the political system works to prevent change. It is why little has changed for the better over half a century and the American empire has expanded. While it may be true that there are signs that this American hegemony is coming to an end (I am not convinced), I would not underestimate the power of the U.S. propaganda apparatus to keep people docile and deluded in the doll's house.

How, for example, is it possible for so many people to see such a stark difference between the despicable Trump and the suave Obama? They are both puppets dancing to their masters' tunes—the same masters. They both front for the empire.

In his excellent new book, *Obama's Unending Wars: Fronting the Foreign Policy of the Permanent Warfare State*, Jeremy Kuzmarov assiduously documents Obama's crimes, including his CIA background.[8] As Glen Ford, of Black Agenda Report, says in the first sentence of his foreword, "Barack Obama may go down in presidential history as the most effective and deceptive imperialist of them all." Read the book if you want all the details. They form an overwhelming indictment of the con artist and war criminal that is irrefutable. But will those who worship at the altar of Barack Obama read it? Of course not. Just as those deluded ones who voted for the reality television flim-flam man, Trump, will ignore all the accumulating evidence that they've been had and are living under a president who is Obama's disguised doppelganger despite the antipathy between them, carrying out the orders of his national security state bosses. This, too, is well documented, and no doubt another writer will arise in the years to come to put it between a book's covers.

Yet even Jeremy Kuzmarov fails to see the link between the JFK assassination and Obama's shilling for the warfare state. His few references to Kennedy are all negative, suggesting he either is unaware of what Kennedy was doing in the last year of his life and why he was murdered by the CIA, or something else. He seems to follow Noam Chomsky, a Kennedy hater, in this regard. I point out this slight flaw in an excellent book because it is symptomatic of certain people on the left who refuse to complete the circle. If, as Kuzmarov, argues, and I agree, Obama was CIA from the start and that explains his extraordinarily close relationship with the CIA's John Brennan, an architect, among many things, of the CIA's extraordinary rendition program, and that Obama told CIA Director Panetta that the CIA would "get everything it wanted," and the CIA killed JFK, well, something's amiss, an enormous gap in the analysis of our current condition. (See chapter 5, The Message From Dallas)

---

8 Jeremy Kuzmarov, *Obama's Unending Wars: Fronting the Foreign Policy of the Permanent Warfare State* (Clarity Press, 2019).

The doll's house is a mind game of extraordinary proportions, orchestrated by the perverted power elites that run the show and ably abetted by their partners in the corporate mass media, even some in the alternative press who either mean well but are confused, or are disinformation agents in the business of sowing confusion together with their mainstream partners. This began with Operation Mockingbird, a secret CIA program begun in the 1950s by Allen Dulles and Cord Meyer and later run by Frank Wisner that recruited journalists and many publications to report what the CIA wanted. It is a spectacle of increasingly open secrecy, in which the CIA has effectively suckered everyone into a game of to and fro in which only they win.

Our only hope for change is to try and educate as many people as possible about the linkages between events that started with the CIA coup d'état in Dallas on November 22, 1963, continued through the killings of Malcolm X, MLK, RFK and on through so much else up to September 11, 2001, which have brought us to the deeply depressing situation we now find ourselves in where truthtellers like Julian Assange, Chelsey Manning, and Edward Snowden are criminalized, while the real perpetrators of terrible evils, no matter how exposed, roam free.

Yes, we must educate but also agitate for the release of Assange, the dropping of all charges and accusations against Snowden so he may return home, and a public apology with recompense for Manning. Their freedom is ours; their imprisonment is ours, whether we know it or not. The walls are closing in.

Lisa Pease is so right: "The way the CIA took over America in the 1960s is *the* story of our time, and too few recognize this. We can't fix a problem we can't even acknowledge exists."

If we don't follow her advice, we will be toyed with like dolls for a long time to come. There will be no one to blame.

What Are We Working For "At Eternity's Gate"?

> *"One also knows from his letters that nothing appeared more sacred to Van Gogh than work."*
>
> —John Berger, "Vincent Van Gogh," ***Portraits***

Ever since I was a young boy, I have wondered why people do the kinds of work they do. I sensed early on that the economic system was a labyrinthine trap devised to imprison people in work they hated but needed for survival. It seemed like common sense to a child when you simply looked at and listened to the adults around you. Karl Marx wasn't necessary for understanding the nature of alienated labor; hearing adults declaim "Thank God It's Friday" spoke volumes.

In my Bronx working class neighborhood I saw people streaming to the subway in the mornings for their rides "into the city" and their forlorn trundles home in the evenings. It depressed me. Yet I knew the goal was to "make it" and move away as one moved "up," something that many did. I wondered why, when some people had options, they rarely considered the moral nature of the jobs they pursued. And why did they not also consider the cost in life (time lost) in their occupations? Were money, status, and security the deciding factors in their choices? Was living reserved for weekends and vacations?

I gradually realized that some people, by dint of family encouragement and schooling, had opportunities that others never received. For the unlucky ones, work would remain a life of toil and woe in which the search for meaning in their jobs was often elusive. Studs Terkel, in the introduction to his wonderful book of interviews, *Working: People Talk About What They Do All Day and How They Feel About What They Do*, puts it this way:

> This book, being about work, is, by its very nature, about violence—to the spirit as well as to the body. It is about ulcers as well as accidents, about shouting matches as well as fistfights, about nervous breakdowns as well as kicking the dog around. It is, above all (or beneath all), about daily humiliations. To survive the day is triumph enough for the walking wounded among the great many of us.

Those words were confirmed for me when in the summer between high school and college I got a job through a relative's auspices as a clerk for General Motors in Manhattan. I dreaded taking it, being apprehensive of being cooped up for the first time in an office building while a summer of my youth passed me by, but the money was too good to turn down (always the bait), and I wanted to save as much as possible for college spending money. So I bought a summer suit and joined the long line of trudgers going to and fro, down and up and out of the underground, adjusting our eyes to the darkness and light.

It was a summer from hell. My boredom was so intense it felt like solitary confinement. How, I kept wondering, can people do this? Yet for me it was temporary; for the others it was a life sentence. But if this were life, I thought, it was a living death. All my co-workers looked forward to the mid-morning coffee wagon and lunch with a desperation so intense it was palpable. And then, as the minutes ticked away to 5 P.M., the agitated twitching that proceeded the mad rush to the elevators seemed to synchronize with the clock's movements. We're out of here!

On my last day, I was eating my lunch on a park bench in Central Park when a bird shat on my suit jacket. The stain was apt, for I felt I had spent my days defiling my true self, and so I resolved never to spend another day of my life working in an office building in a suit for a pernicious corporation. It's a resolution I have kept.

>>>>>>•<<<<<<

"An angel is not far from someone who is sad," says Vincent Van Gogh in the film, *At Eternity's Gate*. For some reason, hearing these words in the darkened theater where I was almost alone, brought me back to that summer and the sadness that hung around all the people that I had worked with. I hoped Van Gogh was right and an angel visited them from time to time. Most of them had no options.

The painter Julian Schnabel's moving picture (moving on many levels since the film shakes and moves with its hand-held camera work and draws you into the act of drawing and painting that was Van Gogh's work) is a meditation on work. It asks the questions: What is work? What is work for? What is life for? Why paint? What does it mean to live? Why do you do what you do? Are you living or are you dead? What are you seeking through your work?

For Vincent the answer was simple: reality. But reality is not given to us and is far from simple; we must create it in acts that penetrate the screens of clichés that wall us off from it. As John Berger writes:

> One is taught to oppose the real to the imaginary, as though the first were always at hand and the second, distant, far away. This opposition is false. Events are always to hand. But the coherence of these events—which is what one means by reality—is an imaginative construction. Reality always lies beyond—and this is as true for materialists as for idealists. For Plato, for Marx. Reality, however one interprets it, lies beyond a screen of clichés.

These screens serve to protect the interests of the ruling classes, who devise ways to trap regular people from seeing the reality of their condition. Yet while working can be a trap, it can also be a means of escape. For Vincent working was the way. For him work was not a noun but a verb. He drew and he painted as he does in this film to "make people feel what it is to feel alive." To be alive is to act, to paint, to write. He tells his friend Gauguin that there's a reason it's called the "act of painting," the "stroke of genius." For him painting is living and living is painting.

The actual paintings that he made are almost beside the point, as all creative artists know too well. It is in the doing where living is found. The completed canvas, essay, or book are what is done. They are nouns, still lifes, just as Van Gogh's paintings have become commodities in the years since his death, dead things to be bought and sold by the rich in a culture of death where they can be hung in mausoleums isolated from the living. It is appropriate that the film ends with Vincent very still in his coffin as "viewers" pass him by and now avidly desire his paintings they once rejected that encircle the room. The poor dead man means nothing to them as they inspect the paintings for a value they never thought they had. The funeral parlor has become a museum.

"Without painting I can't live," he says earlier. He didn't say "without his paintings."

"God gave me the gift for painting," he said. "It's the only gift he gave me. I am a born painter." But his gift has begotten gifts that are still-births that do not circulate and live and breathe to encourage people to find work that will not be, "by its very nature, about violence," as Terkel said. His works, like people, have become commodities, brands to be bought and sold in a world where the accumulation of wealth is frequently accomplished by the infliction of pain, suffering, and death on untold numbers of victims, victims invisible to the wealthy that allow them to maintain their bad-faith innocence. This is often achieved in the veiled shadows of intermediaries such as stock brokers, tax consultants, and financial managers; in the liberal and conservative boardrooms of mega-corporations or law offices; and in the planning sessions of the world's great museums. Like drone killings that distance the killers from their victims, this wealth appropriation allows the wealthy to pretend they are on the side of the angels.

It's called success, and everyone is innocent as they sing, "Hi Ho, Hi Ho, it's off to work we go."

"It is not enough to tell me you worked hard to get your gold," said Henry Thoreau, Van Gogh's soul-mate. "So does the Devil work hard."

Yet while Van Gogh sought reality by breaking the mold, the rich and powerful have devoured the results of his efforts and have transposed them into commodities. Last year, his painting, *Laboureur Dans Un Champ*, painted from an asylum where he had committed himself, sold for $ 81.3 million at Christie's after a frenetic auction.

A humble peasant working in a field becomes a trophy for the rich, who keep the working man slaving away.

And a few years ago there was a major exhibit of Van Gogh's nature paintings at the Clark Museum in Williamstown, Massachusetts—"Van Gogh and Nature"—that aptly symbolized Van Gogh in his coffin. The paintings were exhibited encased in ornate gold frames. Van Gogh in gold. Just perfect. I am reminded of a scene in *At Eternity's Gate* where Vincent and Gauguin are talking about the need for a creative revolution—what we sure as hell need—and the two friends stand side by side with backs to the camera and piss into the wind.

~.~.~.~

But pseudo-innocence dies hard. Not long ago I was sitting in a breakfast room in a bed-and-breakfast in Houston, Texas, sipping coffee and musing myself awake. Two men came in and the three of us got to talking. As people like to say, they were nice guys. Very pleasant and talkative, in Houston on business. Normal Americans. Stressed. Both were about fifty years old with wives and children.

One sold drugs for one of the largest pharmaceutical companies that is known for its very popular anti-depressant drug and its aggressive sales pitches. He travelled a triangular route from Corpus Christi to Austin to Houston and back again, hawking his wares. He spoke about his work as being very lucrative and posing no ethical dilemmas. There were so many depressed people in need of his company's drugs, he said, as if the causes of their depression had nothing to do with the sorry state of the country but were all biological in nature. I thought of recommending a book to him—*Deadly Medicines and Organized Crime: How big pharma has corrupted health care* by Peter Gotzsche—but held my tongue, appreciative as I was of the small but tasteful fare we were being served and not wishing to cause my companions dyspepsia. This guy seemed to be trying to convince me of the ethical nature of the way he panned gold, while I kept thinking of that quote attributed to Mark Twain: "Denial ain't just a river in Egypt."

The other guy, originally from a small town in Nebraska and now living in Baton Rouge, was a former medevac helicopter pilot who had served in the 1st Gulf War. He worked in finance for an equally large oil company. His attitude was a bit different, and he seemed sheepishly guilty about his work with this company as he told me how shocked he was the first time he saw so many oil, gas, and chemical plants lining the Mississippi River from Baton Rouge to New Orleans and all the oil and chemicals being shipped down the river. So many toxins that reminded him of the toxic black smoke rising from all the bombed oil wells in Iraq. Something about it all left him uneasy, but he too said he made a very good "living" and that his wife also worked for the oil company back home.

My childish thought recurred: when people have options, why do they not choose ethical work that makes the world more beautiful and just? Why is money and so-called success always the goal?

Having seen *At Eternity's Gate*, I now see what Van Gogh was trying to tell us, as Julian Schnabel conveys through this moving picture. I see why these two perfectly normal guys I was breaking bread with in Houston are unable to penetrate the screen that lies between them and reality. They have never developed the imaginative tools to go beyond normal modes of perception and conception. Or perhaps they lack the faith to dare, to see the futility and violence in what they are working for and what their companies' products are doing to the world. They think of themselves as hard at work, travelling hither and yon, doing their calculations, "making their living," and collecting their pay. It's their work that has a payoff in gold, but it's not working in the sense that painting was for Vincent, a way beyond the screen. They are mesmerized by the spectacle, as are so many Americans. Their jobs are perfectly logical and allow them a feeling of calm and being in control.

But Vincent, responding to Gauguin, a former stock broker, when he urged him to paint slowly and methodically, said, "I need to be out of control. I don't want to calm down." He knew that to be fully alive was to be vulnerable, to not hold back, to always be slipping away, and to be threatened with annihilation at any moment. When painting, he was intoxicated with a creative joy that belies the popular image of him as always depressed. "I find joy in sorrow," he said, echoing in a paradoxical way Albert Camus, who said, "I have always felt that I lived on the high seas, threatened, at the heart of a royal happiness." Both rebels, one in paint, the other in words: "I rebel: therefore we exist," was how Camus put it, expressing the human solidarity that is fundamental to genuine work in our ephemeral world. Both nostalgic in the present for the future, creating freedom through vision and disclosing the way for others.

And although my breakfast companions felt safe in their calmness on this side of the screen, it was an illusion. The only really calm ones are corpses. And perhaps that's why when you look around, as I did as a child, you see so many of the living dead carrying on as normal.

"I paint to stop thinking and feel I am a part of everything inside and outside me," says Vincent, a self-described exile and pilgrim.

If we could make working a form of such painting, an exhilarating manifestation of human solidarity, what a wonderful world it would be.

The point of rebellion is to get there.

Walking with Fr. Daniel Berrigan, S.J., a Criminal for Peace

Radical dissidents and prophets have never had an easy time of it. When alive, that is. Once safely dead, however, honors and respect are often heaped on their heads. The dead can't talk back, or so it is assumed. Nor can they cause trouble.

Jesuit priest Fr. Daniel Berrigan was one such man. When he died on April 30, 2016, the major media, organs of propaganda and war promotion, noted his death in generally respectful ways. This included *The New York Times*. But back in 1988 when Daniel was a spry 68 years old, the *Times* published a review of his autobiography, *To Dwell in Peace*, which was a nauseating hatchet job aimed at dismissing his anti-war activism through the cheap trick of psychological reductionism and reversal.

How could Berrigan really be a Christian, a man of peace, the reviewer Kenneth Woodward (himself a product of eight years of Jesuit education) asked rhetorically, and be so angry? Wasn't he in truth a bitter, ungrateful, and angry—i.e. violent—"celebrity priest" masquerading as an apostle of peace? And therefore, were not his peace activities, his writings, and his uncompromising critique of American society null and void, the rantings of a disturbed man? Furthermore, by the unspoken intentional logic of such an ad hominem attack, were not those who follow in his footsteps, those who hear his words and—God forbid!—take them seriously, were not they too wolves in sheep's clothing, angry children trying to exact revenge on their parents? "Gratefulness, we learn, is not a Berrigan trait," Woodward concluded in his bilious review of a "pervasively angry autobiography." "The Berrigans [note the plural usage], it seems, never learned to laugh at themselves."

Such character assassination has long been one tool of the power elite. Silence or kill the prophets one way or another.

When Dan and I first met we walked together in the blue cold snowy silence of Ithaca nights. It was December 1967. He was a 46-year-old black-bereted whirling dervish orbiting a profound spiritual and poetic stillness; I, a 23-year-old Marine intent on declaring myself a conscientious objector before my reserve unit was activated and sent to Vietnam.

He had been arrested for the first time at a Pentagon demonstration in late October. A few days later his brother, Philip, together with three others, had upped the ante dramatically by pouring blood on draft files in Baltimore. This action, perpetrated by those who became known as the Baltimore Four, started a chain of draft board raids over the next years. This, and the raging Vietnam War that Johnson was dramatically escalating, were the backdrop for my three-day visit with Dan. The invitation had been arranged by my inspirational college teacher, Bill Frain, Dan's friend.

Walking and talking, talking and walking, we whirled around the Cornell campus where Dan was a chaplain, into and out of town, from apartment to apartment, a gathering here, a Mass there. The intensity was electric. At a party I met and learned from the brilliant Pakistani scholar and activist, Eqbal Ahmad. At an apartment Mass led by Dan in his inimitable style I felt as if we were early Jewish-Christians gathering in secret. There was a sense of foreboding, as if something would soon break asunder as the U.S. rained bombs and napalm down on the Vietnamese.

I recall a sense of intense agitation on Dan's part, as if events were conspiring to push him to answer an overwhelming question. I knew from the first that he was no J. Alfred Prufrock who would sit on the fence. He would never say, "I am no prophet—and here's no great matter/I have seen the moment of my greatness flicker/And I have seen the eternal Footman hold my coat, and snicker/And in short, I was afraid." A poet, yes, a lover of beauty, that I could tell; but I felt his fierceness from the start, and it was something I viscerally connected with. He was preparing for a great leap into the breach; he was Odysseus readying to leave Ithaca, not to wage a violent war against Troy, but to travel to Vietnam to wage a non-violent war against war—part of a lifelong journey. I too felt that my life would never be the same and that I was venturing out onto unchartered waters. His courage rubbed off on me.

In those few days with Dan, I unlearned most of the lessons my Jesuit education had instilled in me. *Deo et Patria* were rent asunder. I had never accepted the Marine slogan that "my rifle is my life," nor had I fully ingested the Jesuits' conservative ideology—what Dan called "consensus, consensus"—that I should become successful through speaking out of both sides of my mouth and serving two masters. But at that point I had no Jesuit mentor who embodied another path. In Dan I found that man, or he found me.

Contrary to some public images of him, he was a man whose bluntness was complemented by his attentive reserve. He had the gift of discernment. Not once during my initial stay with him did he suggest a course of action for me. We talked about the war, of course, of the courage of his brother Phil and others, but we also talked of poetry and art, of the beauty of starry winter nights and the dramatic waterfalls surrounding the Cornell campus. Most of all he wanted to know about me, my family, my background; he listened intently as if he were contemplating his own past as well, weighing the future. I had already decided to leave the Marines one way or the other, but we never discussed this. He arranged for me to speak to a Cornell lawyer who did anti-war work in case I needed legal help. But I felt I was in the presence of a man who knew and respected that such momentous decisions should be made in solitary witness to one's conscience. I felt he would support me whatever I did.

When I set sail from Ithaca, I felt blessed and confirmed. I would never go to war; I knew that. But I also came away with a different lesson: that not participating in the killing wasn't enough. I would have to find ways to resist the forces of violence that were consuming the world. They would have to be my ways, not necessarily Dan's. I was unyielding in my conviction that I would not stay in the Marines no matter what the consequences; but after that I would have to choose and take responsibility for what Dan referred to as "the long haul"—a lifelong commitment to the values we shared. But values are probably too abstract a way to describe what I mean. Dan conveyed to me through his way of being that each of us must follow his soul's promptings—there was no formula. I was young enough to be his son, and yet he spoke to me as an equal. Despite his adamantine strength of purpose and conviction, he let me see the scarecrow man within. No words can describe the powerful stamp this set on my heart that has never left me.

Less than two months later the TET offensive exploded, and Dan was on a night flight to Hanoi with Howard Zinn to bring back three U.S. airmen who had been shot down while bombing North Vietnam. Shortly Dan was invited by Philip to join the Catonsville action. He gave it prayer and thought, and then jumped in, knowing that the children he had met in the North Vietnamese bomb shelters hiding from American bombs were pleading with him. He later wrote of holding a little boy:

In my arms, fathered
In a moment's grace, the messiah
Of all my tears, I bore reborn
A Hiroshima child from hell.

He was a changed man. No longer just a priest-poet, he would now become a revolutionary anti-war activist for life. He wrote in "Mission to Hanoi, 1968":

Instructions for return. Develop for the students the meaning of Ho's "useless years." The necessity for escaping once and for all the slavery of "being useful." On the other hand, prison, contemplation, life of solitude. Do the things that even "movement people" tend to despise and misunderstand. To be radical is habitually to do things which society at large despises.

Shortly after Catonsville I was privileged to be invited by Bill Frain to a meeting at his house in Queens, New York of the Catonsville Nine. The Catonsville Nine were nine Catholic anti-war activists, including Dan and his brother, Philip, who on May 17, 1968 broke into the Selective Service office in Catonsville, Maryland, seized hundreds of draft records, and burned them with homemade napalm in wire baskets in the parking lot, while saying the Lord's Prayer. It was a very dramatic act of civil disobedience in opposition to the Vietnam War, and their action and immediate arrest became front-page news across the country. The great civil rights and anti-war leader, Martin Luther King, was executed by government forces in Memphis six weeks before. The message was clear.

We met deep in his backyard, huddled in a circle away from the prying eyes and listening devices of the FBI. There my education continued. In January I had submitted my request to be discharged from the Marines as a conscientious objector. Now I was gathering with nine incredibly courageous Americans who had taken personal responsibility for the nation's war crimes in an act that sent shock waves around the world. Although I don't recall feeling it at the time, I now realize how blessed I was to have been allowed into that august company. For them to have trusted a 23-year-old whom eight of them had never met takes my breath away. I am sure Dan gave the okay.

Later that night I drove him back to where he was staying in Yonkers. So true to form, as we crossed the Whitestone Bridge in the dark, this beautiful man spoke of the exquisiteness of the sparkling lights and the illuminated Manhattan skyline. He was a hunger artist for beauty. And we talked again of poetry and family, of our relationships, how important they were, and how fractious relationships could get when one stood up for truth and victims everywhere. He asked about my girlfriend: what did she think about these things? As we rolled along in a cocoon of intimate talk, I sensed that without being explicit he was warning me, while simultaneously telling himself that he was in for some sharp criticism from people close to him.

Afterwards, as I drove home, I kept thinking of the great novel by Ignazio Silone, *Bread and Wine,* a book Bill Frain had introduced me to; of Pietro Spina, the revolutionary in hiding disguised as a priest, and of his former teacher, the priest, Don Benedetto. Hunted and surveilled by Italy's fascist government, they secretly meet and talk of the need to resist the forces of state and church collaborating in violence and suppression. Dan and the others had dramatically confronted these twin ogres and were willing to face the consequences. My problem was that Dan was both revolutionary and priest, but I was neither. Who was I? The meaning, if not the exact words, of Don Benedetto came back to me: "But it is enough for one little man to say 'No!' murmur 'No!' in his neighbor's ear, or write 'No!' on the wall at night, and public order is endangered." And Pietro: "Liberty is something you have to take for yourself. It's no use begging it from others."

A few days later another conspiratorial murder took place as Bobby Kennedy was murdered in Los Angeles. First King, then Kennedy. Again I heard Don Benedetto's words: "Killing a man who says 'No!' is a risky business because even a corpse can go on whispering 'No! No! No!' with a persistence and obstinacy that only certain corpses are capable of. And how can you silence a corpse?"

Then the police riots at the Democratic convention followed. Fascist forces had been unleashed. The trial of the Catonsville Nine took place in October, and of course they were convicted and sentenced, as Dan so famously put it, for "the burning of paper instead of children." That fall I received a letter from Marine Headquarters in Washington D.C. informing me that I was being released from the Marine Corps so I "could take final vows in a religious order." It was a complete fabrication since I was engaged to be married, but it was a way to get rid of me without honoring my request as a CO. Yet in its weird way it was true: I was religious and I was trying to follow an order, but as one of the dissenters led by Dan and his brave companions who formed a different corps—one dedicated to life, not death.

In 1970 when Dan had gone underground instead of reporting for prison, I travelled to the big antiwar event, "America is Hard to

Find," at Cornell. Word had gone out that Dan would appear, which he did in Barton Hall in front of a crowd of 15,000, including the FBI who were ready to pounce on him. When Dan appeared on stage and gave a moving speech about the need to oppose the war, silence and a sense of held breath filled the hall. When he finished to thunderous applause, the lights went out and when they came back on, he was gone. It was like being at a magic show. He had escaped inside a puppet of one of the twelve apostles that was part of a group of very large puppets created by the Bread and Puppet Theater, a radical group that opposed the Vietnam War. Oh what great joy and laughter! A circus act! Puckish Dan, imaginative through and through, irreverently funny, later said, "I was hoping it wasn't a puppet of Judas."

That was the man.

Once my wife and I were eating dinner with him at the 98 St. apartment where he lived with other Jesuits. The conversation turned to Dorothy Day, the founder of *The Catholic Worker* and long-time pacifist and servant of the poor. Day had been a mentor to Dan. I told him how I had followed his example when I was teaching in Brooklyn and brought my students to *The Catholic Worker* to meet with Day. Now that Day had died, we asked, what would be the Catholic Church's attitude toward this great dissident? I said that I thought the church would eventually declare her a saint now that she was safely dead. Dan strongly demurred; that would never happen, he said, she was too radical and the institution would not recognize her. Now that Day is being considered for canonization—i.e. declared a saint—I can't help thinking of the ways the powers-that-be, both ecclesiastical and secular, have characterized him before and after his death. Is irony the right word?

I return to a question he had the effrontery to ask, not as an academic exercise but as an existential question demanding a living answer: "What is a human being, anyway?" It is the type of question asked by Emerson and Thoreau, Gandhi and King, dead sages all.

In the truest sense he answered that question with his life. A human being is not cannon fodder, a human being is not a piece of paper, not an abstraction. A human being is not a human being when forced to wage war or live off the spoils of war, a human being is not a human being when in the grip of "Lord Nuke." None of these. A human being is a child of God, and as such is called to resist the rule of human death-dealing in the world, to resist violence with love and non-violence. A human being is a lover.

This means a human being is necessarily at odds with the powers-that-be, the governments and corporations that, in the name of peace, prepare for and wage war. It is a view of human being that is bound to be unpopular, more likely to be affirmed with pieties then contradicted by actions.

Sainthood is a piety, the kiss of death bestowed as a guilt offering by authorities lacking authority. It is the Judas kiss—a cosmic joke made to make God laugh.

Dan wasn't a saint. He was something more—a man—a brave, brilliant, and prophetic inspirational dissident, full of contradictions like us all. He was a true human being of the highest sacramental order—flesh and blood, bread and wine, life and death. At the height of the AIDS crisis in the 1980s, when social panic consumed the nation and people, including the institutional churches, shunned gay men as lepers, only a man of supreme non-judgmental compassion would have befriended and cared for dying patients, as Dan did for many years. This didn't attract headlines as his anti-war activities did, but it symbolized the man. He was a genuine Christian.

Today, he is in death what he was in life—a great spiritual leader. Ever faithful, he leads us on, by deeds and words. There are no bars to manhood (or womanhood), he once wrote. Freedom is our birthright. "This mess of mythological pottage, this self-contradictory dream, makes slaves of us," he wrote, "keeps most of us inert and victimized, makes hostages of our children as well as ourselves. And yet we are instructed by the highly placed smilers to keep smiling through, as if the dollars in our pockets or the brains in our heads were still workable, negotiable, a sound tender. As though, in plain fact, our world was not raving mad in its chief parts. And driving us mad, as the admission price to its Fun House."

On the afternoon of April 30, 2016, I was cleaning out files and had emptied two large drawers of papers. I noticed there was one green sheet left in one drawer. It was a saying Dan had sent to me about death. "Though invisible to us our dead are not absent." I thought how true that was and wondered when Dan would die, knowing he was failing.

The next morning I was informed that Dan had died the previous day. The presence of his absence struck me forcibly. It consoles me in my sadness, as I know it does so many others.

On the morning of his funeral, there was a march around lower Manhattan in his honor. Outside *The Catholic Worker* someone asked me to carry a large photo of Dan, circa 1968. As we proceeded through the rainy streets, it dawned on me that we were walking together again, and although I was now carrying his image, he had carried me for so many years with his indelible stamp on my heart. After stopping at a coffeeshop, some marchers laughed at the incongruous sight of Dan's photo and me emerging from the restroom door. I pointed to Dan's photo and said, "He really had to go." I think I heard Dan laugh and say, "So there you go, shirking responsibility."

I believe he walks beside us still, or in my case, he walks before me, beckoning me on, since I have such a long way to go to learn the lessons that he first taught me long ago on those snowy night walks through Ithaca.

No, you can't silence certain corpses.

The Disappearance of Silence

Silence is a word pregnant with multiple meanings: for many a threat; for others a nostalgic evocation of a time rendered obsolete by technology; for yet others a sentence to boredom; and for the blessed few, devotees of the ancient arts of contemplation, reading, and writing, a word of profound, even sacred importance.

But silence, like so much else in the present world, including human beings, is on the endangered species list. Another rare bird—let's call it the holy spirit of true thought—is slowly disappearing from our midst. The poison of noise and busyness is polluting more than we recognize, but surely our ability to think.

I am sitting on a stone step of a small cabin on an estuary on Cape Cod. All is quiet. Three feet in front of me a baby rabbit nibbles on grass, and that nibbling resounds. Two mourning doves moan intermittently. I see the wind ripple the marsh grass and sense its low humming. I feel at home.

I am dwelling in silent stop-time.

It strikes me how rare silence has become; how doing nothing seems so un-American. Noise and busyness have become our elements. While I watch the rushes sway, I wonder why, wherever you turn, people are rushed and stressed. A frantic anxiety prevails everywhere. Whether you ask the young, the middle-aged, or the retired, they all report stress and lack of time. "It's crazy," you often hear them say. "It" is never defined.

Clearly there are powerful forces that profit from this noisy busyness, this connected way of technological consumption, this contraction of time. Everyone seems to have their reasons why they are in such a state, but few imagine how and why it may be "engineered." They don't have the quiet time to do so.

Or they don't want to.

When I speak of noise, I am not thinking primarily of the din we associate with city life—cars, trucks, taxis, horns, sirens, congestion, etc.—a world rushing to get somewhere for unknown reasons. That noise, alas, is hard to avoid, even in small towns or suburbs. If I travel a half mile from where I sit in silence, I will encounter such noise as people speed by in cars on their search for a vacation from it.

Being in a secluded spot on Cape Cod for a few days is a luxury. I realize that. So too is having these minutes to write these words. Yet I know also that I am choosing to do so, and that for me the luxury is also a necessity. How could I live without "doing nothing" in silence? Even the computer on which I am typing these words tells me I am wrong: it wants to correct my words "doing nothing" to "doing anything." I'm surprised it doesn't tell me that I should be having "fun," though perhaps doing anything is the equivalent.

The noise of modern life is hard to avoid completely, and, in any case, it is the least disruptive of the silence I have in mind. There is another kind of noise that is self-imposed and whose purpose, consciously or not, is to make sure one is not "caught" by silence. As those who flee from silence know, it can be dangerous to one's reigning assumptions about self and the world. Noise seems more comforting.

We all know people who go from morning till night, day in and day out, without ever pausing to enter the zone of slow silence. One doesn't have to look far for them; technology has made them the rule. They race through their lives in a cocoon of technological noise. They're informed, in touch, tuned in to everything but their own souls. They drown themselves in the incessant noise of televisions and radios, or the busyness of telephone calls, texting, or trivia "that has to be done." They are always planning, going, organizing, and scheduling activities. Or talking—endless chatter about the weather or shopping or the latest mainstream media's blaring headlines.

They choose to fill their lives with distracting noise in order to avoid the silence that might force them to confront issues of self-knowledge that are the stuff of great books, true art, a fully human life; self-knowledge that connects the individual to his social circumstances in his historical period; knowledge that might allow them to grasp the sources of the profound anxiety and despair that induces their franticness. This is what C. Wright Mills called the sociological imagination.

Since 9/11, nearly two decades ago at this writing, the United States has been living under an official state of national emergency and constant, paralyzing fear—a fear that keeps people moving as fast as they can so they don't stop and look back and see what has happened to them and why and where they are heading—over the cliff.

It is another day now and I am sitting in the shade of a tree looking out on a beautiful harbor filled with sailboats. A seagull swoops and sails before me. A strong wind picks up from the west. This water is the playground of the wealthy. Unlike the poor, they can buy outer silence. They seem to have plenty of time to think deep thoughts, such as where did all their money come from. From corporations that are part of the military-industrial complex? By exploiting others? I suspect they use their "free" time to think of other things.

For some reason the rough water reminds me of all those refugees fleeing war and chaos on the Mediterranean Sea. Desperate people. Why must they die seeking refuge? Why must they flee their homelands? Who drove them to the boats? The sea and silence brings these thoughts to my mind. Silent reverie can do that. It can conjure up disturbing thoughts.

I often write about such matters. Most of what I write is serious stuff, what people refer to as "heavy" writing: wars, assassinations, coups, etc.—a lot of history, social issues, philosophical and theological questioning. And I find that many people find it tough to take. They can't find the time or silent concentration to read it closely and study to see if my analyses are correct. I think they choose not to take the time to enter the cocoon of silent concentration it demands. They will nod or demur, but not delve any deeper. Deeper means danger.

Those hundreds of thousands of fleeing boat people, for example; who is responsible for their fate? Who started the wars that drove them from their homes? Might we be implicated? Do we bear responsibility? Can we be silently attentive enough to hear their cries and explore the facts? Is the noisy busyness a self-imposed distraction from the truth? Do we live in bad faith?

Can we stop talking, stop moving, and stop doing long enough to contemplate such matters?

Can we shut up long enough to listen to what the silence might reveal?

What are we running away from? Are there truths so deep and so disturbing that they must be "silenced"?

I think so.

Slow silence would allow us to understand how the leaders of the United States are pushing the world toward the ultimate silence of nuclear conflagration by provoking war with Russia and China. Most people are too "busy" and too distracted—and therefore too ignorant—to notice. So for them it's not happening. It's not happening, as Harold Pinter said of all the countless war crimes committed by the United States while the American people were hypnotized into thinking otherwise: "It never happened. Nothing ever happened. Even while it was happening it wasn't happening. It didn't matter. It was of no interest."

We were too busy to notice. All we could hear was the noise, the propagandistic bedlam.

A society suffering from socially induced attention-deficit disorder is a society in a state of disintegration. Focused on the noisy foreground of conventional thinking fueled by a mass media spewing out endless distractions and pseudo-events, most people are lost in a cacophonous mental chaos.

I'm not sure if there is any point in writing these words.

But I am sure that the art of writing implies the art of reading. The writer creates and the reader recreates. Both demand silence, a not-doing, the cessation of all noise that serves to prevent true thought. Can you hear me?

The machines must be turned off. "Our inventions," Thoreau noted, "are wont to be pretty toys, which distract our attention from serious things."

It is not hard to turn a switch, pull a plug, or press a button; the hard part is wanting to. Harder still, but equally necessary, is the quieting of the mind, the silencing of the incessant internal chatterboxes that accompany us everywhere.

Unless by some miracle we reject the bill of goods of noisy busyness that has been sold to us to sow confusion, we are doomed. That might sound hyperbolic, but it is not. We are being led to the slaughter by crazed elites who are pushing for a world war. We are drowning in lies and more lies, lies compounded by noisy repetition.

"There ain't nothing more powerful than the odor of mendacity. . . . You can smell it. It smells like death." That's what I recently heard Big Daddy say in a production of *Cat on a Hot Tin Roof*.

The Trappist monk Thomas Merton once wrote that someday they will sell us the rain; in saying that he implied that any essential, beautiful aspect of life could be destroyed by a society hell-bent on destruction through war, the search for profit, and consumerism. Now that they have succeeded in selling us noise and speed to eliminate slow silence, we are in far deeper trouble. We can't think straight, if we can think at all. And clear thinking has never been more important.

Gandhi, the revolutionary, put it perfectly, "In the attitude of silence the soul finds the path in a clearer light, and what is elusive and deceptive resolves itself into crystal clearness. Our life is a long and arduous quest after Truth."

The Message from Dallas: JFK and The Unspeakable

Despite a treasure-trove of new information having emerged over the last fifty-seven years, there are many people who still think who killed President John Fitzgerald Kennedy and why are unanswerable questions. There are others who cling to the Lee Harvey Oswald "lone-nut" explanation proffered by the Warren Commission. Both groups agree, however, that whatever the truth, it has no contemporary relevance but is old-hat, history, stuff for conspiracy-obsessed people with nothing better to do. The general thinking is that the assassination occurred almost a half-century ago, so let's move on.

Nothing could be further from the truth, as James W. Douglass shows in his extraordinary book, *JFK and the Unspeakable: Why He Died and Why It Matters*. It is clearly one of the best books ever written on the Kennedy assassination and deserves a vast readership. It is bound to roil the waters of complacency that have submerged the truth of this key event in modern American history.

It's not often that the intersection of history and contemporary events poses such a startling and chilling lesson as does the contemplation of the murder of JFK on November 22, 1963 when juxtaposed with the situations addressed by President Obama, a liberal icon of a later era. Obama's behavior mirrored Johnson's, not Kennedy's, as he escalated the war in Afghanistan, inflamed a New Cold War, and used mercenaries and Islamic jihadists to assault Libya and Syria, among others. One might wonder if the thought of JFK's fate might not have been far from Obama's mind as he contemplated his next move in these places.

Douglass presents a very compelling argument that Kennedy was killed by "unspeakable" (the Trappist monk Thomas Merton's term) forces within the U.S. national security state *because* of his conversion from a cold warrior into a man of peace. He argues, using a wealth of newly uncovered information, that JFK had become a major threat to the burgeoning military-industrial complex and was eliminated through a conspiracy that had to have been planned by the CIA—"the CIA's fingerprints are all over the crime and the events leading up to it"—not by a crazed individual, the Mafia, or disgruntled anti-Castro Cubans, though some of these may have been used in the execution of the plot.

Why and by whom? These are the key questions. If it can be shown that Kennedy did, in fact, turn emphatically away from war as a solution to political conflict—did, in fact, as he was being urged by his military and intelligence advisers to up the ante and use violence, reject such advice and turn toward peaceful solutions—then, a motive for his elimination is established. If, furthermore, it can be clearly shown that Oswald was a dupe in a deadly game and that forces within the military/intelligence apparatus were involved with him from start to finish, then who perpetrated the crime is solved, not by fingering an individual who may have given the order for the murder or pulled the trigger, but by showing that the coordination of the assassination had to involve U.S. intelligence agencies, most notably the CIA. Douglass does both, providing highly detailed and intricately linked evidence based on his own research and a vast array of the best scholarship by persons who have been working on this issue for decades.

We are then faced with the assassination's contemporary relevance. Since we know that every president since JFK has refused to confront the growth of the national security state and its call for violence, one can logically assume a message was sent and heeded. In this regard, it is not incidental that former twenty-seven-year CIA analyst Raymond McGovern, in a recent interview, warned of the "two CIAs,"[9] one the analytic arm providing straight scoop

---

9 Brad Friedman, "Ray McGovern Warns of 'Two CIAs,'" *Consortium News*, Sept. 13, 2009, https://www.consortiumnews.com/2009/091309a.html.

to presidents, the other the covert action arm which operates according to its own rules. "Let me leave you with this thought," he told his interviewer, "and that is that I think Panetta (current CIA Director), and to a degree Obama, are afraid—I never thought I'd hear myself saying this—I think they are afraid of the CIA." He then recommended Douglass' book, "It's very well-researched and his conclusion is very alarming."

Let's look at the history marshaled by Douglass to support his thesis.

First, Kennedy, who took office in January 1961 as somewhat of a Cold Warrior, was quickly set up by the CIA to take the blame for the Bay of Pigs invasion of Cuba in April 1961. The CIA and generals wanted to oust Castro, and in pursuit of that goal, trained a force of Cuban exiles to invade Cuba. Kennedy refused to go along and the invasion was roundly defeated. The CIA, military, and Cuban exiles bitterly blamed Kennedy. But it was all a sham.

Though Douglass doesn't mention it, and few Americans know it, classified documents uncovered in 2000 revealed that the CIA had discovered that the Soviets had learned of the date of the invasion more than a week in advance and then the Soviets had informed Castro,[10] but—and here is a startling fact that should make people's hair stand on end—the CIA never told the President. The CIA knew the invasion was doomed before the fact but went ahead with it anyway. Why? So they could and did afterwards blame JFK for the failure.

This treachery set the stage for events to come. For his part, sensing but not knowing the full extent of the set-up, Kennedy fired CIA Director Allen Dulles (who, as in a bad joke, was later to be named to the Warren Commission investigating his death) and his assistant General Charles Cabell (whose brother Earle Cabell, to make a bad joke absurd, was the mayor of Dallas on the day Kennedy was killed) and said he wanted "to splinter the CIA in a thousand pieces and scatter it to the winds." Not the sentiments to

---

10 Vernon Loeb, "Soviets Knew Date of Cuba Attack," *Washington Post*, April 29, 2000.

endear him to a secretive government within a government whose power was growing exponentially.

The stage was now set for events to follow as JFK, in opposition to nearly all his advisers, consistently opposed the use of force in U.S. foreign policy.

In 1961, despite the Joint Chief's demand to put troops into Laos, Kennedy bluntly insisted otherwise as he ordered Averell Harriman, his representative at the Geneva Conference, "Did you understand? I want a negotiated settlement in Laos. I don't want to put troops in."

Also in 1961, he refused to accede to the insistence of his top generals to give them permission to use nuclear weapons in Berlin and Southeast Asia. Walking out of a meeting with top military advisors, Kennedy threw his hands in the air and said, "These people are crazy."

He refused to bomb and invade Cuba as the military wished during the Cuban missile crisis in 1962. Afterwards he told his friend John Kenneth Galbraith that "I never had the slightest intention of doing so."[11]

Then in June 1963 he gave an incredible speech at American University in which he called for the total abolishment of nuclear weapons, the end of the Cold War and the "Pax Americana enforced on the world by American weapons of war," and movement toward "general and complete disarmament."

A few months later he signed a Limited Test Ban Treaty with Nikita Khrushchev.

In October 1963 he signed National Security Action Memorandum 263 calling for the withdrawal of 1,000 U. S. military troops from Vietnam by the end of the year and a total withdrawal by the end of 1965.

All this he did while secretly engaging in negotiations with Soviet Premier Nikita Khrushchev via the KGB, Norman Cousins, and Pope John XXIII, and with Cuba's Prime Minister Fidel Castro through various intermediaries, one of whom was French

---

11 See James K. Galbraith, "Exit Strategy," *Boston Review,* October/November 2003.

Journalist Jean Daniel. In an interview with Daniel on October 24, 1963 Kennedy said, "I approved the proclamation Fidel Castro made in the Sierra Maestra, when he justifiably called for justice and especially yearned to rid Cuba of corruption. I will go even further: to some extent it is as though Batista was the incarnation of a number of sins on the part of the United States. Now we will have to pay for those sins. In the matter of the Batista regime, I am in agreement with the first Cuban revolutionaries. That is perfectly clear." Such sentiments were anathema, shall we say treasonous, to the CIA and top generals.

These clear refusals to go to war with Cuba and his decision to engage in private, back-channel communications with Cold War enemies marked Kennedy as an enemy of the national security state. They were on a collision course. As Douglass and others have pointed out, every move Kennedy made was anti-war. This, Douglass argues, was because JFK, a war hero, had been deeply affected by the horror of war and was severely shaken by how close the world had come to destruction during the Cuban missile crisis. Throughout his life he had been touched by death and had come to appreciate the fragility of life. Once in the Presidency, Kennedy underwent a deep metanoia, a spiritual transformation, from Cold Warrior to peace maker. He came to see the generals who advised him as devoid of the tragic sense of life and as hell-bent on war. And he was well aware that his growing resistance to war had put him on a dangerous collision course with those generals and the CIA. On numerous occasions he spoke of the possibility of a military coup d'etat against him. On the night before his trip to Dallas, he told his wife, "But, Jackie, if somebody wants to shoot me from a window with a rifle, nobody can stop it, so why worry about it." And we know that nobody did try to stop it because they had planned it.

But who killed him?

Douglass presents a formidable amount of evidence, some old and some new, against the CIA and covert action agencies within the national security state, and does so in such a logical and persuasive way that any fair-minded reader cannot help but be taken aback—stunned, really. And he links this evidence directly to JFK's actions on behalf of peace.

He knows, however, that to truly convince he must break the "conspiracy of silence that would envelop our government, our media, our academic institutions, and virtually our entire society from November 22, 1963, to the present." This "unspeakable," this hypnotic "collective denial of the obvious," is sustained to this day by a mass-media whose repeated message is that the truth about such significant events is beyond our grasp, that we will have to drink the waters of uncertainty forever. As for those who don't, they are relegated to the status of conspiracy nuts.

Fear and uncertainty block a true appraisal of the assassination—that plus the dismissal that it no longer matters.

It matters. For we know that no president since JFK has dared to buck the military-intelligence-industrial complex. We know a Pax Americana has spread its tentacles across the globe with U.S. military in over 130 countries on 750 plus bases. We know that the amount of blood and money spent on wars and war preparations has risen astronomically.

There is a great deal we know but even more that we don't want to know, or at the very least, investigate.

If Lee Harvey Oswald was connected to the intelligence community, the FBI and the CIA, then we can logically conclude that he was not "a lone-nut" assassin. Douglass marshals a wealth of evidence to show how from the very start Oswald was moved around the globe like a pawn in a game, and when the game was done, the pawn was eliminated in the Dallas police headquarters. As he begins to trace Oswald's path, Douglass asks this question: "Why was Lee Harvey Oswald so tolerated and supported by the government he betrayed?" After serving as a U.S. Marine at the CIA's U-2 spy plane operating base in Japan with a Crypto clearance (higher than top secret, a fact suppressed by the Warren Commission), Oswald left the Marines and defected to the Soviet Union. After denouncing the U.S., working at a Soviet factory in Minsk, and taking a Russian wife—during which time Gary Powers' U-2 spy plane is shot down over the Soviet Union—he returned to the U.S. with a loan from the American Embassy in

Moscow, only to be met at the dock in Hoboken, New Jersey by a man, Spas T. Raikin, a prominent anti-communist with extensive intelligence connections, recommended by the State Department. He passed through immigration with no trouble, was not prosecuted, moved to Fort Worth, Texas where, at the suggestion of the Dallas CIA Domestic Contacts Service chief, he was met and befriended by George de Mohrenschildt, an anti-communist Russian, who was a CIA asset. De Mohrenschildt got him a job four days later at a graphic arts company that worked on maps for the U.S. Army Map Service related to U-2 spy missions over Cuba. Oswald was then shepherded around the Dallas area by de Mohrenschildt who, in 1977, on the day he revealed he had contacted Oswald for the CIA and was to meet with the House Select Committee on Assassinations' investigator Gaeton Fonzi, allegedly committed suicide. Oswald then moved to New Orleans in April 1963 where he got a job at the Reilly Coffee Company owned by CIA-affiliated William Reilly. The Reilly Coffee Company was located in close vicinity to the FBI, CIA, Secret Service, and Office of Naval Intelligence offices and a stone's throw from the office of Guy Bannister, *a former Special Agent in Charge of the FBI's Chicago Bureau*, who worked as a covert action coordinator for the intelligence services, supplying and training anti-Castro paramilitaries meant to ensnare Kennedy. Oswald then went to work with Bannister and the CIA paramilitaries.

From this time up until the assassination Oswald engaged in all sorts of contradictory activities, one day portraying himself as pro-Castro, the next day as anti-Castro, many of these theatrical performances being directed from Bannister's office. It was as though Oswald, on the orders of his puppet masters, was enacting multiple and antithetical roles in order to confound anyone intent on deciphering the purposes behind his actions and to set him up as a future "assassin." Douglass persuasively argues that Oswald "seems to have been working with both the CIA and FBI," as a provocateur for the former and an informant for the latter. Jim and Elsie Wilcott, who worked at the CIA Tokyo Station from 1960-64, in a 1978 interview with the *San Francisco Chronicle*, said,

"It was common knowledge in the Tokyo CIA station that Oswald worked for the agency."

When Oswald moved to New Orleans in April 1963, de Mohrenschildt exited the picture, having asked the CIA for and been indirectly given a $285,000 contract to do a geological survey for Haitian dictator "Papa Doc" Duvalier, which he never did, but for which he was paid. Ruth and Michael Paine then entered the picture on cue. She had been introduced to Oswald by de Mohrenschildt. In September 1963 Ruth Paine drove from her sister's house in Virginia to New Orleans to pick up Marina Oswald and bring her to her house in Dallas to live with her. Back in Dallas, Ruth Paine conveniently got Oswald a job in the Texas Book Depository where he began work on October 16, 1963. Ruth later was the Warren Commission's critically important witness against Oswald. Dulles questioned the Paines in front of it, studiously avoiding any revealing questions.

Douglass illuminatingly traces their intelligence connections. Thirty years after the assassination a document was declassified showing Ruth Paine's sister Sylvia worked for the CIA. Her father traveled throughout Latin America on an Agency for International Development (notorious for CIA front activities) contract and filed reports that went to the CIA. Her husband Michael's step-father, Arthur Young, was the inventor of the Bell helicopter and Michael's job there gave him a security clearance. Her mother was related to the Forbes family of Boston and her lifelong friend, Mary Bancroft, worked as a WW II spy with Allen Dulles and was his mistress.

From late September until November 22, various Oswalds are later reported to have simultaneously been seen from Mexico City to Dallas. Two Oswalds were arrested in the Texas Theatre, the real one taken out the front door and an impostor out the back. As Douglass says, "There were more Oswalds providing evidence against Lee Harvey Oswald than the Warren Report could use or even explain." Even J. Edgar Hoover knew that Oswald impostors were used, as he told LBJ concerning Oswald's alleged visit to the Soviet Embassy in Mexico City. He later called this CIA ploy, "the false story re Oswald's trip to Mexico . . . their (CIA's) double-dealing," something that he couldn't forget. It was apparent that a very intricate and deadly game was being played out at high levels in the shadows.

We know Oswald was blamed for the President's murder. But if one fairly follows the trail of the crime it becomes blatantly obvious that government forces were at work. Douglass adds layer upon layer of evidence to show how this had to be so. Oswald, the mafia, anti-Castro Cubans could not have withdrawn most of the security that day. The Sheriff Bill Decker withdrew all police protection. The Secret Service withdrew the police motorcycle escorts from beside the president's car where they had been the day before in Houston; took agents off the back of the car where they were normally stationed to obstruct gunfire. They approved the fateful, dogleg turn (on a dry run on November 18) where the car came almost to a halt, a clear security violation. The House Select Committee on Assassinations concluded this, not some conspiracy nut.

Who could have squelched the testimony of all the doctors and medical personnel who claimed the president had been shot from the front in his neck and head, testimony contradicting the official story? Who could have prosecuted and imprisoned Abraham Bolden, the first African-American Secret Service agent personally brought on to the White House detail by JFK, who warned that he feared the president was going to be assassinated? (Douglass interviewed Bolden seven times and his evidence on the aborted plot to kill JFK in Chicago on November 2—a story little known but extraordinary in its implications—is riveting.) The list of all the people who turned up dead, the evidence and events manipulated, the inquiry squelched, distorted, and twisted in an ex post facto cover-up clearly point to forces within the government, not rogue actors without institutional support.

The evidence for a conspiracy organized at the deepest levels of the intelligence apparatus is overwhelming. James Douglass presents it in such depth and so logically that only one hardened to the truth would not be deeply moved and affected by his book.

Douglass says it best:

The extent to which our national security state was systematically marshaled for the assassination of President John F. Kennedy remains incomprehensible to us. When we live in a system, we absorb and think in a system. We lack the independence needed to judge the system around us. Yet the evidence we have seen points toward our national security state, the systemic bubble in which we all live, as the source of Kennedy's murder and immediate cover-up.

Speaking to his friends Dave Powers and Ken O'Donnell about those who planned the Bay of Pigs invasion of Cuba, JFK said, "They couldn't believe that a new president like me wouldn't panic and try to save his own face. Well, they had me figured all wrong."

Soon we would learn, to our chagrin and his glory, that the president's younger brother, Senator Robert F. Kennedy, equally brave and unintimidated, would take a bullet to the back of his head in 1968 as he was headed to the presidency and the pursuit of his brother's killers. The same cowards struck again. They still run the country.

WHY I DON'T SPEAK OF 9/11 ANYMORE

Tuesday, September 11, 2001, was a non-teaching day for me. I was home when the phone rang at 9 A.M. It was my daughter, who was on a week's vacation with her future husband. "Turn on the TV," she said. "Why?" I asked. "Haven't you heard? A plane hit the World Trade Tower."

I turned the TV on and watched a plane crash into the Tower. I said, "They just showed a replay." She quickly corrected me, "No, that's another plane." And we talked as we watched in horror, learning that it was the South Tower this time. Sitting next to my daughter was my future son-in-law; he had not had a day off from work in a year. He had finally taken a week's vacation so they could go to Cape Cod. He worked on the 100th floor of the South Tower. By chance, he had escaped the death that claimed 176 of his co-workers.

That was my introduction to the attacks. Nineteen years have disappeared behind us, yet it seems like yesterday. And yet again, it seems like long, long ago.

Over the next few days, as the government and the media accused Osama bin Laden and 19 Arabs of being responsible for the attacks, I told a friend that what I was hearing wasn't believable; the official story was full of holes. It was a reaction that I couldn't fully explain, but it set me on a search for the truth. I proceeded in fits and starts, but by the fall of 2004, with the help of the extraordinary work of David Ray Griffin (see *How Bush and Cheney Ruined America and The World*) and other early skeptics, I could articulate the reasons for my initial intuition. I set about creating a college course on what had come to be called 9/11.

But I no longer refer to the events of that day by those numbers. Let me explain why.

By 2004 I was convinced that the U.S. government's claims (and *The 9/11 Commission Report*) were fictitious. They seemed so blatantly false that I concluded the attacks were a deep-state intelligence operation whose purpose was to initiate a national state of emergency to justify wars of aggression, which came to be known euphemistically as "the war on terror." The sophistication of the attacks, and the lack of any proffered evidence for the government's claims, suggested that a great deal of planning had been involved.

Yet I was chagrined and amazed by so many people's insouciant lack of interest in researching arguably the most important world event since the assassination of President Kennedy. I understood the various psychological dimensions of this denial, the fear, cognitive dissonance, etc., but I sensed something else as well. For so many people their minds seemed to have been "made up" from the start. I found that many young people were the exceptions, while most of their elders dared not question the official narrative. This included many prominent leftist critics of American foreign policy. Now that nearly two decades have elapsed, this seems truer than ever.

So with the promptings of people like Graeme MacQueen, Lance deHaven-Smith, T.H. Meyer, et al., I concluded that a process of linguistic mind-control was in place before, during, and after the attacks. As with all good propaganda, the language had to be insinuated over time and introduced through intermediaries. It had to seem "natural" and to flow out of events, not to precede them. And it had to be repeated over and over again.

In summary form, I will list the language I believe "made up the minds" of those who have refused to examine the government's claims about the September 11 attacks and the subsequent anthrax attacks.

Pearl Harbor. As pointed out by David Ray Griffin and others, this term was used in September 2000 in The Project for the New American Century's report, "Rebuilding America's Defenses" (p.51). Its neo-con authors argued that the U.S. wouldn't be able to attack Iraq, Afghanistan, etc. "absent some catastrophic event—like a new Pearl Harbor." Coincidentally or not, the film Pearl Harbor, made with Pentagon assistance and a massive budget, was released on May 25, 2001 and was a box office hit. It was in the theatres throughout the summer. The thought of the attack on Pearl Harbor (which was not a surprise to the Roosevelt government, but was presented as such) was in the air despite the fact that the 60th anniversary of that attack was not until December 7, 2001, a more likely release date. Once the September 11 attacks occurred, the Pearl Harbor comparison was "plucked out" of the social atmosphere and used innumerable times, beginning immediately. Even George W. Bush was widely reported to have had the time that night to allegedly use it in his diary. The examples of this comparison are manifold, but I am summarizing, so I will skip giving them. Any casual researcher can confirm this.

Homeland. This strange un-American term, another WW II word associated with another enemy—Nazi Germany—was also used many times by the neo-con authors of "Rebuilding America's Defenses." I doubt any average American had referred to this country by that term before. Of course it became the moniker for the Department of Homeland Security, marrying home with security to form a comforting name that simultaneously and unconsciously suggests a defense against Hitler-like evil coming from the outside. Not coincidentally, Hitler introduced it into the Nazi propaganda vernacular at the 1934 Nuremberg rally. Both usages conjured up images of a home besieged by alien forces intent on its destruction making preemptive action in order.

Ground Zero. This is a third WWII ("the good war") term first used at 11:55 A.M. on September 11 by Mark Walsh (aka "the Harley Guy" because he was wearing a Harley-Davidson tee shirt) in an interview on the street by a Fox News reporter, Rick Leventhal. Identified as a Fox free-lancer, Walsh also explained the Twin Towers collapse in a precise, well-rehearsed manner that would be the same illogical and anti-scientific explanation later given by the government: "mostly due to structural failure because the fire was too intense." Ground zero—a nuclear bomb-related term first used by U.S. scientists to refer to the spot where they exploded the first nuclear bomb in New Mexico in 1945—became another meme adopted by the media that suggested a nuclear attack had occurred or might in the future if the U.S. didn't act. The nuclear scare was raised again and again by George W. Bush and U.S. officials in the days and months following the attacks, although nuclear weapons were beside the point. But the conjoining of "nuclear" with "ground zero" served to raise the fear factor dramatically. Ironically, the project to develop the nuclear bomb was called the Manhattan Project and was headquartered at 270 Broadway, NYC, a few short blocks north of the World Trade Center.

The Unthinkable. This is another nuclear term whose usage as linguistic mind control and propaganda is analyzed by Graeme MacQueen in the penultimate chapter of his very important book, *The 2001 Anthrax Deception*. He notes the patterned use of this term before and after September 11, while saying "the pattern may not signify a grand plan.... It deserves investigation and contemplation." He then presents a convincing case that the use of this term couldn't be accidental. He notes how George W. Bush, in a major foreign policy speech on May 1, 2001, "gave informal public notice that the United States intended to withdraw unilaterally from the ABM Treaty"; Bush said the U.S. must be willing to "rethink the unthinkable." This was necessary because of terrorism and rogue states with "weapons of mass destruction." PNAC also argued that the U.S. should withdraw from the treaty. A signatory to the treaty could only withdraw after giving six months' notice and because of "extraordinary events" that "jeopardized its supreme interests." Once the September 11 attacks occurred, Bush rethought the unthinkable and officially gave formal notice on December 13 to withdraw the U.S. from the ABM Treaty. MacQueen specifies the many times different media used the term "unthinkable" in October 2001 in reference to the anthrax attacks. He explicates its usage in one of the anthrax letters—"The Unthinkabel" [sic]. He explains how the media that used the term so often were at the time unaware of its usage in the anthrax letter since that letter's content had not yet been revealed, and how the letter writer had mailed the letter before the media started using the word. He makes a rock-solid case showing the U.S. government's complicity in the anthrax attacks and therefore in the Sept 11 attacks. While calling the use of the term "unthinkable" in all its iterations "problematic," he writes, "The truth is that the employment of 'the unthinkable' in this letter, when weight is given both to the meaning of this term in U.S. strategic circles and to the other relevant uses of the term in 2001, points us in the direction of the U.S. military and intelligence communities." I am reminded of Orwell's point in 1984: "a heretical thought—that is, a thought diverging from the principles of Ingsoc—should be literally *unthinkable*, at least as far as thought is dependent on words." Thus the government and media's use of "unthinkable" becomes a classic case of "doublethink." The unthinkable is unthinkable.

9/11. This is the key usage that has reverberated down the years around which the others revolve. It is an anomalous numerical designation applied to an historical event, and obviously also is the emergency telephone number. Try to think of another numerical appellation for an important event in American history. The future editor of *The New York Times* and Iraq war promoter, Bill Keller, introduced this connection the following morning in a *NY Times* op-ed piece, "America's Emergency Line: 911." The linkage of the attacks to a permanent national emergency was thus subliminally introduced, as Keller mentioned Israel nine times and seven times compared the U.S. situation to that of Israel as a target for terrorists. His first sentence reads: "An Israeli response to America's aptly dated wake-up call might well be, 'Now you know.'" By referring to September 11 as 9/11, an endless national emergency became wedded to an endless war on terror aimed at preventing Hitler-like terrorists from obliterating us with nuclear weapons that could create another ground zero or holocaust. It is a term that pushes all the right buttons evoking unending social fear and anxiety. It is language as sorcery; it is propaganda at its best. Even well-respected critics of the U.S. government's explanation use the term that has become a fixture of public consciousness through endless repetition. As Condoleeza Rice would later put it as she connected Saddam Hussein to "9/11" and pushed for the Iraq war, "We don't want the smoking gun to become a mushroom cloud." All the ingredients for a linguistic mind-control smoothie had been blended.

I have concluded—and this is impossible to prove definitively at this time because of the nature of such propagandistic techniques—that the use of all these words/numbers is part of a highly sophisticated linguistic mind-control campaign waged to create a narrative that has lodged in the minds of hundreds of millions of people and is very hard to dislodge. That is why I don't speak of "9/11" anymore. I refer to those events as the attacks of September 11, 2001, which is a mouthful and not easily digested in the age of Twitter and texting. But I am not sure how to be more succinct or how to undo the damage.

Lance deHaven-Smith puts it well in *Conspiracy Theory in America*:

> The rapidity with which the new language of the war on terror appeared and took hold; the synergy between terms and their mutual connections to WW II nomenclatures; and above all the connections between many terms and the emergency motif of "9/11" and "9-1-1"—any one of these factors alone, but certainly all of them together—raise the possibility that work on this linguistic construct began long before 9/11 . . . . It turns out that elite political crime, even treason, may actually be official policy.

Needless to say, his use of the words "possibility" and "may" are in order when one sticks to strict empiricism. However, when one reads his full text, it is apparent to me that he considers these "coincidences" part of a conspiracy. I have also reached that conclusion. As Thoreau put in his underappreciated humorous way, "Some circumstantial evidence is very strong, as when you find a trout in the milk."

The evidence for linguistic mind control, while the subject of this essay, does not stand alone, of course. It underpins the actual attacks of September 11 and the subsequent anthrax attacks that are linked. The official explanations for these events by themselves do not stand up to elementary logic and are patently false, as proven by thousands of well-respected professional researchers from all walks of life—i.e. engineers, pilots, architects, and scholars from many disciplines. To paraphrase the prescient Vince Salandria, who said it long ago concerning the assassination of President Kennedy, the attacks of 2001 are "a false mystery concealing state crimes." If one objectively studies the 2001 attacks together with the language adopted to explain and preserve them in social memory, the "mystery" emerges from the realm of the unthinkable and becomes utterable. "There is no mystery." How to communicate this when the corporate mainstream media serve as the government's mockingbird (as in Operation Mockingbird), repeating and repeating and repeating the same narrative in the same language. That is the difficult task we are faced with, but there are signs today that breakthroughs are occurring.

Words have a power to enchant and mesmerize.

We need a new vocabulary to speak of these terrible things.

The Sexual Passion of Winston Smith

> "Christianity gave Eros poison to drink; he did not die of it, certainly, but degenerated to Vice."
>
> —**Frederick Nietzsche,** *Beyond Good and Evil*

> "Ours is essentially a tragic age, so we refuse to take it tragically. The cataclysm has happened, we are among the ruins, we start to build up new little habitats, to have new little hopes. It is rather hard work: there is now no smooth road into the future: but we go round, or scramble over the obstacles. We've got to live, no matter how many skies have fallen."
>
> —**D. H. Lawrence,** *Lady Chatterley's Lover*

> "The so-called consumer society and the politics of corporate capitalism have created a second nature of man which ties him libidinally and aggressively to the commodity form. The need for possessing, consuming, handling and constantly renewing gadgets, devices, instruments, engines, offered to and imposed upon the people, for using these wares even at the danger of one's own destruction, has become a 'biological' need."
>
> —**Herbert Marcuse,** *One Dimensional Man*

There is a vast literature analyzing the political prophecy of George Orwell's *Nineteen Eighty-Four*—Big Brother, double-speak, telescreens, crimestop, etc.—all applied to our current political situation. The language has become part of our popular lexicon, and as such, has become clichéd through overuse. Blithe, habitual use of language robs it of its power to crack open the safe that hides the realities of life.

There is no doubt that Orwell wrote a brilliant political warning about the methods of totalitarian control. But hidden at the heart of the book is another lesson lost on most readers and commentators. Rats, torture, and Newspeak resonate with people fixated on political repression, which is a major concern, of course. But so too is privacy and sexual passion in a country of group-think and group-do, where "Big Brother" poisons you in the crib and the entertainment culture then takes over to divorce intimacy from sexuality by selling it as another public commodity.

The United States is a pornographic society. By pornographic I do not just mean the omnipresent selling of exploitative sex through all media to titillate a voyeuristic public living in the unreality of screen "life" and screen sex through television, movies, and online obsessions. I mean a commodified consciousness, where everyone and everything is part of a prostitution ring in the deepest sense of pornography's meaning—for sale, bought. And consumed by getting, spending, and selling. Flicked into the net of Big Brother, whose job is to make sure everything fundamentally human and physical is debased and mediated, until people become consumers of the unreal and discouraged from direct experience. The natural world becomes an object to be conquered and used. Animals are produced in chemical factories to be slaughtered by the billions only to appear bloodless under plastic wrap in supermarket coolers. The human body disappears into hypnotic spectral images. One's sex becomes one's gender as the words are transmogrified and as one looks in the mirror of the looking-glass self and wonders how to identify the one looking back.

Streaming life from Netflix or Facebook becomes life the movie. The brilliant perverseness of the mediated reality of a screen society—what Guy Debord calls *The Society of the Spectacle*—is that as it distances people from fundamental reality, it promotes false reality through its screen fantasies. "Get away from it all and restore yourself at our spa in the rugged mountains where you can hike in pristine woods after yoga and a breakfast of locally sourced eggs and artisanally crafted bread." Such garbage would be funny if it weren't so effective. Debord writes:

> The spectacle is not a collection of images, but a social relation among people, mediated by images.... Where the real-world changes into simple images, the simple images become real beings and effective motivations of hypnotic behavior.

Thus two recent items in the news—sex with robots and marrying yourself—are not aberrations but logical extensions of a society where solipsism meets machine in the American dream.

As this happens, words and language become corrupted by the same forces that Orwell called Big Brother, whose job is total propaganda and social control. Just as physical reality now mimics screen reality and thus becomes chimerical, language, through which human beings uncover and articulate the truth of being, becomes more and more abstract. People don't die; they "pass on" or "pass away." Dying, like real sex, is too physical. Wars of aggression don't exist; they are "overseas contingency operations." Killing people with drones isn't killing; it's "neutralizing them." There are a "ton" of examples, but I am sure "you guys" don't need me to list any more.

Orwell called Big Brother's language Newspeak, and Hemingway preceded him when he so famously wrote in disgust in *A Farewell to Arms*, "I was always embarrassed by the words sacred, glorious, and sacrifice, and the expression in vain.... Abstract words such as glory, honor, courage, or hallow were obscene...." This destruction of language has been going on for a long time, but it's worth noting that from Hemingway's WW I through Orwell's WW II up until today's endless U.S. wars against Afghanistan, Iraq, Yemen, Syria, Libya, etc., there has been the parallel development of screen and media culture, beginning with silent movies through television and on to the total electronic media environment we now inhabit—the surround sound and image bubble of literal abstractions that inhabit us, mentally and physically. In such a society, to feel what you really feel and not what, in Hemingway's words, "you were supposed to feel, and had been taught to feel" has become extremely difficult.

Language, as the Greeks told us, should open up a clearing for the truth (Greek *aleitheia*, unhiddenness) to emerge so we can grasp the essence of life. And so it is ironically appropriate that Orwell's Winston Smith discovers such essence, not in analyzing Crimestop, his tormenter O'Brien, or Doublethink, but "in a natural clearing, a tiny grass knoll surrounded by tall saplings that shut it in completely" where he secretly meets a young woman who had passed him a note saying she loved him. Away from the prying eyes of Big Brother and his spies, amidst bluebells and a torrent of song from a thrush, they come together almost wordlessly. "Winston and Julia clung together, fascinated" as the thrush sang madly. "The music went on and on, minute after minute, with astonishing variations, never once repeating itself, almost as if the bird were deliberately showing off its virtuosity . . . . He stopped thinking and merely felt." Here the secret lovers affirm their humanity, the truth of sexual intimacy that is the enemy of all abstractions used by the powerful to control and manipulate normal people and to convince them to participate in killing others. "Almost as swiftly as he had imagined it, she had torn her clothes off, and when she flung them aside it was with that same magnificent gesture by which a whole civilization seemed to be annihilated." Reveling in love-making in a free space outside the Party's control, they felt they had triumphed.

But as we learn in *1984* and should learn in the USA today, "seemed" is the key word. Their triumph was temporary. For sexual passion reveals truths that need to be confirmed in the mind. In itself, sexual liberation can be easily manipulated, as it has been so effectively in the United States. "Repressive de-sublimation" Herbert Marcuse called it fifty years ago. You allow people to act out their sexual fantasies in commodified ways that can be controlled by the rulers, all the while ruling their minds and diverting potential political rebelliousness. Sex becomes part of the service economy where people service each other while serving their masters. Using pseudo-sex to sell them a way of life that traps them in an increasingly totalitarian social order that only seems free.

This has been accomplished primarily through screen culture and the concomitant confusion of sexual and gender identity. Perhaps you have noticed that over the past twenty-five years of growing social and political confusion, we have witnessed an exponential growth in "the electronic life," the use of psychotropic drugs, and sexual disorientation. This is no accident. Wars have become as constant as Eros—the god of love, life, joy, and motion—has been divorced from sex as a stimulus and response release of tension in a "stressed" society. Rollo May, the great American psychologist, grasped this:

> Indeed, we have set sex over against eros, used sex precisely to avoid the anxiety-creating involvements of eros.... We are in flight from eros and use sex as the vehicle for the flight.... Eros [which includes, but is not limited to, passionate sex] is the center of vitality of a culture—its heart and soul. And when release of tension takes the place of creative eros, the downfall of the civilization is assured.

Because Julia and Winston cannot permanently escape Oceania, but can only tryst, they succumb to Big Brother's mind control and betray each other. Their sexual affair can't save them. It is a moment of beauty and freedom in an impossible situation. Of course the hermetically sealed world of *1984* is not the United States. Orwell created a society in which escape was impossible. It is, after all, an admonitory novel—not the real world. Things are more subtle here; we still have some wiggle room—some— although the underlying truth is the same: the U.S. oligarchy, like "The Party," "seeks power entirely for its own sake" and "are not interested in the good of others," all rhetoric to the contrary. Our problem is that too many believe the rhetoric, and those who say they don't really do at the deepest level. Fly the flag and play the national anthem and their hearts are aflutter with hope. Recycle old bromides about the next election when your political enemies will be swept out of office and excitement builds as though you had met the love of your life and all was well with the world.

But an understanding of the history of public relations, advertising, propaganda, the CIA, the national security apparatus, technology, etc., makes it clear that such hope is baseless. For the propaganda in this country has penetrated far deeper than anyone can imagine, and it has primarily done this through advanced technology and the religion of technique—machines as pure abstractions—that has poisoned not just our minds, but the deepest wellsprings of the body's truths and the erotic imagination that links us in love to all life on earth.

In "Defence of Poetry," Percy Bysshe Shelley writes:

> The great secret of morals is love; or a going out of our nature, and an identification of ourselves with the beautiful which exists in thought, action, or person, not our own. A man, to be greatly good, must imagine intensely and comprehensively; he must put himself in the place of another and of many others; the pains and pleasure of his species must become his own. The great instrument of moral good is the imagination.

We are now faced with the question: Can we escape the forces of propaganda and mind control that run so very deep into American life? If so, how? Let's imagine a way out.

Orwell makes it very clear that language is the key to mind control, as he delineates how Newspeak works. I think he is right. And mind control also means the control of our bodies, Eros, our sex, our physical connections to all living beings and nature. Today the U.S. is reaching the point where "Oldspeak"—Standard English—has been replaced by Newspeak, and just "fragments of the literature of the past" survive here and there. This is true for the schooled and unschooled. In fact, those more trapped by the instrumental logic, disembodied data, and word games of the power elite are those who have gone through the most schooling, the indoctrination offered by the so-called "elite" universities. I suspect that more working-class and poor people still retain some sense of the old language and the fundamental meaning of words, since it is with their sweat and blood that they "earn their living."

Many of the highly schooled are children of the power elite or those groomed to serve them, who are invited to join in living the life of power and privilege if they swallow their consciences and deaden their imaginations to the suffering their "life-styles" and ideological choices inflict on the rest of the world. In this world of *The New York Times*, Harvard, *The New Yorker*, Martha's Vineyard, The *Washington Post*, Wall St., Goldman Sachs, the boardrooms of the ruling corporations, all the corporate media, etc., language has become debased beyond recognition. Here, as Orwell said of Newspeak, "a heretical thought . . . should be literally unthinkable, at least as far as thought is dependent on words. Its vocabulary was so constructed as to give exact and often very subtle expression to every meaning that a Party member could properly wish to express." The intelligently orthodox, he adds, must master the art of "doublethink" wherein they hold two contradictory ideas in their minds simultaneously, while accepting both of them. This is the key trick of logic and language that allows the power elites and their lackeys in the U.S. today to master the art of self-deception and feel good about themselves as they plunder the world. In this "Party" world, the demonization, degradation, and killing of others is an abstraction; their lives are spectral. Orwell describes doublethink this way:

> To tell deliberate lies while genuinely believing in them, to forget any fact that has become inconvenient, and then, when it becomes necessary again, to draw it back from oblivion for just so long as it is needed, to deny the existence of objective reality and all the while to take account of the reality one denies—all this is indispensably necessary. Even in using the word doublethink it is necessary to exercise doublethink. For by using the word one admits one is tampering with reality; by a fresh act of doublethink one erases this knowledge; and so on indefinitely, with the lie always one leap ahead of the truth.

It may sound silly to say, but language, as its etymology tells us, begins with the tongue (Latin, lingua). And the tongue is a bell, tolling out its meaning. Indeed, all language springs from the body—is body language. And when language becomes abstract and devoid of blood, it becomes etiolated and unable to convey the truth that is the mystical body of the world. It becomes a viper's tongue, dividing the "good" people from the "bad" so the good can eliminate the bad who have become abstractions.

When Winston Smith and Julia hid in the arbor and for once felt free and alive as they made passionate love—despite its transitoriness—Orwell was suggesting something that his dystopian novel denies is possible: that we can escape our own *1984* in 2020 by returning to fundamentals. Whitman told us that if anything is sacred it is the human body, and he sang "the body electric." This is the task of artists: to sing the words that tell the truth the propagandists try to deny.

James Joyce writes in *The Portrait of the Artist as a Young Man:*

> Welcome, oh life! I go to encounter for the millionth time the reality of experience and to forge in the smithy of my soul the uncreated conscience of my race.

Perhaps we should add: in the smithy of our souls and bodies. His fellow Irishman, William Butler Yeats, brings us down to earth with the words:

> *Now that my ladder's gone*
> *I must lie down where all the ladders start*
> *In the foul rag and bone shop of the heart.*

And Joyce has Molly Bloom, as she lies in bed awaiting Leopold to return to her, end *Ulysses* with the passionate words:
"Yes I said yes I will Yes."

Gina Haspel and Pinocchio from Rome

Being in Rome, Italy and thinking of Gina Haspel, the CIA nominee and admitted torturer who says her "moral conscience" has changed after the fact, seems most fitting. Wherever you go in central Rome, you seem to hear the screams and smell the blood of those tortured and killed by the Roman Empire and those who ably followed in their stead. And you can see the crumbled stones and the pathetic architectural remains of those who thought they had triumphed. Their triumph turned to dust, despite their belated *mea culpas*, if and when these ever came, they always rang as hollow as those of Gina Haspel, Lt. William Calley, and Adolph Eichmann who claimed that they were only doing their jobs and following orders.

Throughout Rome there are hawkers dangling Pinocchio trinkets in your face, constant reminders of the cost of lying. Or perhaps more aptly, the fame that ensues from lying followed by a childish semi-apology, even when it's as obvious as the nose on your face that you are lying still. So in the Senate Intelligence Committee hearing Haspel was asked by Senator Mark Warner, D-VA., the kind of question that allows a respondent to answer in a deceptive way that means nothing, but seems profoundly sincere. Warner asked:

> If this president asked you to do something that you find morally objectionable, even if there is an [Office of Legal Counsel] opinion, what will you do? Will you carry out that order or not?

To which Haspel replied:

> Senator, my moral conscience is strong. I would not allow the CIA to carry out any activity that I thought was immoral—even if it was technically legal. I would absolutely not permit it.

From all reports, neither Warner's nor Haspel's noses grew longer, but perhaps such deceptive phrasing slyly falls beyond the parameters of Pinocchio's sins and the Blue Fairy's sanctions.

So the woman who oversaw detainee torture at a CIA "black site" in Thailand tells us she has a strong moral conscience, but she doesn't tell us what that conscience considers intrinsically evil, if anything. Nor what that "strong" moral conscience considers moral or immoral in any way, just that the "CIA must undertake activities that are consistent with American values," whatever they might be. And if she were ordered to carry out an action—let's say kill a foreign agent or assassinate a political leader—that was technically illegal but accorded with her strong moral conscience, would she do so? Don't ask—she wasn't. Even Pinocchio would get confused by this legerdemain.

The good Senator, adept at playing deceptive verbal games as befits his stature, is happy to have his non-question answered with a non-answer, leaving both he and Haspel content. Good question, good answer, good conscience. Nothing bad about that. Then Warner goes and votes for Haspel, whom he says is "among the most experienced people to be nominated" to head the CIA, and Haspel says she thinks torture—"enhanced interrogation"—doesn't work anyway. Practicality wins the day.

But here in Rome in May 2018, so many regular people are not so practical. They seem to relish life, not as a task to accomplish, but as a pleasure to enjoy. Despite the history that surrounds them, and the dismal political economy that weighs heavy on their country, they seem less anxious and terrorized than Americans. Of course this may be a visitor's myopic vision, and when seen clearly, Romans might be as stressed as Americans. But I doubt it. For this visiting American, it is hard to dismiss thoughts about the disgraceful charade happening back in Washington D.C. Thinking here in Rome of the Haspel vote, I am reminded of the "ratlines" organized by ex-CIA Director Allen Dulles and long-time Chief of Counterintelligence James Jesus Angleton. These were escape routes for Nazi and fascist killers and torturers, so many of whom were brought to the United States and other countries after World War II through Italy to help the newly formed CIA torture the truth out of detainees and assassinate opponents. Our post September 11 torture is nothing new.

Is this what Haspel meant by "American values"? Many victims would attest to that.

In an old city like Rome one tends to think old thoughts: that the history of torture, human treachery, lying, and violence is long; that secular and religious fanatics are nothing new; and that empires rise and fall and everyone dies, even those who build monuments to their own "glorious" deeds.

But if one wanders around with no itinerary, one also encounters beautiful people and small pockets of faith, love, and devotion. One encounters magnificent art that embodies the heights to which the human imagination can aspire. One realizes that despite the gory history of the human race, the killers and torturers, humans have and do rise above their worst inclinations and do the work of angels.

As we were sitting at a café in the Piazza della Rotonda, my wife said to me, "You have your back to the Pantheon." It was true. Those monumental gods bored me. My glass of vino rosso whirled my mind to better things. Lighter. Not stone idolatry. Not empires, except their death. Not stone gods, nor inquisitors or black sites or hooded torturers with PhDs from Harvard. Not palaces for Renaissance princes or Central Intelligence agents, corrupt bastards of different times and places. Not the Wall Street/CIA nexus. Not dastardly gross, stupid, rich Trump with his orange hair and phallic towers, nor his doppelganger, Berlusconi, here in Italy.

Gina Haspel seemed so far away—yet near. I kept thinking of all those U.S. Senators who would go on to vote for this torturer to lead the CIA. Will they say they were only doing their jobs and following orders? Do they think of themselves as civilized?

I then looked up as the bird took flight, and saw a cross silhouetted against the blue sky. I wondered.

Will these torturers and war criminals ever face justice?

Without Poetry We are Dead: With It We Die Living

Most Americans dislike poetry, or at least are indifferent to it. That is probably an understatement. We live in an age of prose, of journalese, and advertising jingles. Poetry, the most directly indirect, mysterious, condensed, and passionate form of communication, is about as American as socialism or not shopping. Unlike television, texting, or scrolling the internet, it demands concentration; that alone makes it suspect. Add silent, calm surroundings and a contemplative mind, and you can forget it, which is what most people do. Silence, like so much else in the present world, including human beings, is on the endangered species list. Another rare bird—let's call it the holy spirit of true thought—is slowly disappearing from our midst.

How, for example, could a noisy mind hovering in a technological jangling begin to grasp these lines from Federico Garcia Lorca's poem "New York"?

> *The mountains exist. I know that*
> *And the lenses ground for wisdom.*
> *I know that. But I have not come to see the sky.*
> *I have come to see the stormy blood,*
> *the blood that sweeps the machines on to the*
>   *waterfalls,*
> *and the spirit on to the cobra's tongue.*

Can you imagine telling someone in the U.S. what you did for a living was write poems (as if this were possible)? They'd look at you as if you were from outer space, some weirdo, probably a secret Russian agent, out to corrupt the youth of the land.

Long dead poets are okay in school, of course. They're safe, since what they have to say is assumed to have no direct bearing on the present. They call their work "classics," and force you to read and dissect a few before you can pass an English course. They sterilize them and create immunity to their power in students. As one of our great poets and man of letters, Kenneth Rexroth, has written, "The entire educational system is in a conspiracy to make poetry as unpalatable as possible . . . . everybody is out to depoetize the youth of the land." In this regard, the schools do a terrific job. Most students graduate with the firm intent never to open another book of poems, and they don't.

There are minor exceptions to this dismal picture of schools and poetry. There is a national program in the U.S. called Poetry Out Loud that introduces a small percentage of high school students to poetry. It is a program that individual schools can adopt and takes place a few weeks every fall. Being voluntary, it depends on the motivation of the country's best English teachers (my wife being one) and enlightened administrators for support. Highly motivated students choose from an extensive list of poems. They must memorize their selections, and then recite them before their respective schools. Their recitations must convey the inner meaning of the poem, and their performances are judged on that and stage presence. The winners advance from schools to counties to states to national winners. One hopes that many of these students carry a love of poetry into adult life, although I would add a few caveats as it concerns competition, performance, and winning. Great poets, while not immune to those twin vices, are primarily devoted to art as a vocation. They compose in the spirit of inspiration. Nevertheless, Poetry Out Loud is a positive development.

But the vast majority of students are not part of this program, which is a shame. From their meagre education about poetry's importance to their lives, perhaps this would be the only echo they would remember: "Two roads diverged in a yellow wood, and I took the one to the mall."

Poetry, they've learned, has no bearing on life; it's impractical, too meditative, nor will it get you a job. These condemnations follow them to college, and their parents usually reinforce them. Poetry is not one of the highly funded and promoted STEM (Science, Technology, Engineering, and Mathematics) disciplines that will supposedly lead to the gravy train. Students' minds and emotions, following the corporatization of schooling, have been digitized. Their faces often reflect the affectless nature of the little machines they are constantly fingering and assiduously searching, as if for secret messages. They meditate on Facebook as nuns do on their rosary beads and a few poetry lovers still do on lines from Rilke:

> *Sometimes a man stands up during supper*
> *and walks outdoors, and keeps on walking,*
> *because of a church that stands somewhere in the*
>   *East.*

In this the young are like their poetry-avoiding parents and teachers who have not walked out but have walked into a technological labyrinth that devours their spirits—consumes them as they consume. It is no wonder that a company has been formed to study and report to the corporations on their emotions. Affectiva (no, not a yogurt) describes its mission as follows:

> Our mission is to bring emotional intelligence to the digital world. When we digitize emotion it can enrich our technology, for work, play and life . . . . Spun out of MIT Media Lab, our company is leading the effort to emotion-enable technology. From understanding how consumers engage with digital content, to enabling developers to add emotion sensing and analytics technology to their own apps and digital experiences.

Reading faces, not poetry, is their business. They measure and analyze facial expressions of emotion with the assistance of The National Science Foundation. They have no clue that the living poems that are persons need to be pondered intimately to be known; that behind every expression is a meaning. Their manipulative stupidity is so great, and their clients' faith in technology so touching, that they both assume the outer is the inner, that faces tell the story of the spirit's truth, the living meaning of a person's heart. They read the face on the book's cover—as with Facebook—for its contents. They seem ignorant of Shakespeare or the actor's art. They are killers of the spirit and typify the anti-poetic ethos that reigns in the U.S.

Compare the technological face-readers' manipulations with the truth of these lines from Galway Kinnell's poem, "The Fundamental Project of Technology":

> *To de-animalize human mentality, to purge it of*
>   *obsolete,*
> *evolutionary characteristics, in particular of*
>   *death,*
> *which foreknowledge terrorizes the content of*
>   *skulls with,*
> *is the fundamental project of technology;*

Here in a few lines a poet tells us why Americans are addicted to technology and where this is leading—nuclear annihilation. He reveals the death fear at the heart of the technological obsession and its self-defeating consequences. He tells a truth few want to hear, and in doing so fulfills the age-old prophetic function of art—poetry, drama, painting, etc. Acting as "antennae of the race," in Ezra Pound's words, genuine artists grasp by their art the unconscious conflicts most prefer to avoid at their peril. In a country addicted to ingesting technologically produced mind-altering drugs and to being consumed by machines, it is no wonder that poetry is considered irrelevant.

In many other countries, poets are held in high esteem and their poems affect people's lives. People know their national poets' work by heart. The Russians know Pushkin; the Irish can recite Yeats; the Chileans revere Neruda. They find hope and joy and the passion to resist oppression in their verses. Their poets take them to places where passionate love of the world can be awakened in their hearts and minds. In the U. S. they are ignored, at best. Why bother with them is the unspoken assumption. What good is poetry? We have our machines.

And if by some small chance Americans do bother, they find that a great deal of what passes for poetry is worthless drivel churned out according to formula by "creative writing" students and their mentors who have carved out a safe place for themselves in American colleges. Behind a façade of seeming profundity and studied ambiguity hides a nihilism that can best be described as a bad joke. Much of this academic poetry is just plain trivial, devoid of ideas and any lived encounter with world events that so deeply influence our lives. So much of it is solipsistic in the extreme—"selfies" in verse written from within a bubble.

I will elide Hallmark poetry at the risk of ridicule.

There are, however, many profound and wonderful contemporary poets, and it is a shame they are not read. They work in the shadows. They are not household names as in the past when literature meant something to Americans and they weren't despondently depressed and drugged into a zombie-like passivity. Perhaps this is because, as the philosopher/psychologist Rollo May puts it, "The poet's way is the opposite to the opaque, placid life. In authentic poetry we find a confrontation which does not involve repression nor covering up nor sacrifice of passion in order to avoid despair, nor any of the other ways most of us use to avoid direct acknowledgment of our destiny."

In an age of constant death and war and smiling killers sitting in the White House, who seeks out today's Kenneth Rexroth? "Thou Shalt Not Kill" was written in the "placid" 1950s. A few lines follow:

> *You,*
> *The hyena with the polished face and bow tie,*
> *In the office of a billion dollar*
> *Corporation devoted to service;*
> *The vulture dripping with carrion,*
> *. . .*

> *You, the finger man of behemoth,*
> *The murderer of the young men.*

The work of our best poets confronts us with our deepest anxieties and the questions that hover over our lives like a held breath. Since the late 19th century, our finest poets and thinkers have devoted themselves to the Herculean task of undercutting the false distinction between thought and emotion (passion being a more inclusive word) that has been a mainstay, not only of rationalism and romanticism, but of the way we live. This invalid distinction goes back to Plato, who wanted poetry banned because he said it was imitative and did not possess ideas, as philosophy did. He said poetry was irrationally emotional and dealt in illusions.

This critique of poetry is paralleled at the individual level by the saying, "I know that intellectually, but emotionally . . ."—as if emotions were irrational and seize one like a *worry* dog seizes a duck shot by a hunter and strangles it to death with its teeth (Middle English *wirien* [c. 1300], "to slay, kill or injure by biting and shaking the throat"). This belief regards people as becoming victims of their emotions, and victims of poetry and the arts that are assumed to be devoid of ideas. This schizoid attitude lies at the heart of issues of faith and responsibility that plague our times, and it is against this ongoing myth that the most astute poets aim their art.

This effort is linked to the increasingly widespread disbelief in the reality of the objective world and the growing acceptance of the idea from the sociology of knowledge of the "social construction of reality" (even if one never heard of the term), an idea co-terminus with the movement from modern to "postmodern society" and the development of sophisticated technologies of mind control. It has led to the devaluation of our senses, our divorce from the reality of the natural world, and the diminution of direct personal experience. While understanding how powerful elites manipulate "reality" perception can lead to liberating truth, it has primarily led to widespread skepticism and confusion as technology has grown exponentially more sophisticated and the modern corporate state's propaganda machines have laced it with lies and deceptions in the service of empire. When people believe that "everything is relative" and socially constructed, the assumption that there are no facts or truths seeps into public consciousness and corrupts people's sense of reality at the deepest level. It is soul murder. Of course, that "everything is relative" is an absolute statement that contradicts itself is usually lost on true believers. Or is it true doubters?

Modern propaganda is reality construction. People like Dick Cheney and his innumerable ilk throughout the U.S. government bluntly crow that while others may report the facts, they create them—they create reality and what people think is reality. At this point, it's impossible to even find out who actually said this highly memorable quote, "We're an empire now, and when we act, we create our own reality. And while you're studying that reality—judiciously as you will—we'll act again, creating other new realities, which you can study too, and that's how things will sort out." Nonetheless, the stenographers in the mainstream corporate media continue to report this created reality that most distracted, hypnotized, and ignorant Americans take for reality.

So what at first glance may seem a small issue of concern only to poets and assorted eggheads, is actually everyone's. Against a steady devaluation of the created world—poetry stands opposed. The poet's fight is against the heightened emphasis on pure form over content, as if the world existed as a palette for one's inward paintings, a recording of precious images, stylistic performances, or fake news.

I am not arguing that poetry and all the arts should be didactic or political tracts. Far from it.

No Theory

No theory will stand up to a chicken's guts
being cleaned out, a hand rammed up
to pull out the wriggling entrails,
the green bile and the bloody liver;
no theory that does not grow sick
at the odor escaping.

—David Ignatow

Poetry is the search for truth. It marries outer to inner. It probes reality with words. It suggests, states, intimates, inviting the reader to raid what was previously unspeakable. This exploration is composed of ideas, images, and words arranged in ways that engender powerful emotions and thoughts. Like life, a poem swims in mystery. Sometimes it carries a tune that moves the words, and the reader is moved in return. Sometimes it is out of tune to jar the reader out of a life of complacency where no questions are asked, no disruptions faced. True poetry startles. It inspires. It enlivens.

It is a distillation of the human spirit, as essential as bread. It is composed of a few simple ingredients, as is bread. They are: the real, actually existing, outside world, and us; the outside world that we are in and that is in us, and our emotional thoughts about our condition. Flour, water, and yeast. The bread rises, the poem forms. They are good or bad, depending on taste. They nourish or don't. But we cannot live without them. Thomas McGrath writes:

> *On the Christmaswhite plains of the floured and*
> *flowering kitchen table*
> *The holy loaves of bread are slowly being born:*
> *Rising like low hills in the steepled pastures of*
> *light-*
> *Lifting the prairie farmhouse afternoon on their*
> *arching backs.*

While academic hucksters churn out reams of solipsistic verse of hallucination and artifice, true poets passionately address questions of value and ultimate concern, of life and death, of meaning or meaninglessness, of truth and lies.

In a screen and selfie culture, these matters are irrelevant. In a robotized world, technology is king.

Great poets say otherwise.

If such poetry needs a defense, let me leave the final words to Caroline Forché, an authentic poet if there ever were one. The following is from her poem "Ourselves or Nothing" and cuts to the heart of the matter.

There is a cyclone fence between
Ourselves and the slaughter and behind it
We hover in a calm protected world like
Netted fish, exactly like netted fish.
It is either the beginning or the end
Of the world, and the choice is ourselves or
   nothing.

AMERICAN VALUES: LESSONS I LEARNED FROM MY FAMILY

When a book as fascinating, truthful, beautifully written, and politically significant as *American Values: Lessons I Learned from My Family,* written by a very well-known author by the name of Robert F. Kennedy, Jr. and published by a prominent publisher (HarperCollins), is boycotted by mainstream book reviewers, you know it is an important book and has touched a nerve that the corporate mainstream media wish to anesthetize by eschewal.

The Kennedy name attracts the mainstream media only when they can sensationalize something "scandalous"—preferably sexual or drug related—whether false or true, or merely innocuous that can lend credence to the myth that the Kennedys are lightweight, wealthy celebrities descended from Irish mobsters. This has been going on since the 1960s with the lies and cover-ups of the assassinations of President Kennedy and his brother Robert, propaganda that continues to the present day, always under the aegis of the CIA-created phrase "conspiracy theory." A thinking person might just get the idea that the media are in league with the CIA to bury the Kennedys.

Such disinformation has been promulgated by many sources, prominent among them from the start in the 1960s was the CIA's Sam Halpern, a former Havana bureau chief for *The New York Times,* who was CIA Director Richard Helms's deputy and the key source for Seymour Hersh's Kennedy hatchet job, *The Dark Side of Camelot,* who began spreading lies about the Kennedys that have become ingrained in the minds of leftists, liberals, centrists, and conservatives to this very day. Fifty years later, after decades of reiteration by the CIA's Wurlitzer machine (the name given by the CIA's Frank Wisner to the CIA's penetration and control of the mass media, Operation Mockingbird), Halpern's lies have taken on mythic proportions. Among them: that Joseph. P. Kennedy, the patriarch, was a bootlegger and Nazi lover; that he was Mafia connected and fixed the 1960 election with Chicago mobster Sam Giancana; and that JFK and RFK knew of and approved the CIA plots to assassinate Fidel Castro.

Of course, whenever a writer extolls the Kennedy name and legacy, he is expected to add the caveat that the Kennedys, especially JFK and RFK, were no saints. Lacking this special talent to determine sainthood or its lack, I will defer to those who feel compelled to temper their praise with a commonplace slander. Let me say at the outset that I greatly admire President John Kennedy and his brother, Robert, as very courageous men who both died in a war to steer this country away from the nefarious path of war-making and deep-state control that it has followed with a vengeance since their murders.

And I admire Robert F. Kennedy, Jr. for writing this compelling book that is a tour de force on many levels.

Part memoir, part family history, part astute political analysis, and part-confessional, it is in turns delightful, sad, funny, fierce, and frightening in its implications. From its opening sentence—"From my youngest days I always had the feeling that we were all involved in some great crusade, that the world was a battleground for good and evil, and that our lives would be consumed in the conflict."—to its last—"'Kennedys never give up,' she [Ethel Kennedy] chided us. 'We have to die with our boots on!'"—the book is imbued with the spirit of the eloquent, romantic Irish-Catholic rebels whose fighting spirit and jaunty demeanor the Kennedy family has exemplified. RFK, Jr. tells his tales in words that honor that literary and spiritual tradition.

So what is it about this book that has caused the mainstream press to avoid reviewing it?

Might it be the opening chapter devoted to his portrait of his grandfather, Joseph P. Kennedy, who comes across as a tender and doting grandpa, who created an idyllic world for his children and grandchildren at "The Big House" on Cape Cod? We see Grandpa

Joe taking the whole brood of Kennedys, including his three famous political sons, for a ride on his cabin cruiser, the *Marlin*, and JFK (Uncle Jack) singing "The Wearing of the Green" and, together with his good friend, Dave Powers, teaching the kids to whistle "The Boys of Wexford" (Wexford being the Kennedy's ancestral home), an Irish rebel tune, all of whose words John Kennedy knew by heart:

> *We are the boys of Wexford*
> *Who fought with heart and hand*
> *To burst in twain*
> *The galling chain*
> *And free our native land.*

We see Joseph P. Kennedy sitting on the great white porch, holding hands with his wife Rose Kennedy, as the kids played touch football on the grass beyond. We read that "Grandpa wanted his children's minds unshackled by ideology" and that his "overarching purpose was to engender in his children a social conscience" and use their money and advantages to make America and the world a better place. We learn, according to Joe's son, Senator Robert Kennedy, that he loved all of them deeply, "not love as it is described with such facility in popular magazines, but the kind of love that is affection and respect, order, encouragement and support." We hear him staunchly defended from the political criticisms that he was a ruthless, uncaring, and political nut-case who would do anything to advance his political and business careers. In short, he is presented very differently here from the popular understanding of him as a malign force and a ruthless bastard.

Portraying his grandfather as a good and loving man may be one minor reason that Robert Jr.'s book is being ignored.

No doubt it is not because of the picture he paints of his paternal grandmother, Rose Kennedy, who comes across similarly to her husband as a powerful presence and as a devoted mother and grandmother who expected much from her children and grandchildren but gave much in return. Robert Jr. writes that "Grandpa and Grandma were products of an alienated Irish generation that kept itself intact through rigid tribalism embodied in the rituals and mystical cosmologies of medieval Catholicism," but that both believed the Church should be a champion of the poor as Christ taught. The glowing portrait of Grandmother Rose could not be the reason the book has not been reviewed.

Nor can the chapter on Ethel Kennedy's family, the Skakels, be the reason. It is a fascinating peek into certain aspects of Ethel's character—the daring, outrageous, fun-loving, and wild side—from her upbringing in a wild and crazy family, together with the Kennedys one of the richest Catholic families in the U.S. in days past. But there their similarities end. The Skakels were conservative Republicans in the oil, coal, and extraction business, who "reveled in immodest consumption," were huge into guns and "more primitive weaponry like bows, knives, throwing spears and harpoons," and "pretty much captured shot, stabbed, hooked, or speared anything that moved, including each other." The Skakel men worked as informers for the CIA wherever their businesses took them around the world and they worked very hard to sabotage JFK's run for the presidency. Ethel's brother George was a creepy and crazy wild man. Once Ethel met RFK, she switched political sides for good, embracing the Kennedys' liberal Democratic ethos.

A vignette of Lemoyne Billings, JFK's dear friend, who after RFK's assassination took Robert Jr. under his wing, can't be the reason. It too is a loving portrait of the man RFK Jr. says was "perhaps the most important influence in my life" and also the most fun. In his turn Billings said that JFK was the most fun person he had ever met. They referred to each other as Johnny and Billy and both were expelled from Choate for hijinks. But such stories about Lem, JFK, and RFK Jr.'s wayward youth should have attracted, not repelled, the mainstream press's book reviewers.

Similarly, the chapter about Robert Jr.'s early bad behavior, his drug use, and his conflicted relationship with his mother should have been fuel for the Kennedy haters. "I seem to have been at odds with my mother since birth," he writes. "My mere presence seemed to agitate her." Mother and son were at war for decades, and his father's murder sent him on a long downward spiral into self-medicating that inflamed their relationship. Moving from school to school and keeping away from home as much as possible, his "homecomings were like the arrival of a squall. With me around to provoke her, my mother didn't stay angry very long—she went straight to rage." His victory over drugs through Twelve Step meetings and his reconciliation with his mother are also the stuff that the mainstream press revels in, yet they ignored the book.

The parts about his relationship with his father, his father's short but electrifying presidential campaign in 1968, his death, and funeral are deeply moving and evocative. Deep sadness and lost hope accompanies the reader as one revisits RFK's funeral and the tear-filled eulogy given by his brother Ted, then the long, slow train ride bearing the body from New York to Washington, D.C. as massive crowds lined the tracks, weeping and waving farewell. As was Robert, Jr., now a 66-year-old-man, but then a 14-year-old-boy, named after his look-alike father, the father who supported and encouraged him despite his difficulties in school, the father who took the son on all kinds of outdoor adventures—sailing, white water canoeing, mountain climbing—always reminding him to "always do what you are afraid to do." This, the son understood to be "boot camp for the ultimate virtue—moral courage. Despite his high regard for physical bravery, my father told us that moral courage is the rarer and more valuable commodity." Such compelling, heartfelt writing, with not a word of speculation about who might have killed his father, is another reason why the mainstream press would have no problem reviewing this book.

But it is the heart of this book that has the reviewers avoiding it like the plague, perhaps a plague introduced by a little mockingbird.

American Values revolves around the long war between the Kennedys and the CIA that resulted in the deaths of JFK and RFK. All the other chapters, while very interesting personal and family history, pale in importance.

No member of the Kennedy family since JFK or RFK has dared to say what RFK, Jr. does in this book. He indicts the CIA.

While some news outlets have mentioned the book in passing because of its assertion of what has been known for a long time to historically aware people—that RFK immediately suspected that the CIA was involved in the assassination of JFK—Robert Jr.'s writing on the war between the CIA and his Uncle Jack and father is so true and so carefully based on the best scholarship (see *Brothers* and *The Devils Chessboard* by David Talbot, and *JFK and The Unspeakable* by James W. Douglass, among many others) and family records that the picture he paints fiercely indicts the CIA in multiple ways while also indicting the mass media that have been its mouthpieces. These sections of the book are masterful lessons in understanding the history and machinations of "The Agency" that the superb writer and researcher, Douglas Valentine, refers to as "organized crime"—*The CIA as Organized Crime*.

A careful reading of RFK Jr.'s critical history leads to the conclusion that the CIA and the Mafia are not two separate murderers' rows, but one organization that has corrupted the country at the deepest levels and is, as Robert, Jr. quotes his father—"a dark force infiltrating American politics and business, unseen by the public, and out of reach of democracy and the justice system"—posing "a greater threat to our country than any foreign enemy." The CIA's covert operations branch has grown so powerful that it feels free to murder its opponents at home and abroad and make sure "splendid little wars" are continually waged around the globe for the interests of its patrons. As Robert Jr. puts it, "A permanent state of war abroad and a national security surveillance state at home are in the institutional self-interest of the CIA's clandestine services."

No Kennedy has dared speak like this since Senator Robert Kennedy last did so—but privately—and paid the price. His son tells us:

> Days before his murder, as my father pulled ahead in the California polls, he began considering how he would govern the country. According to his aide Fred Dutton, his concerns often revolved around the very question that his brother asked at the outset of his presidency,

"What are we going to do about the CIA?" Days before the California primary, seated next to journalist Pete Hamill on his campaign plane, my father mused aloud about his options. "I have to decide whether to eliminate the operations arm of the Agency or what the hell to do with it," he told Hamill. "We can't have those cowboys wandering around and shooting people and doing all those unauthorized things."

Then Robert Kennedy was shot dead.

For whatever their reasons, for fifty plus years the Kennedy family has kept silent on these matters, including the death of JFK, Jr. in 1999. Now Senator Robert Kennedy's namesake has picked up his father's mantle and dared to tell truths that take courage to utter. By excoriating the secret forces that seized power, first with the murder of his Uncle Jack when he was a child, and then his father, he has exhibited great moral courage and made great enemies who wish to ignore his words as if they were never written. But they have been. They sit between the covers of this outstanding and important book, a book written with wit and eloquence, a book that should be read by any American who wants to know what has happened to their country.

There is a telling anecdote that took place in the years following JFK's assassination when RFK was haunted by his death. It says so much about Senator Robert Kennedy and now his son, a son who, in many ways for many wandering years, became a prodigal son lost in grief and drugs only to return home to find his voice and tell the truth for his father and his family. He writes:

> One day he [RFK] came into my bedroom and handed me a hardcover copy of Camus' *The Plague*. "I want you to read this," he said with particular urgency. It was the story of a doctor trapped in a quarantined North African city while a raging epidemic devastates its citizenry; the physician's small acts of service, while ineffective against the larger tragedy, give meaning to his own life, and, somehow, to the larger universe. I spent a

lot of time thinking about that book over the years, and why my father gave it to me. I believe it was the key to a door that he himself was then unlocking . . . . It is neither our position nor our circumstances that define us . . . but our response to those circumstances; when destiny crushes us, small heroic gestures of courage and service can bring peace and fulfillment. In applying our shoulder to the stone, we give order to a chaotic universe. Of the many wonderful things my father left me, this philosophical truth was perhaps the most useful. In many ways, it has defined my life.

By writing *American Values: Lessons I Learned from My Family*, Robert F. Kennedy, Jr. has named the plague and entered the fight. His father would be very proud of him. He has indeed defined his life.

Will NPR Now Officially Change Its Name to National Propaganda Radio?

Back in the 1960s, CIA official Cord Meyer said the agency needed to "court the compatible left." He knew that drawing liberals and leftists into the CIA's orbit was the key to efficient propaganda. Right-wing and left-wing collaborators were needed to create a powerful propaganda apparatus that would be capable of hypnotizing audiences into believing the myth of American exceptionalism and its divine right to rule the world. The CIA therefore secretly worked to influence American and world opinion through the literary and intellectual elites.

Frances Stonor Saunders comprehensively covers this in her 1999 book, *The Cultural Cold War: The CIA And The World Of Arts And Letters*, and Joel Whitney followed this up in 2016 with *Finks: How the CIA Tricked the World's Best Writers*, with particular emphasis on the complicity between the CIA and the famous literary journal, *The Paris Review*. By the mid-1970s, as a result of the Church Committee hearings, it seemed as if the CIA, NSA, FBI, etc. had been caught *in flagrante delicto* and disgraced, had confessed their sins, and resolved to go and sin no more.

Then in 1977, Carl Bernstein wrote a long piece for *Esquire*—"The CIA and the Media"—naming names of journalists and media (*The New York Times, CBS*, etc.) that worked hand-in-glove with the CIA, propagandizing the American people and the rest of the world. It seemed, per the intent of a "limited hangout," as if all would be hunky-dory now with the bad boys purged from the American "free" press. Seemed to the most naïve, that is, by which I mean the vast numbers of people who wanted to re-stick their heads in the sand and believe, as Ronald Reagan's team of truthtellers would announce, that it was "Morning in America" again with the free press reigning and the neo-conservatives, many of whom had been "converted" from their leftist views, running things in Washington.

So again it is morning in America this September 6, 2019, as the headline from National Public Radio announces the glad tidings that NPR has named a new CEO. His name is John Lansing, and the headline says he is a "veteran media executive." We are meant to be reassured. It goes on to say that Mr. Lansing, 62, is currently the chief executive of the government agency, The U.S. Agency for Global Media, that oversees Voice of America, Radio and Television Marti, and Radio Free Europe/Radio Liberty, among others. We are furthermore reassured by NPR that Lansing "made his mark in his current job with stirring defenses of journalism, free from government interference." The announcement goes on to say:

> Lansing has earned an advanced degree in political agility. At the U.S. Agency for Global Media, Lansing championed a free press even as leaders of many nations move against it.
>
> "Governments around the world are increasingly cracking down on the free flow of information; silencing dialogue and dissent; and distorting reality," Lansing said in a speech he delivered in May to the Media for Democracy Forum. "The result, I believe, is a war on truth."
>
> He continued: "Citizens in countries from Russia to China, from Iran to North Korea, have been victimized for decades. But now we're seeing authoritarian regimes expanding around the globe, with media repression in places like Turkey and Venezuela, Cambodia and Vietnam."

Doubtless we are reassured that the new head of NPR, the former chief of all U.S. government propaganda, is a champion of a free press.

Perhaps NPR will soon enlighten the American public by interviewing its new head honcho and asking him if he thinks Julian Assange and Chelsey Manning, by exposing America's war crimes, and Edward Snowden, by exposing the U.S. government's vast electronic surveillance programs of its own citizens, deserve to be jailed and exiled for doing the job the American mainstream "free press" failed to do. What NPR failed to do.

Perhaps NPR will ask him if he objects to the way his own government "interfered" in the lives of these three courageous people who revealed truths that every citizen of a free country is entitled to.

Perhaps NPR will ask him if the U.S. government's persecution of these truthtellers is what he means by there being "a war on truth." Perhaps they will ask him if he thinks the Obama and Trump administrations have been "distorting reality" and waging a war on truth.

Perhaps not. Of course not.

Don't laugh, for the joke will be on you if you listen to NPR and its sly appeal to "liberal" sensibilities. If you are wondering why we have had the Russia-gate hoax and who was responsible (read the work of Russia expert Prof. Stephen Cohen) and are now involved in a new Cold War and a highly dangerous nuclear confrontation with Russia, don't wait for NPR. Go straight to Lansing's July 10, 2019 testimony before the House Appropriations Sub-Committee on State, Foreign Operations and Related Programs: *"United Sates Efforts to Counter Russian Disinformation and Malign Influence."*

Here is an excerpt:

> USAGM provides consistently accurate and compelling journalism that reflects the values of our society: freedom, openness, democracy, and hope. Our guiding principles—enshrined in law—are to provide a reliable,

authoritative, and independent source of news that adheres to the strictest standards of journalism. . . .

Russian Disinformation. And make no mistake, we are living through a global explosion of disinformation, state propaganda, and lies generated by multiple authoritarian regimes around the world. The weaponization of information we are seeing today is real. The Russian government and other authoritarian regimes engage in far-reaching malign influence campaigns across national boundaries and language barriers. The Kremlin's propaganda and disinformation machine is being unleashed via new platforms and continues to grow in Russia and internationally. Russia seeks to destroy the very idea of an objective, verifiable set of facts as it attempts to influence opinions about the United States and its allies. It is not an understatement to say that this new form of combat on the information battlefield may be the fight of the 21st century.

Then research the history of Radio Free Europe/Radio Liberty, the Voice of America, Radio and Television Marti, etc. You will be reassured that Lansing's July testimony was his job interview to head National Propaganda Radio.

Then sit back, relax, and tune into NPR's Morning Edition. It will be comforting to know that it is "Morning in America" once again.

The Art of Doublespeak: Bellingcat and Mind Control

In the 1920s, the influential American intellectual, Walter Lippman, argued that the average person was incapable of seeing or understanding the world clearly and needed to be guided by experts behind the social curtain. In a number of books he laid out the theoretical foundations for the practical work of Edward Bernays, who developed "public relations" (aka propaganda) to carry out this task for the ruling elites. Bernays had honed his skills while working as a propagandist for the United States during World War I as a member of the Committee on Public Information, and after the war he set himself up as a public relations counselor in New York City.

There is a fascinating exchange at the beginning of Adam Curtis's documentary, *The Century of Self*, where Bernays, then nearly 100 years old but still very sharp, reveals his manipulative mindset and that of so many of those who have followed in his wake. He says the reason he couldn't call his new business "propaganda" was because the Germans had given propaganda a "bad name," and so he came up with the euphemism "public relations." He then adds that "if you could use it [i.e. propaganda] for war, you certainly could use it for peace." Of course, he never used PR for peace but just to manipulate public opinion (he helped engineer the CIA coup against the democratically elected Arbenz government in Guatemala in 1954 with fake news broadcasts). He says "the Germans gave propaganda a bad name," not Bernays himself and the United States with their vast campaign of lies, mainly aimed at the American people to get their support for going to a war they opposed (think "weapons of mass destruction in Iraq" nearly a century later). Bernays sounds proud of his war propaganda work, felt it resounded to his credit since it led to support for the "war to end all wars" and subsequently to a hit movie about WWI, *Yankee Doodle Dandy*, made in 1942 to promote the second world war, since the first one somehow didn't achieve its lofty goal.

As Bernays has said in his book, *Propaganda*, "The American motion picture is the greatest unconscious carrier of propaganda in the world today."

He was a propagandist to the end. I suspect most viewers of the film are taken in by these softly spoken words of an old man sipping a glass of wine at a dinner table with a woman who is asking him questions. I have shown this film to hundreds of students and none has noticed his legerdemain. It is an example of the sort of hocus-pocus I will be getting to shortly, the sly insertion into seemingly liberal or matter-of-fact commentary of statements that imply a different story: the placement of convincing or confusing disingenuous ingredients into a truth sandwich—for Bernays knew that a few slices from the bread of truth is essential to conceal the lies.

In the following years, Bernays, Lippman, and their ilk were joined by social "scientists," psychologists, and sundry others intent on making a sham out of the idea of democracy by developing strategies and techniques for the engineering of social consensus consonant with the wishes of the ruling classes. Their techniques of propaganda developed exponentially with the development of technology, the creation of the CIA, its infiltration of all the major media, and that agency's courting of what CIA official Cord Meyer called in the 1950s "the compatible left," having already had the right in its pocket. Today most people are, as is said, "wired," and they get their information from the electronic media that is mostly controlled by giant corporations in cahoots with government propagandists. Ask yourself: Has the power of the oligarchic, permanent warfare state with its propaganda and spy networks increased or decreased over your lifetime? The answer is obvious: the average people that Lippman and Bernays trashed are losing and the ruling elites are winning.

This is not just because powerful propagandists are good at controlling so-called "average" people's thinking, but perhaps more importantly, because they are also adept—probably more so—at confusing or directing the thinking of those who consider themselves *above* average, those who still might read a book or two or have the concentration to read multiple articles that offer different perspectives on a topic. This is what some call the professional and intellectual classes, perhaps 10–15% of the population, most of whom are not among the ruling elites but are directly or indirectly their employees and sometimes their mouthpieces. It is this segment of the population that considers itself "informed," but the information they imbibe is often sprinkled with bits of misdirection, both intentional and not, that beclouds their understanding of important public matters while still leaving them with the false impression that they are in the know.

Recently I have noticed a group of interconnected examples of how this group of the population that exerts influence incommensurate with their numbers has contributed to the blurring of lines between fact and fiction. Within this group there are opinion makers who are often journalists, writers, and cultural producers of some sort or other, and then there is the larger number of the intellectual or schooled class who follow their opinions. This second group then passes on their received opinions to those who look up to them.

There is a notorious propaganda outfit called Bellingcat, started by an unemployed Englishman named Eliot Higgins, that has been funded by The Atlantic Council, a think-tank with deep ties to the U.S. government, NATO, war manufacturers and their allies, and the National Endowment for Democracy (NED), another infamous U.S. front organization heavily involved in so-called color revolution regime change operations all around the world. A film celebrating Bellingcat, with the Orwellian title, *Bellingcat: Truth in a Post-Truth World,* has won and just received in New York City the International Emmy Award for best documentary.

Allegedly composed of a group of amateur online researchers, Bellingcat has spent years shilling for the U.S.-instigated war against the Syrian government, blaming the Douma chemical attack and others on the Assad government, and for the anti-Russian propaganda connected, among other things, to the Skripal poisoning case in England, and the downing of the flight MH17 plane in Ukraine. It has been lauded by the corporate mainstream media in the west. Its support for the equally fraudulent White Helmets in Syria (also funded by the U.S. and the UK) has also been praised by the western corporate media.

Bellingcat's fraudulent narratives have been ably dissected as propaganda by many excellent independent journalists such as Eva Bartlett, Vanessa Beeley, Catte Black, among others, and skewered by the likes of Seymour Hersh and MIT professor Theodore Postol. Its U.S. government connections have been pointed out by many others, including Ben Norton and Max Blumenthal at The Gray Zone. And now once again we have the mainstream media's wall of silence on the leaks from the Organization for the Prohibition on Chemical Weapons (OPCW) concerning the Douma chemical attack by OPCW scientists protesting the doctoring of their report that provided a pretext for the illegal U.S. bombing of Syria in the spring of 2018. Bellingcat was at the forefront of providing justification for such bombing, and now the journalists Peter Hitchens, Tareq Harrad (who recently resigned from *Newsweek* after accusing the publication of suppressing his revelations about the OPCW scandal) and others are fighting an uphill battle to get the truth out.

Yet *Bellingcat: Truth in a Post-Truth World* won the Emmy, fulfilling Bernays' point about films being the greatest unconscious carriers of propaganda in the world today.

Who presented the Emmy Award to the film makers, but none other than the left-wing journalist Chris Hedges. Why he did so, I don't know. But that he did so clearly sends a message to those who follow his work and trust him that Bellingcat is a trustworthy and even heroic force.

So, one presumes, does *The Intercept*, the billionaire Pierre Omidyar-owned publication associated with Glen Greenwald and Jeremy Scahill, and also read by many progressive-minded people. *The Intercept* that earlier this year disbanded the small team that was tasked with reviewing and releasing more of the massive trove of documents they received from Edward Snowden six years ago, a minute number of which have ever been released or probably ever will be. As Whitney Webb pointed out last year, *The Intercept* hosted a workshop for Bellingcat. She wrote:

> *The Intercept,* along with its parent company First Look Media, recently hosted a workshop for pro-war, Google-funded organization Bellingcat in New York. The workshop, which cost $2,500 per person to attend and lasted five days, aimed to instruct participants in how to perform investigations using "open source" tools —with Bellingcat's past controversial investigations for use as case studies.... Thus, while *The Intercept* has long publicly promoted itself as an anti-interventionist and progressive media outlet, it is becoming clearer that—largely thanks to its ties to Omidyar—it is increasingly an organization that has more in common with Bellingcat, a group that launders NATO and U.S. propaganda and disguises it as "independent" and "investigative journalism."

Then we have Jefferson Morley, the editor of T*he Deep State,* former *Washington Post* journalist, and JFK assassination researcher, who has written a praiseworthy review of the Bellingcat film and who supports Bellingcat. "In my experience, Bellingcat is credible," he writes in an *Alternet* article, the "Bellingcat documentary has the pace and plot of a thriller."

Morley has also just written an article for *Counterpunch*— "Why the Douma Chemical Attack Wasn't a 'Managed Massacre'"—in which he disputes the claim that the April 7, 2018 attack in the Damascus suburb was a false flag operation carried out by Assad's opponents. "I do not see any evidence proving that Douma was a false flag incident," he writes in this article that is written in a style that leaves one guessing as to what exactly he is saying. It sounds convincing unless one concentrates, and then his double messages emerge. Yet it is the kind of article that certain "sophisticated" left-wing readers might read and feel is insightful. But then Morley, who has written considerably about the CIA, edits a website that advertises itself as "the thinking person's portal to the world of secret government," and recently had an exchange with former CIA Director John Brennan where "Brennan put a friendly finger on my chest," said in February 2017, less than a month after Trump was sworn in as president, that:

> With a docile Republican majority in Congress and a demoralized Democratic Party in opposition, the leaders of the Deep State are the most—perhaps the only—credible check in Washington on what Senator Bob Corker (R-Tenn.) calls Trump's "wrecking ball presidency."

Is it any wonder that some people might be a bit confused?

"I know what you're thinking about," said Tweedledum; "but it isn't so, nohow."

"Contrariwise," continued Tweedledee, "if it was so, it might be; and if it were so, it would be; but as it isn't, it ain't. That's logic."

As a final case in point, there is a recent book by Stephen Kinzer, *Poisoner in Chief: Sidney Gottlieb And The CIA Search For Mind Control*, the story of the chemist known as Dr. Death who ran the CIA's MK-ULTRA mind control project, using LSD, torture, electric shock therapy, hypnosis, etc.; developed sadistic methods of torture still used in black sites around the world; and invented various ingenious techniques for assassination, many of which were aimed at Fidel Castro. Gottlieb was responsible for brutal prison and hospital experiments and untold death and suffering inflicted on all sorts of innocent people. His work was depraved in the deepest sense; he worked with Nazis who experimented on Jews despite being Jewish himself.

Kinzer writes in depth about this man who considered himself a patriot and a spiritual person—a humane torturer and killer.

It is an eye-opening book for anyone who does not know about Gottlieb, who gave the CIA the essential tools they use in their "organized crime" activities around the world—in the words of Douglas Valentine, the author of *The CIA as Organized Crime* and *The Phoenix Program*. Kinzer's book is good history on Gottlieb; however, he doesn't venture into the present activities of the CIA and Gottlieb's patriotic followers, who no doubt exist and go about their business in secret.

After recounting in detail the sordid history of Gottlieb's secret work that is nauseating to read about, Kinzer leaves the reader with these strange words:

> Gottlieb was not a sadist, but he might well have been.... Above all he was an instrument of history. Understanding him is a deeply disturbing way of understanding ourselves.

What possibly could this mean? Not a sadist? An instrument of history? Understanding ourselves? These few sentences, dropped out of nowhere, pull the rug out from under what is generally an illuminating history and what seems like a moral indictment. This language is pure mystification.

Kinzer also concludes that because Gottlieb said so, the CIA failed in their efforts to develop methods of mind control and ended MK-ULTRA's experiments long ago. Why would he believe the word of a man who personified the agency he worked for: a secret liar? He writes:

> When Sydney Gottlieb brought MK-ULTRA to its end in the early 1960s, he told his CIA superiors that he had found no reliable way to wipe away memory, make people abandon their consciences, or commit crimes and then forget them.

As for those who might think otherwise, Kinzer suggests they have vivid imaginations and are caught up in conspiracy thinking: "This [convincing others that the CIA had developed methods of mind control when they hadn't] is Sydney Gottlieb's most unexpected legacy," he asserts. He says this although Richard Helms, the CIA Director, destroyed all MK-Ultra records. He says that Allen Dulles, Gottlieb, and Helms themselves were caught up in a complete fantasy about mind control because they had seen too many movies and read too many books; mind control was impossible, a failure, a myth, he maintains. It is the stuff of popular culture, entertainment.

In an interview with Chris Hedges, interestingly posted by Jefferson Morley at his website, *The Deep State*, Hedges agrees with Kinzer. Gottlieb, Dulles, et al. were all deluded. Mind control was impossible. You couldn't create a Manchurian Candidate—by implication, someone like Sirhan Sirhan could not have been programmed to be a fake Manchurian Candidate and to have no memory of what he did, as Sirhan claims. He could not have been mind-controlled by the CIA to perform his part as the seeming assassin of Senator Robert Kennedy, while the real killer shot RFK from behind. All eyewitnesses asserted that Sirhan was many feet in front of Kennedy when he fired, while the official autopsy report, handed to the defense by the prosecution half-way through the trial, makes it emphatically clear that RFK was shot from behind at point-blank range with the fatal bullet entering his head behind his right ear from a forty-five degree angle from below. All three bullets that entered his body from the rear were not from Sirhan's gun. Anyone who wishes to check this information that has even been reported in *The Washington Post* can do so easily. What do they say: Google it? It's not a mystery unless you check. So if the whole story about Sirhan killing Bobby Kennedy is bogus, where does that leave those who think a fake Manchurian Candidate could not be created?

Furthermore, as is so common in books such as Kinzer's, he repeats the canard that JFK and RFK knew about and pressured the CIA to assassinate Fidel Castro. This is demonstrably false, as shown by the Church Committee and the Assassinations Record Review Board, among many others. That Kinzer takes the word of notorious liars like Richard Helms and the top-level CIA operative Samuel Halpern is simple incredible, something that is hard to consider a mistake. Slipped into a truth sandwich, it is devoured and passed on. But it is false.

But this is how these games are played. If you look carefully, you will see them widely. Inform, enlighten, while throwing in doubletalk and untruths. The small number of people who read such books and articles will come away knowing some history that has no current relevance and being misinformed on other history that does. They will then be in the know, ready to pass their "wisdom" on to those who care to listen. They will not think they are average.

But they will have been mind controlled, and the killer cat will roam freely without a bell, ready to devour the unsuspecting mice.

Lost in the Theatre of Data, Dada, and Emotional Manipulation

> "It is not only information that they need—in this Age of Fact, information often dominates their attention and overwhelms their capacities to assimilate it . . . . What they need, and what they feel they need, is a quality of mind that will help them to use information and to develop reason in order to achieve lucid summations of what is going on in the world and of what may be happening within themselves . . . what may be called the sociological imagination."
>
> —**C. Wright Mills,** *The Sociological Imagination,* **1959**

> "'Our own death is indeed, unimaginable,' Freud said in 1915, 'and whenever we make the attempt to imagine it we can perceive that we really survive as spectators.' It is thus the very habit of military situations that turn them theatrical. And it is their utter unthinkableness: it is impossible for a participant to believe that he is taking part in such murderous proceedings in his own character. The whole thing is too grossly farcical, perverse, cruel, and absurd to be credited as a form of 'real life.' Seeing warfare as theatre provides a psychic escape for the participant: with a sufficient sense of theatre, he can perform his duties without implicating his 'real' self and without impairing his innermost conviction that the world is still a rational place. Just before the attack on Loos, Major Pilditch testifies to 'a queer new feeling these last few days, intensified last night. A sort of feeling of unreality as if I were acting on a stage. . . .'"
>
> —**Paul Fussell,** *The Great War and Modern Memory*

> "The society whose modernisation has reached the stage of integrated spectacle is characterised by the combined effect of five principal factors: incessant technological renewal, integration of state and economy, generalised secrecy, unanswerable lies, and eternal present. . . ."
> —**Guy Debord, *The Society of the Spectacle***

> "Hi-diddle-dee-dee
> An actor's life for me..
> Hi-diddle-dee-dum
> An actor's life is fun"
> —**Walt Disney, "Pinocchio"**

It was 102 years ago this November 11th when World War I ended. This "War to End All Wars" resulted in the death of approximately 9 million soldiers and 9 million civilians. The brilliant leaders who waged this war—the crème de la crème—men who, in their own warped minds, possessed impeccable logic and rigorous reasoning, expected the war to be over in a few months. It lasted four years. Like their more current American counterparts before they launched the war against Iraq in 2003, they expected a "cakewalk" or a "slam-dunk" (the former term is racist and the latter a sports term, perfect unconscious verbiage for the slaughter of "lesser" humans). All these principals were data demented, they had lined up their little toy ducks in a row and expected a neat and logical outcome. Or so they said. The new weapons would quickly make mincemeat of the enemy. Technology would expeditiously destroy to expeditiously save.

Nothing has changed in one hundred years

Such instrumental logic and its positivistic data reductionism has now deeply infected the popular mind, as common sense has been destroyed by government and mass media propaganda so blatantly ridiculous that only a hypnotized person could believe it. But so many have been hypnotized and follow the repetitive and overwhelming streaming of each day's markedly ad hoc "news," following the Pied Piper to their doom via the wizardry of digital technology. Raptly attentive to the "politainment" that passes for journalism, they pinball between alleged assertions of fact cobbled together with tendentious and faulty logic and theatrical displays of emotion meant to manipulate an audience of spectators in the national theatre of absurdity. It is all show and tell in which the audience is expected to react emotionally rather than think, with images and feelings having replaced concentrated reflection, and facts and evidence having disappeared like a coin from a magician's hand.

This technological surround-sound theatre has reduced everything to play-acting, with audiences and their puppeteers playing reciprocal parts. Theodor Adorno analogizes thus:

> Real life is becoming indistinguishable from the movies. The sound film, far surpassing the theatre of illusion, leaves no room for imagination or reflection on the part of the audience, who is unable to respond within the structure of the film, yet deviate from its precise detail without losing the thread of the story; hence the film forces its victims to equate it directly with reality. The stunting of the mass-media consumer's powers of imagination and spontaneity does not have to be traced back to any psychological mechanisms; he must ascribe the loss of those attributes to the objective nature of the products themselves, especially to the most characteristic of them, the sound film. They are so designed that quickness, powers of observation, and experience are undeniably needed to apprehend them at all; yet sustained thought is out of the question if the spectator is not to miss the relentless rush of facts.

Meanwhile, the real business of murder, mayhem, and economic exploitation continues apace. As one "small" example of a fact relegated to oblivion by our mainstream media, in Gaza this past week, Israeli occupation forces killed Nasser Azim Musabeh (12), Mohammed Nayef Ai (14), Mohammed Ali Mohasmmed

Anshasi, (18), Iyar Khalil Al-Sha'er (18), Mohasmmed Bassam Mohammed (24), Mohammed Walid Haniyeh (23), and Mohammed Ashraf Awawdeh (23). But such facts don't matter since these dead young people were already reduced to invisible people not worthy of a mention. For the U.S. government, Palestinians are not human and can be treated accordingly.

Rather, pseudo-debates and pseudo-events are created by media and political magicians whose goal is to confuse the audience through information (data) and emotional overload into thinking that they are "freely" choosing what is always the same, to paraphrase Theodor Adorno. It is a conjurer's act of mind manipulation in support of a repressive political and economic ideology built on false dichotomies. The political/media empire creates its own "reality" that the captivated audience takes as reality, as their emotions swing from outrage to laughter and their electronic clickers jump them from show to show, from CNN or Fox or *The New York Times* to Saturday Night Live in the land where there is no business but show business. "Amusing ourselves to death," as Neal Postman so aptly put it. To which I would add: As we put others to death outside the show.

The other day I was in a library and was looking through a large book of World War I photographs from the Imperial War Museum that I found lying on a table. They were arranged chronologically from the start of the war in 1914 to its end in 1918. Fascinating photos, I thought. I went through the book page by page, examining the photos one by one, beginning with the assassination of Archduke Ferdinand by a young guy, on through the photos of stiff British war-hawk leaders in double-breasted suits, through photos of the trenches and the new weapons until I reached photos of the treaty to "end" it. By the conclusion, I felt exhausted and knew nothing new. Photos as data. Click, click, click: How many are enough? It was like spending an hour with the mainstream corporate media, and much of the alternative press. It was like a black and white movie in no motion. "Same old, same old," as a young man I know often says when I ask him what's new. Same old data via photographs. War is hell. Ditto. Bodies get blown to bits and decompose in mud. Ditto. Heads get separated from necks and blood pours forth. Ditto. War is hell. Ditto. Great leaders meet and end the carnage. Ditto.

Ditto Data Dada. I had to imagine the subsequent pages and years as these great leaders, so disgusted by war, prepared for the next one, and the one following, etc. Ditto, data, dada.

I understood then why the first famous Dadaist piece of art that emerged from absolute disgust with the data driven crazies who started and waged WW I was Marcel Duchamp's 1917 "Fountain," a porcelain urinal signed by R. Mutt, a message to tell the "great" leaders to piss off.

But Dadaist art, like all avant-garde art, gets quickly sucked into the maw of the entertainment complex, which is another name for the propaganda complex. As the word media means etymologically—magicians—these sorcerer's have developed and use every bit of black magic to engineer the consent of the bewildered herd, to blend the words of two of America's key propagandists from the past: Edward Bernays, Freud's American nephew and President Woodrow Wilson's master propagandist for WW I, and the famous journalist Walter Lippman. Bernays put it straight and succinctly:

> It is impossible to overestimate the importance of engineering of consent. The engineering of consent is the very essence of the democratic process. It affects almost every aspect of our daily lives.

Last week I attended a production of the play *Annie* in a community theatre in a liberal town in the northeast. The show was sold out, and I was there because my lovely granddaughter was performing in the play, one whose story and music I was very familiar with. The show was delightful and the audience was enraptured by the performances and the wonderful music. If you are not familiar with the story, it is about an 11-year-old orphan named Annie who, in 1933 when FDR has assumed the presidency, is in search of her biological parents. Together with other orphans in a NYC orphanage, she is treated miserably by a character named Miss Hannigan. By the play's end, Annie is adopted by a wealthy man to presumably live happily ever after. At one point in the play, this wealthy man brings Annie to Washington D. C. to meet his friend, President Roosevelt. He says to FDR, Franklin, you need to do something and get my factories humming again. In this scene, Roosevelt and his cabinet, the wealthy man, and Annie sing the very upbeat song—"Tomorrow"—which Roosevelt loves since it offers hope in the dark time of the great depression. Everyone sings the stirring song, many in the audience silently singing along and the mood in the theater elevates. By the play's end Annie is adopted by the wealthy man, whose name is Daddy Warbucks. This super-capitalist billionaire with a mansion on Fifth Avenue and a heart of gold has made his riches making weapons for WW I, though this is not spelled out in the show. I kept wondering what the audience of liberal-minded people were thinking, or if they were, about the strange fact the hero of the show was a man with a warmonger's name whose factories had produced armaments that had created tens of thousands of war orphans and who was urging the liberal Roosevelt to get his munitions factories up and running again in 1933. I suspected they weren't thinking about this at all and that the work of subtle propaganda was being magically induced at an unconscious level. For how could such a nice, caring guy, who adopts the cute Annie and who sings such tuneful songs, be a killer?

I guiltily thought: I shouldn't be thinking such thoughts, even as I also thought, how can I not think them. Emotionally I felt one thing, and intellectually another. This was the classic double-bind.

Upon further reflection, I realized that this is how the finest propaganda works. It splits people in two and works subtly. Emotionally you are pulled one way, and intellectually another, if you are thinking at all. There are certain connections you are not supposed to make or verbalize, as if to oppose the powerful sway of the media's emotional appeals is a betrayal of your humanity and certain victims, such as a cute orphan or other (happy, acceptable) victims, even when that doesn't follow logically.

But in the Magic Theatre that is American life, false choices are the essence of the show. Democrats vs. Republicans, Clinton vs. Bush, Bush vs. Obama, Obama vs. Trump, liberals vs. conservatives, and on and on endlessly. It's Dada, my friends, all theater. The next election will change everything, right? "The sun'll come out/Tomorrow, So ya gotta hang on/'Till tomorrow/Come what may."

Only when we leave the theatre can we see the real play. But that's a bold act for which no Oscars, Tonys, or Emmys are handed out. And outside the theater's warm embrace, it's cold, and you feel like an orphan looking for a home, no matter how much blood-money purchased it. But don't go back in; it's a trap.

Albert Camus and Our Haunted World

Not many writers stand the test of time. One that has, whose work has indeed grown more significant since his death in 1960, is the French Nobel Laureate, Albert Camus.

On January 4, 1960, Albert Camus died in a car crash at a point when he thought his true work had not even begun. He was 46 years old. He had already written *The Stranger*, *The Fall*, and *The Plague*, among other works. He had won the Nobel Prize for Literature. Yet he felt that in his writing he had to hide behind a mask that stifled him. After all these successes, as well as criticism from the left and right French intelligentsia, he was looking forward to a time when he would be able to speak his own truth without the mask of depersonalization—to enter a period of *création en liberté*.

He was finding a new voice beyond the prison of a classical form he felt he needed to escape. In his briefcase was the uncompleted manuscript of that effort, the autobiographical and posthumously published novel, *The First Man*, written in a new lyrical and powerfully emotional style. It is a beautiful book.

A true artist, Camus tried to serve both beauty and suffering. He confronted issues that continue to haunt our plague-stricken world. In particular, I think his ideas of measure (*mesure*, f) and limits, rooted as they were in nature and people of flesh and blood, not some abstractions or pseudo-realities, speak to us today in a profound way.

Were Camus alive today, he would no doubt be struck by the constant stream of news reports exemplifying the hubris of our technological rationality, a mode of thinking that has made a fetish out of technology, worships efficiency, and considers any critical protest as irrational. For Camus was deeply influenced by ancient Greek philosophy. "Greek thought was always based on the idea of limits," he wrote. "Nothing was carried to extremes, neither religion nor reason, because Greek thought denied nothing, neither reason nor religion . . . . And, even though we do it in diverse ways, we extoll one thing and one alone: a future world in which reason will reign supreme."

He would be appalled by the arrogance of a nation led by technocratic experts and politicians who claim to have embraced the power of pure reason devoid of values. Despite all rhetoric to the contrary, the embrace of technical reason, which is innately amoral, has caused many of the problems we seem unable to remedy. These include environmental catastrophe, high-tech wars, GM foods, drone killings, drug addiction, biological and nuclear weapons, to name but a few. To address such problems created by technology, our esteemed leaders pursue technological solutions. The high-priests of this technological complex—organization types all—use the technology and control the information which they then present as "facts" to justify their actions. The absurdity of this vicious circle is lost on them. Their unstated assumption: We are prohibited to prohibit. If it can be done, it will be done. We have no limits.

Camus thought differently: "In our madness, we push back the eternal limits, and at once Furies swoop down upon us to destroy. Nemesis, the goddess of moderation, not of vengeance, is watching. She chastises, ruthlessly, all those who go beyond the limit."

Genetically modified babies, the manufacture of babies without biological parents, part-human part-animal creatures, robots powered by artificial intelligence—these are on the drawing board or already a reality. While the elite media report these developments, they try simultaneously to discount the possibility that the most extreme of these technological discoveries will ever become realities. Yet average people sense otherwise: that the theology of technological "progress" operates according to the law of can do, will do.

Camus, who grew up poor and in love with nature, would no doubt see in these developments our bewitchment by the Promethean god of reason and progress. God being dead since we have murdered him—as he was fond of quoting Nietzsche—our scientists and political leaders think of themselves as gods. "We have conquered in our turn, have set aside the bounds, mastered heaven and earth. Our reason has swept everything away. Alone at last, we build our empire upon a desert."

Of course such rationally organized experts in a technocracy never say that what they are doing harms people's lives since their reasoning is circular. They always claim they are intent on preserving life while fighting death. What they "have developed" must be good and for the improvement of humanity since they developed it out of good intentions. That they might be Dr. Frankensteins, developing monsters in their labs is beyond their ken. No deadly pathogens will ever escape their tight controls.

Birth's conjoined opposite, death, has traditionally been the other limit to human control. It, too, has come to be seen by the technocrats as simply another obstacle to be overcome. The high-tech guru, Ray Kurzweil, is one among many high priests of the scientific/technological faith for whom death is simply another limit to surpass. They expect to accomplish this in the relatively near future. That they are serious would make Camus grin or grimace with irony.

For Camus, as for so many of our greatest writers of the past, his work revolved around the issue of death and the human need to face it lucidly. That meant not explaining it away or justifying it; in short, not presuming to know the unknowable but accepting limits to human knowledge. That was—and is—a tall order in this "century of fear," as Camus dubbed the 20th century (an appellation perfectly apt for the 21st as well), but which also could be called the time of knowledge lust, the time in which human presumptuousness has reached new heights.

The uncanny Romanian-born writer, E. M. Cioran, author of *The Trouble with Being Born*, presciently wrote in 1973 that "when we have worn out the interest we once took in death, when we realize we have nothing more to gain from it, we fall back on birth, we turn to a much more inexhaustible abyss."

This turn to birth has happened, and Camus would notice. I think he would feel compelled to link the current technological obsession to control birth via cloning, genetic research, eugenics, test tube babies, etc. with the inevitability of death, and would have linked both to our prohibition to prohibit. Nothing is off-limits today, since there are no limits to be off. People who think they are gods have none.

For in our great uncertainty, we have sought knowledge, not wisdom, as an end in itself. Afraid at the loss of God and the traditional consolation of personal immortality, we have, through our scientific and technological obsessions, transgressed ancient limits and usurped the traditional power of God over life and death. "While the Greeks used reason to restrain the will," Camus wrote, "we have ended by placing the impulse of the will at the heart of reason, and reason has therefore become murderous." A world verging on nuclear annihilation is the logical consequences of such scientific willfulness. Avid for the conquest of totality, we have become the children of excess.

Camus would take note of Barack Obama's speech on his visit to Hiroshima. He would note the great irony of the president of the only country that has used nuclear weapons—the ultimate technological achievement of a society unmoored from limits—saying that "death fell from the sky and the world was changed." Yes, death just fell. No one dropped nuclear bombs to kill as many people as possible. No one was responsible. Things happen. Death falls.

Camus would observe with Gallic irony the use of an abstraction by a technocratic leader whose hubris knew no limit; who, while saying that the souls of the victims "ask us to look inward," outwardly oversaw a trillion dollars investment in new nuclear weapons while continuing the Bush administration's pursuit of a working ABM system. He would note the hypocrisy of Obama's statement that "we must have the courage to escape the logic of fear and pursue a world without them [nuclear weapons]," even as he embraced them and provoked Russia with military moves into Eastern Europe.

It is worth noting that with the invention of nuclear weapons, the power over birth, life, and death so many people believe belonged to God, was commandeered by those who invented the weapons. No doubt to "help people." With that bit of technological magic, they became as gods. The sacred canopy that once gave people religious consolation was replaced by a mushroom cloud in a symbolic transfer of unimaginable consequences.

Camus, quintessentially a man of his era, was haunted by the image of the world as a prison, exemplified in his great novel, *The Plague*, the tale of a town cut off from the world by a pestilence, whose residents lack the imagination to foresee. Even as it happens, they remain oblivious, for they "work hard, but solely with the object of getting rich." Bored by their habits, heavily drugging themselves with drink, and watching many movies to distract themselves, they fail to grasp the significance of "the squelchy roundness of a still-warm body" of the plague-bearing rats that emerge from their underworld to die in their streets. "It was as if the earth on which our houses stood were being purged of their secret humors; thrusting up to the surface the abscesses and pus-clots that had been forming in its entrails." To them the plague is "unthinkable," an abstraction, until all their denials are swept aside as the truth emerges from the sewers and their neighbors and families die from the disease. "Stupidity has a way of getting its way," the narrator, Dr. Rieux tells us, "as we should see if we were not always so wrapped up in ourselves . . . . plagues and wars take people equally by surprise."

The Plague is often read as a metaphorical depiction of the German occupation of France during World War II. While this is true to the extent that Camus had lived through that experience as a member of the French Resistance and writer and editor of the underground newspaper *Combat*, his artistry makes it a revelatory read for today, especially for citizens of the United States, the greatest purveyor of the plague of violence in the world. We are all infected with the soul-destroying evil that our leaders have loosed upon the world.

For we live in plague time, and the plague lives in us. Like the inhabitants of the novel's French-Algerian city of Oran, the United States is "peopled with sleepwalkers," pseudo-innocents, who are "chiefly aware of what ruffled the normal tenor of their lives or affected their interests." That their own government, no matter what political party is in power (both working for deep-state, elite interests led by the organized criminals of the CIA), is the disseminator of a world-wide plague of virulent violence, must be denied and divorced from consensus reality. These plague-stricken deaths visited on millions around the world—by Clinton, by the Bushes, by Obama, and by Trump—must be denied by diverting attention to the kind of partisan politics that elicits outrage after outrage by the various factions and their minions against each other, policies be damned. The true plague, the bedrock of a nation continually waging wars against the world, is avoided. Presently, it is the liberals that are "shocked" that Trump was elected President. These are the same people who went silent for the last eight years as Obama ravaged the world and lied about his cruel policies. Their shock over the Trump victory reeks of bad faith, with most of them supporting Hillary Clinton, Obama's presumed heir apparent and a neo-liberal war-monger par excellence. Further "shocks" will follow when Trump leaves office and the latest neo-liberal avatar succeeds him; conservatives will resume their harangues and protestations, just as they have done during Obama's reign. The two war parties will exchange insults as their followers are outraged and the American Empire, built on the disease of violence, will roll along. The plague will rage on and the mainstream corporate media will play along.

For "decent folks must be allowed to sleep at night," says the character Tarrou sarcastically; he is a man who has lost his ability to "sleep well" since he witnessed a man's execution where the "bullets make a hole into which you could thrust your fist." He awakens to the realization that he "had an indirect hand in the deaths of thousands of people." He loses any peace he had and vows to resist the plague in every way he can. "For many years I've been ashamed," he says, "mortally ashamed, of having been, even with the best intentions, even at many removes, a murderer in my turn."

The rats are dying in the streets. They are our rats, diseased by us. They have emerged from the underworld of a nation plagued by its denial. Unconscious evil bubbles up. We are an infected people. Worry and irritation—"these are not feelings with which to confront plague." But we don't seem ashamed of our complicity in our government's crimes around the world. Camus knew better. He warned us, "It's a wearying business being plague-stricken. But it's still more wearying to refuse to be it. That's why everybody in the world looks so tired; everyone is more or less sick of plague. But that is why some of us, those who want to get the plague out of their systems, feel such desperate weariness."

Yet the fight against the plague must go on. Tarrou puts it thus:

> All I maintain is that on this earth there are pestilences and there are victims, and it's up to us, as far possible, not to join forces with the pestilences. That may sound simple to the point of childishness; I can't judge if it's simple, but I know it's true. You see, I'd heard such quantities of arguments, which very nearly turned my head, and turned other people's heads enough to make them approve of murder; and I'd come to realize that all our troubles spring from our failure to use plain, clear-cut language. So I resolved always to speak—and to act—quite clearly, as this was the only way of setting myself on the right track.

Although his life and work were cut short by an absurd automobile accident with an unused train ticket in his pocket, Camus stood with the victims. He was on the right track. He left us a living lesson in integrity in the face of violence.

Refuse it always. If not, you will be destroyed by your own complicity in evil. You will be plagued by your own hand, was his message to us.

In his last novel, *The Fall*, he left us Jean Baptiste Clamence, a nihilist worthy of our times, a lawyer dedicated to abstract justice, a phony actor who, in the name of absolute sincerity, lies in order to mask his destructive nihilism that knows no bounds. He reminds me of our power elites. His maxim cuts to the heart of our modern madness:

When one has no character, one has to apply a method.

Denying the Obvious: Leftists and Crimestop

> *"And thus the U.S. left leadership sits in the left chamber of the hall of mirrors, complaining about conspiracy theories while closing its eyes to actual conspiracies crucial to contemporary imperialism."*
>
> —Graeme MacQueen, "Beyond Their Wildest Dreams: September 11, 2001 and the American Left"

It is well known that effective propaganda works through slow, imperceptible repetition. "The slow building up of reflexes and myths" is the way Jacques Ellul put it in his classic, *Propaganda*. This works through commission and omission.

I was reminded of this recently after I published a newspaper editorial for Martin Luther King Day, January 15, 2018, stating the fact that the United States' government had assassinated Dr. King. To the best of my knowledge, this has been the only newspaper op-ed to say that. I discovered that many newspapers and other publications (with very rare exceptions), despite a plethora of articles and editorials praising King, ignored this "little" fact as if it were inconsequential. No doubt they wish it were, or that it were not true, just as many hoped that repeating the bromide that James Earl Ray killed Dr. King would reinforce the falsehood they've been selling for fifty years, despite overwhelming evidence to the contrary that is available to anyone wishing to investigate the truth.

William Pepper, an attorney who represented the King family in the 1999 trial that found U.S. officials of the federal (in particular, the FBI and Army Intelligence), state, and local governments responsible for King's assassination, has worked on the King case since 1977. He has written three books on the case, culminating with *The Plot to Kill King*, a voluminously documented book. In it he resurrects the revolutionary MLK, and in doing so shows in striking and definitive detail why elements within the U.S. government executed him. After reading this book, no fair-minded reader can reach any other conclusion. It consists of slightly less text than supporting documentation in its appendices, which include numerous depositions and interviews that buttress Pepper's thesis on the why and how of this horrible murder. It demands a close reading that should put to rest any pseudo-debates about the essentials of the case.

But the general attitude seemed to be: Let's just appreciate MLK on his birthday and get on with it. Don't be a spoil-sport.

That this is the approach of the mainstream corporate media (MSM) should not be surprising, for they are mouthpieces for official government lies. But when the same position is taken by so many liberal and progressive intellectuals and publications who are otherwise severely critical of the MSM for their propaganda in the service of empire, it gives pause. Like their counterparts in the MSM, these liberals shower King with praise, even adding that he was more than a civil rights leader, that he opposed war and economic exploitation as well, but as to who killed him, and why, and why it matters today, that is elided. Amy Goodman at *Democracy Now!*, in a recent piece about an upcoming documentary about King, is a case in point. Not once in this long conversation about a film about the last few years of King's life and his commitment to oppose the Vietnam War and launch the Poor People's Campaign is the subject of who killed him and why broached. It is a perfect example of the denial of the truth through omission.

Propaganda, of course, comes in many forms: big lies and small; half-truths, whispers, and rumors; slow-drip and headlong; misinformation and disinformation; through commission and omission; intentional and unintentional; cultural and political, etc. Although it is omnipresent today—24/7 surround sound—when it comes from the mouths of government spokespeople or corporate media the average person, grown somewhat suspicious of official lies, has a slight chance of detecting it. This is far more difficult, however, when it takes the form of a left-wing critique of U.S. government policies that subtly supports official explanations through sly innuendos and references, or through omission. Reading an encomium to Dr. King that attacks government positions on race, war, and economics from the left will often get people nodding their heads in agreement while they fail to notice a fatal flaw at the heart of the critique. The *Democracy Now!* piece is a perfect example of this legerdemain.

I do not know the motivations or intentions of many prominent leftist intellectuals and publications, but I do know that many choose to avoid placing certain key historical events at the center of their analyses. In fact, they either avoid them like the plague, dismiss them as inconsequential, or use the CIA's term of choice and call them "conspiracy theories" and their proponents "conspiracy nuts." The result is a powerful propaganda victory for the power elites they say they oppose.

Orwell called it "Crimestop: [it] means the faculty of stopping short, as though by instinct, at the threshold of any dangerous thought. It includes the power of not grasping analogies, of failing to perceive logical errors, of misunderstanding the simplest arguments if they are inimical to Ingsoc, and of being bored or repelled by any train of thought which is capable of leading in a heretical direction. Crimestop, in short means protective stupidity."

There are many fine writers and activists who are very frustrated by their inability, despite a vast and continuous outpouring of excellent critiques of the machinations of the oligarchical rulers of the U.S., to convince people of the ways they have been brainwashed by government/media propaganda. Most of their anger is directed toward the most obvious sources of this intricate psychological warfare directed at the American people. They often fail to realize, however—or fail to say—that there are leftists in their ranks who, whether intentionally or not, are far more effective than the recognized enemies in government intelligence agencies and their corporate accomplices in the media in convincing people that the system works and that it is not run by killers who will go to any lengths to achieve their goals. These leftist critics, while often right on specific issues that one can agree with, couch their critiques within a framework that omits or disparages certain truths without which nothing makes sense. By truths I do not mean debatable matters, but key historical events that have been studied and researched extensively by reputable scholars and have been shown to be factual, except to those who fail to fairly do their homework, purposely or through laziness.

There is no way to understand today's world without confronting five key historical events out of which spring today's conditions of oligarchic rule, constant war, and the growth of an intelligence apparatus that makes Orwell's 1984 look so anachronistic.

They are: the assassinations of JFK, Malcom X, MLK, and RFK by elements within the U.S. intelligence services, and the insider attacks of September 11, 2001. Discussing these is anathema to a group of very prominent left-wing intellectuals and liberal publications. It is okay for them to attack Bush, Obama, Clinton, Trump, the Democratic Party, Bernie Sanders, liberals in general, creeping fascism, capitalism, the growth of the intelligence state, etc.; but to accept, or even to explore fairly in writing, what I assert as factual above, is verboten. Why?

When President Kennedy was murdered by the CIA, the United States effectively suffered a coup d'état that resulted in years of savage war waged against Vietnam, resulting in the deaths of millions of Vietnamese and more than fifty-eight thousand American soldiers. The murder of JFK in plain sight sent a message in clear and unambiguous terms to every President that followed: toe the line or else. They have toed the line. The message from the coup planners and executioners was clear: we run the show. They have been running it ever since.

When Malcom X spoke so loudly and eloquently and said "I believe that there will ultimately be a clash between the oppressed and those that do the oppressing. I believe that there will be a clash between those who want freedom, justice and equality for everyone and those who want to continue the systems of exploitation," he had to go. So they killed him.

When Martin Luther King declared his opposition to the Vietnam War and joined it to his espousal of a civil rights and an anti-capitalist program, he had to go. So they killed him.

Then, when the last man standing who had a chance to change the direction of the JFK coup—Robert Kennedy—seemed destined to win the presidency, he had to go. So they killed him.

To ignore these foundational state crimes for which the evidence is so overwhelming and their consequences over the decades that have been so noxious—well, what explanation can the purportedly white-hat leftist critics offer for doing so?

And then there are the attacks of September 11, 2001, the fifth foundational event that has brought us to our present abominable condition. One has to be very ignorant to not see that the official explanation is a fiction conjured up to justify an endless "war on terror" planned as perhaps the prelude to the use of nuclear weapons, those weapons that JFK in the last year of his life worked so hard to eliminate after the Cuban Missile Crisis of 1962.

In refusing to connect the dots from November 22, 1963 through February 21, 1965 through April 4 and June 5, 1968 and September 11, 2001 until today, prominent leftists continue to do the work of Crimestop. For the moment I will leave it to readers to identify who they are, and the numerous leftist publications that support their positions. There are two famous left-wing American intellectuals, one living and one dead, who are often intoned to support this work of propaganda by omission: Noam Chomsky and Howard Zinn, both of whom dismissed the killing of JFK and the attacks of September 11 as inconsequential and not worthy of their attention. They have quite a few protégés whose work you probably read and agree with, despite this void at the heart of their critiques. Why they avoid accepting the truth and significance of the five events I have mentioned, only they can say. That they do is easy to show, as are the dire consequences for a united front against the deep-state forces intent on reducing this society and the world to rubble. Their refusal to confront the systemic evil renders it unspeakable.

In his groundbreaking book on the assassination of John Kennedy, *JFK And The Unspeakable: Why He Died & Why It*

Matters, James Douglass quotes his guide into the dark underworld of radical evil and our tendency to turn away from its awful truths, the Trappist Monk Thomas Merton, who said of the Unspeakable:

> It is the void that contradicts everything that is spoken even before the words are said; the void that gets into the language of public and official declarations at the very moment when they are pronounced and makes them ring dead with the hollowness of the abyss.

Can you hear it on your left?

A Do-Nothing Anti-Labor Day: A Modest Proposal

Perhaps the word "ironic" begins to describe the following essay in light of the Covid-19 lockdowns.

In a country with a Mount Rushmore that celebrates the ruthless and frenetic westward expansion, it might be a bit naïve to suggest a Do-Nothing Day. I have nothing against laboring men and women having their day. I am a laborer myself, and national holidays are great—so many sales for stuff no one needs, and far too many people working on an ostensible holiday. But I have this ridiculous dream of a day when everyone just does nothing.

To rush less, to idle, and to do nothing sounds so un-American, yet it might be a solution to many of our country's problems. Quixotic as it may sound, if every person in the country could be convinced to lay aside his compulsive busyness for one day per month, for starters, this not-doing would paradoxically accomplish so much.

Nothing is a funny word, as Shakespeare well knew. There is so much to it; "much ado" as he put it. It is the great motivator. While it frightens people, it is also the spur to creativity. Samuel Beckett once astutely said, "Nothing is more real than nothing." It is the void, the womb, the empty space out of which we come and live out our days. It is the background silence for all our noise. Like the rain, it is purely gratuitous. Such a gift should not be shunned.

By doing nothing I mean the following: no work, just free play; no travel, except by foot or bicycle; no use of technology of any sort except stoves for cooking meals to share; no household repairs or projects; no buying or selling of any kind, including thinking of buying and selling. You get the point. This not-doing doing could be called dreaming or simply being. It's a tough task indeed, but fitting for the paradoxical creatures that we are. And that's just for individuals.

Nationally, all businesses would be closed, factories would be idled, planes and trains grounded. Only emergency services—hospitals, police, etc. would be allowed to operate. Quixotic, yes, but our national leaders, Republicans and Democrats alike, are surely apt to agree since it would add one more day to their monthly schedules of doing "nothing."

Making my point in a slightly different way, Mark Twain said, "Suppose you were an idiot and suppose you were a member of Congress. But I repeat myself."

Think of how much we would accomplish by doing nothing! People might dream and think; they might hear birds singing or even sing themselves; they might have real conversations; they might feel the peace of a wild idleness; our ecological matrix would have a brief chance to catch its breath; a massive amount of energy would be saved and little carbon would be spewed into the atmosphere (a rather startling statistic could be inserted here). The benefits are endless—and all from doing nothing.

The immediate downside would be millions of mental breakdowns of the do-something addicts. Their agony from trying to do nothing would be excruciating. A friend from another country where they still take siestas and celebrate doing nothing was kind enough to suggest a rapid resolution to this mass madness. Kill these do-somethings. Since they are not good for nothing while alive, she said, and can't help contaminating the earth with their compulsive busyness, why keep them around. She advocated enlisting the help of the Pentagon for this work since killing is their business and they are good at it. While acknowledging the aptness of her suggestion, I told her I thought the Pentagon was much too busy killing foreigners to get involved in a domestic caper at this time. It also raises a number of other practical problems, the biggest being how and where to bury so many busybodies all at once.

Furthermore, people who have so utterly forgotten their childhood's lovely ability to do nothing are far too old and tough and set in their skins to be used as food, as another wag of my acquaintance suggested. Even trying a little tenderizer on their frazzled flesh wouldn't work. After all, when Jonathan Swift had that profound idea of how to solve the Irish famine problem, he was suggesting soft and tender one-year-olds be slaughtered and sold to the wealthy since they would make "delicious, nourishing, and wholesome food, whether stewed, roasted, baked, or boiled." But older, compulsive, do-something people, set in their ways, while seemingly organic—a good thing these days—are tough and sinewy—a not very appetizing thought. I doubt there would be much demand for their meat.

Therefore, in all due respect, let me suggest another way to proceed. I think it best to just let them go mad on Do Nothing Days. They will bounce back on the intervening go-go days but should eventually get so discouraged by having to stop once a month that they will do us the favor of committing suicide. That way they'll get what they didn't want—a quite long stretch of days doing nothing, if eternity has days. And the survivors can live guilt-free, since all they did was nothing to stop them.

As you can see, the downsides to Do-Nothing Days are small compared to the benefits. But convincing people to adopt my plan won't be easy. Long ago I stopped giving advice to friends and family since whatever I suggested seemed to encourage them to do the opposite. Yet here I go again, suggesting this big Do-Nothing Day. So I will desist in the name of the law of reversed effort.

I really don't want to organize a movement to establish particular days for this not-doing. I don't want to establish a cult and be a cult leader. I'm really too busy for that. My schedule is too packed for such a job. Maybe you have time. I have too much to do.

I say, "Nothing doing."

I was once rushing to take groceries to my elderly mother when I ran into the sharp metal edge of a stop sign. Stunned and coming to on my back on the pavement with blood dripping down my face, it bemused me to think how fast I was stopped. Ever since, I've been on the go, laboring away.

Nothing showed me its face.

Yet here and there I have this dream of a Do-Nothing Day. It's the dream of a ridiculous man, isn't it?

Looking Through the Screen at the World's Suffering

> *"If you are really going to be free, you have to overcome the love of wealth and the fear of death."*
> —Martin Luther King, Jr. as quoted by Andrew Young in the documentary, *King in the Wilderness*

Most people on this earth live on the edge of an abyss. Life is a daily struggle to stay alive, to acquire enough to eat and drink, rudimentary health care, housing, and protection from murderous government forces, their various death-squads, and their economic vultures. The gap between the rich and poor, while always great, has grown even more obscenely vast, and lies at the core of what so many face daily. Their perilous conditions are sustained by imperial nations, led by the United States, who, together with its minions, buy and bribe and butcher overtly and covertly all around the world. The love of wealth and the fear of death drive these power-mad marauders and divert the gazes of their citizens from the slaughter. It's an old story.

I am probably not telling you anything new. You know this, as do I, as I sit safely behind a screened-in table on a beautiful spring day in the hills of western Massachusetts. I have had some soup and bread for lunch and there are no bombers overhead or death-squads cruising the roads here. While my family and I live a simple life, compared to the world's poor and persecuted, we are privileged. One does not have to be rich to be privileged. The advantages granted to those like me who can securely sit and pen words about the fate of the poor and persecuted victims of my country's endless violence weighs heavy on my conscience, as they have done since I was young.

I am ashamed to say that in the early morning of May 1, as I lay in bed musing, I thought I would like to stay in bed all day, a depressed feeling that I had never had before. Discouragement enveloped me: I was being forced out of my teaching job; I felt that my dissident writing and teaching had made no difference in a world where injustice and violence are endemic and without end; and the forces of evil seemed to be triumphing everywhere. Self-pity mixed with an angry sadness that disgusted me. I disgusted myself. So I jumped out of bed and prepared to go and teach some of my last classes. But I was lost in gloom as I drove along the winding roads.

When I arrived at the college and checked my mail, there was a package waiting for me. It was a review copy of the poet Carolyn Forché's startling new memoir (*What You Have Heard Is True: A Memoir of Witness and Resistance*) about her youthful transformative experiences in El Salvador in the late 1970s as U.S. trained and supported death-squads brutally murdered poor peasants and priests, and guerrilla resistance was growing prior to the outbreak of civil war. I opened the book to the epigraph, which reads:

> *Hope also nourishes us. Not the hope of fools.*
> *The other kind. Hope, when everything is clear.*
> *Awareness.*

The quotation is from the Salvadorian writer Manlio Argueta, whose deeply moving novel, *One Day of Life* (1980), banned by the Salvadorian government, takes the reader through one terrifying and bloodstained day in the life of peasants struggling to stay alive as they are tortured and slaughtered with impunity. We hear the voices of the poor tell a story of the growth of conscience ("God is conscience. And conscience is we, the ones forgotten now, the poor."), the discovery of rights, and the awareness of exploitation. Despite the terrifying evil that pervades this book—now considered one of the greatest Latin American novels of the

20th century—there is a luminous spirit of hope and resistance that miraculously prevails, that is passed on from person to person despite death, torture, and immense suffering. Argueta fulfills the words of the tortured Jose to Lupe: "Don't worry, if those of us with understanding failed to act, we would all be in real trouble."

I remembered that I had reviewed this book in the early 1980s at a time when 100 or more very poor *campesinos* were being murdered every week, a few years after Archbishop Oscar Romero, the courageous defender of the poor who spoke out against the killers, had been gunned down while saying Mass. The Roman Catholic Church has subsequently declared him a saint.

Yet decades later, despite the extraordinary efforts of awakened souls like Carolyn Forché, it still seems true that Americans can't visualize, no less believe in or care about, the death and suffering their government is inflicting on innocent people all around the world. Today's screen culture—I Phone therefore I Am—while seemingly allowing for the visualization of the suffering of the world's poor, has rendered all reality more abstract and unreal, inducing a collective hallucination sustained by media and machines that divorces us from flesh and blood, our own and others. All the disembodied data that is daily disgorged through these screens seems to me to have rendered the world disincarnate through the metastasizing of a digital dementia tied to death denial.

Awareness? I sit here looking through the screen that encloses the little porch where my table rests. MLK's words reverberate in my mind as I watch a grey fox slink across the grass in search of prey. What is it about the love of money and the fear of death that so cripples people's care and compassion? I know I don't want to see that fox seize a screaming rabbit and worry (to kill by biting and shaking the throat; strangle) it to death. Unlike Forché, I have not physically seen the dead and mutilated bodies of Salvadorian victims of death squads, nor been threatened by them, as she was. Nevertheless, thanks to her and others like Manlio Argueta, I have seen them in my imagination and heard the screams, and they have haunted me. Ghosts.

But why are some so haunted and others not?

The foreknowledge that terrorizes the contents of skulls, as the poet Galway Kinnell puts it—our ultimate powerlessness—overwhelms humans from childhood unless they can find a way forward that discovers power in powerlessness. When one's "well-being" is dependent on the death of others, as is the case for most Americans and others in the so-called first world, people tend to repress the terror of death by building various types of culturally induced defenses that allow them to shakily believe they are in control of life and death. One's natural impotence is then hidden within what Ernest Becker called "the vital lie of character," and in what, by extension, is the lie of American character that rests on money and military might. One lives within the manageable cultural world that helps blot out existential awareness by offering various social games, agreed forms of "madness" that narcotize. One learns to adjust, to use all sorts of techniques to blot out the awareness that each of us is essentially exposed and mortal, flesh and blood. The aim is clearly to cut life down to manageable proportions, domesticate terror, and learn to think we are captains of our fate. Inevitably, however, not all these social "tricks" work equally well. Life's terrors have a way of breaking through to dim awareness, and therefore more drastic measures are needed. So after having lived the cultural lie uncritically, one tries to blot out awareness itself. If shopping to forget doesn't work, if obsessive work doesn't do it, one turns to drugs or drink, anything to forget, anything to assuage our fears, anything to deny our need for courage. Anything to help us refuse the truth that our lives are built on the blood of others.

The ineluctable reality of uncertainty is our fate. I have always known that, but I forget. I have also long known that we live by faith of one kind or another, and whatever name we give it, it is by faith we enter into the holy mystery of existence. We are carried forward by the spirit that binds us in solidarity to all human struggles for freedom and dignity, for bread and justice. The day I wished to stay in bed and wallow in self-pity and depression came as a shock to me. It revealed to me my hubris, my sense of self-importance, as if my efforts were not just a drop in the sea, seeds scattered that may or may not take root. I was afraid to accept possible defeat, despite my best efforts. I was afraid of death and lacked courage. Like those I criticize for turning their faces away from the suffering faces of America's victims, I lost my courage that morning in bed. And hope.

But later that day I would awaken and see through the screen of my self-importance when I leafed through Carolyn Forché's book and chanced upon her quoting Fr. Romero's words: "We must hope without hoping. We must hope when we have no hope."

Then her poem "Ourselves or Nothing" bubbled up in memory:

> *There is a cyclone fence between*
> *Ourselves and the slaughter and behind it*
> *We hover in a calm protected world like*
> *Netted fish, exactly like netted fish.*
> *It is either the beginning or the end*
> *Of the world, and the choice is ourselves or nothing.*

Priest and poet, reminding us to fight lucidly on. Hope when everything is clear. Awareness.

THE LIES OF 9/11
MIRACLE WORKERS

"America's fate was sealed when the public and the antiwar movement bought the government's 9/11 conspiracy theory. The government's account of 9/11 is contradicted by much evidence. Nevertheless, this defining event of our time, which has launched the U.S. on interminable wars of aggression and a domestic police state, is a taboo subject for investigation in the media. It is pointless to complain of war and a police state when one accepts the premise upon which they are based."

—Paul Craig Roberts, *How America Was Lost*

David Ray Griffin is an international treasure and truth teller, who, while being ignored by the mainstream corporate media (MSM) for his extraordinary series of books exposing the false flag attacks of September 11, 2001, will someday be lauded as a modern prophet. To those who know and have studied his work, he is an inspiration for his persistent insistence in more than a dozen books since 2004 that the truth about the U.S. treachery of that infamous day is essential for understanding the violence, planned by neo-conservatives and embraced by neo-liberals, that the United States has subsequently inflicted on the world. He has consistently argued that to believe in the government's explanation for 9/11, one has to reject logic, scholarship, and the basic laws of modern science.

Bush and Cheney: How They Ruined America and the World is Griffin's latest, and maybe his last, effort to reach those people who, out of fear, ignorance, or laziness, have walled themselves into a cyclopean labyrinth of denial about the defining event of our time. Without the clarifying truth about the attacks of September 11, 2001, there will be no exit from the continuing nightmare the world is experiencing.

If you are reading this review, you are probably not one of those people Griffin is trying to reach. Ay, there's the rub! As the title of his book suggests, he is using reversed logic to try and reach those who have accepted the official fiction that is *The 9/11 Commission Report* (no doubt without having read it; outside of serious researchers, I have never met a person who has, except for some of my students) and all the antecedent and subsequent government and MSM propaganda.

To this end, the first three-quarters of the book is devoted to the "destructive transformations of America and the world as a whole" that were initiated and justified by 9/11, many of which have been accepted by innumerable people as being based on government lies, most notably the war against Iraq. Griffin's hope is that if he can convince skeptical readers that the government would lie about Iraq, Libya, Ukraine, Syria, Yemen, etc., resulting in the deaths and maiming of millions of innocent people and the destruction of their countries, it would also lie about the attacks of September 11 that "legitimized" such carnage and the ongoing shredding of the U.S. Constitution.

The Will to Examine Miracles?

It's an ingenuous and compelling method, culminating with his concluding section on "15 major miracles" of 9/11, by which he means "violations of the laws of nature" in the strictest scientific sense. Astutely logical, deeply sourced, and scientifically compelling, the book's conclusion can only be rejected by one adamantly closed to accepting the ugly truth about the U.S. government and its media accomplices.

But getting skeptical people to read the book is the trick. I think that is very hard but much easier than to get the MSM to do so and give it a fair shake. People have friends whom they trust, and sometimes friends can convince friends to at least take a look. Speaking of the MSM, Griffin puts it thus:

> However, while granting that the Bush-Cheney administration told big and disastrous lies, which led to millions of deaths, most mainstream commentators have considered the idea that this administration engineered the 9/11 attack to be so absurd that they can render judgment without checking the evidence.

"Judging without checking the evidence" is the job of the MSM, who are stenographers for the government, but regular people might be persuaded to check the evidence before reaching a conclusion, if they can be led to that assessment one logical step after another. One can even hope that left-wing alternative media critics of the government, many of whom avoid this issue like the plague, might find the courage to reassess their anti-scientific denials in light of Griffin's work. After all, "the laws of physics don't lie," and logical reasoning has generally been a strength of many dissenters, especially those well-skilled in the art of disputation.

The Birth of the Tangled Web

Griffin is a master logician, so he begins with the obvious fact that the Bush-Cheney administration failed to prevent 9/11 and therefore failed to keep America safe that day, as Donald Trump said in a 2016 election debate, for which he was castigated by his opponents and the media. But he was right; it is a fact, whatever Bush-Cheney's deceptive excuses. As a result of those attacks, the U.S. attacked Afghanistan, claiming that was because Osama bin Laden orchestrated the attacks from that country. No evidence of bin Laden's guilt was ever presented, though Colin Powell initially said it would be shortly forthcoming (he quickly reneged on the promise). The invasion of Afghanistan, planned well in advance of 9/11, was the start of the war on terror that's been going on for 19 years with no end in sight. A 19-year-old war based on no evidence, just lies. Griffin shows how the alleged "evidence" that was eventually produced—the bin Laden videos—were fraudulent; that they were indeed "produced," and not by bin Laden; they were "bogus" according to Professor Bruce Lawrence of Duke University, the leading academic expert on bin Laden. And the FBI reported that it had "no hard evidence connecting Bin Laden to 9/11." But the administration and the media sang of bin Laden's guilt in unison. The public, beaten down in fear and trembling, accepted the claim as a fact, as they were further traumatized by additional lies about the anthrax attacks that are a key component of the entire propaganda campaign of fear and intimidation that resulted in The Patriot Act. (Graeme MacQueen's masterful analysis, *The 2001 Anthrax Deception*, should be required reading; for he shows how the often-forgotten anthrax attacks are intimately linked to those of September 11 and when studied closely, prove that 9/11 was an inside job.)

So Griffin begins with the lie about bin Laden that led to the lie about Afghanistan that led to the illegal and immoral and ongoing war against Afghanistan and all the millions of deaths and destruction that have ensued.

So knowing how lie leads on to lie, let us count some of the lies that followed. Griffin documents these in deeply sourced details, but I will list them concisely:

U.S. Government Lies Subsequent to the 9/11 Attacks:

- That the 9/11 attacks were surprises, a "New Pearl Harbor."
- That there was solid evidence for bin Laden's guilt.
- That the invasion of Afghanistan (and Pakistan) was therefore justified.
- That the "war on terror" and therefore The Patriot Act were necessary.
- That Saddam Hussein was connected to 9/11, was developing nuclear weapons, and had weapons of mass destruction
- That the attacks on Muslim countries were not based on Islamophobia

- That the chaos and destruction unleashed throughout the Middle East were not pre-planned and intentional.
- That the Obama administration's attack on Libya was a humanitarian response to the "madman" Gaddafi, who adopted a rape policy fueled by Viagra drugged troops ready to unleash a blood bath.
- That the war against Syria was not a CIA-instigated plan to overthrow Assad under the guise of "liberating" the Syrian people.
- That the jihadists in Syria, including ISIS, were not armed and supported by the U.S., with many of those arms being shipped out of Benghazi, Libya, under the direction of Hillary Clinton, Barack Obama, General David Petraeus, and Chris Stevens, the U.S. ambassador to Libya.
- That the Syrian "White Helmets" are independent volunteer do-gooders, not a propaganda outfit funded by the U.S. and UK governments.
- That the wars against Muslim countries throughout the Greater Middle East are not connected to the Israeli occupation of Palestine and serve as American support for Israel's agenda in the region.
- That drone killings are legal and morally justified.
- That the U.S. Constitution has not been shredded.
- That the coup d'état in Ukraine was not a U.S. operation as part of a continuing U.S. aggression toward Russia and a growing threat of a nuclear annihilation.
- That the U.S. buildup of military forces along Russia's western borders and the massive transfer of U.S. Naval forces to China's east are not U.S. acts of aggression making nuclear war more likely, but are acts of self-defense.
- That the threat of ecological holocaust is not connected to a 770 billion dollar "defense" budget, a trillion-dollar nuclear weapons modernization program, and U.S. wars against countries containing vast amounts of fossil fuels and rare minerals.

- That is only a sample of the lies that Griffin uses to lead the reader back to 9/11, the alleged reason for the death and destruction justified by such lies. If the U.S. government would lie in all these ways, he is saying, why would they not have lied with the Big Lie that started this string of destructive deceptions?

September 11, 2001

Thus the last section of the book (a little more than 25%) is devoted to "9/11: A Miraculous Day." Herein he explains why George W. Bush and Dick Cheney should not be trusted on 9/11. They did not want an investigation into the September 11 attacks; wanted the public to just trust them. They were eventually forced into an investigation by public pressure; originally named Henry Kissinger to head it (don't laugh—ha! ha!); rigged its makeup and had Philip Zelikow, arch neo-con and Bush insider, appointed its Executive Director. In short, they did everything possible to prevent an honest investigation. And we know that the result was *The 9/11 Commission Report* that is a piece of legerdemain on a par with *The Warren Commission Report*. In other words, a cover-up.

Griffin shows that "Bush and Cheney lied about their activities on 9/11" and that their relationship to the subsequent anthrax attacks, a key motivator for The Patriot Act and "the war on terror," suggest that their administration was the source of those attacks and therefore the 9/11 attacks. (See Graeme MacQueen's *The 2001 Anthrax Deception*). Griffin further notes how declassified official accounts refute "central features of the Bush-Cheney account of 9/11."

And then—the coup de grace—he shows how the official account of 9/11 depends on "miracle stories." Yet, "a look at the evidence shows that many people who accept science on tobacco, evolution, and global warming, accept miracles, implicitly, on the subject of 9/11, especially in relationship to the World Trade Center (WTC)." Herein lies the great stumbling block to convincing people of the truth of 9/11. Science, logic, careful reasoning, evidence, documentation, what you can observe with your own eyes, etc.—none of this matters when you are intent on being deceived (or pretending to be) because of the implications of examining the evidence and reaching conclusions that are deeply disturbing to your world view, ideology, or sense of self. To admit that you have believed a pack of lies for years is very difficult to accept. But regular people of good will can do so. These are the people Griffin is trying to reach. To convince those who have for years publicly and professionally dismissed those who have questioned the official version of 9/11 as conspiracy nuts is probably an impossible task. To convince the MSM that have worked hand-in-glove with the government to conceal the truth is preposterous. To convince those fine people who are devoted to truth in other areas to reconsider their positions on this core issue is conceivable. Surely the world is full of weird events that logic and science cannot explain. But when the defining event of recent history that has resulted in the world teetering on the edge of final destruction is explained by at least the following 15 miracles that Griffin lists, only a delusional person or one whose will to untruth is set in stone would not be moved to ask how these could be possible, and draw the obvious conclusions.

A Miraculous Precedent: The Assassination of JFK

I am reminded of that other foundational case in modern American history: the CIA-directed assassination of JFK. Dan Rather, the famous CBS news anchor, was in Dallas that day, and after seeing the Zapruder film (which was then kept from the American public for a decade), went on television to say that when the president was shot in the head he violently lurched forward, clearly implying that the shot came from Oswald from the rear. Of course once the public was able to see the film, it was obvious to anyone with eyes that he was violently thrown back and to his left, therefore having been shot from his front right, not by Oswald. Bingo: a conspiracy. Then in 2012, another famous TV personality, Bill O'Reilly wrote a book called *Killing Kennedy* in which he claims that he and his co-author watched the Zapruder film "time after time to understand the sequence of events," but still concluded that The Warren Commission was correct and that Oswald shot

Kennedy from behind despite the obvious visual evidence to the contrary. Miracles then, miracles now—they seem to define the two key events of modern American history for those wanting to obfuscate the truth.

Do you believe in miracles?

A Summation of Griffin's 15 Major Miracles

1. The Twin Towers and WTC 7 were the only steel-framed high-rise buildings ever to come down without explosives or incendiaries.
2. The Twin Towers, each of which had 287 steel columns, were brought down solely by a combination of airplane strikes and jet-fuel fires.
3. WTC 7 was not even hit by a plane, so it was the first steel-framed high-rise to be brought down solely by ordinary building fires.
4. These World Trade Center buildings also came down in free fall—the Twin Towers in virtual free fall, WTC 7 in *absolute* free fall—for over two seconds.
5. Although the collapses of the of the WTC buildings were not aided by explosives, the collapses imitated the kinds of implosions that can be induced only by demolition companies.
6. In the case of WTC 7, the structure came down symmetrically (straight down, with an almost perfectly horizontal roofline), which meant that all 82 of the steel support columns had to fall simultaneously, although the building's fires had a very *asymmetrical pattern.*
7. The South Tower's upper 30-floor block changed its angular momentum in midair.
8. This 30-floor block then disintegrated in midair.
9. With regard to the North Tower, some of its steel columns were ejected out horizontally for at least 500 feet.

10. The fires in the debris from the WTC buildings could not be extinguished for many months.

11. Although the WTC fires, based on ordinary building fires, could not have produced temperatures above 1,800°F, the fires inexplicably melted metals with much higher melting points, such as iron (2,800°F) and even molybdenum (4,753°F).

12. Some of the steel in the debris had been sulfurized, resulting in Swiss-cheese-appearing steel, even though ordinary building fires could not have resulted in the sulfidation.

13. As a passenger on AA Flight 77, Barbara Olson called her husband, telling him about hijackers on her plane, even though this plane had no onboard phones and its altitude was too high for a cell phone call to get through.

14. Hijacker pilot Hani Hanjour could not possibly have flown the trajectory of AA 77 to strike Wedge 1 of the Pentagon, and yet he did.

15. Besides going through an unbelievable personal transformation, ringleader Mohamed Atta also underwent an impossible physical transformation.

Griffin examines each of these "miracles" in detail. Taken together, they reduce the official explanation of 9/11 to a story told to credulous children who are afraid of the dark. One can only hope that Americans are ready to grow up and accept that the bogeyman is real and that he is out to devour them and the rest of the world if they don't awaken from their hypnotic sleep.

The Overwhelming Consensus of Experts

It is important to note that David Ray Griffin is not alone in his assessment that 9/11 was an inside job done to legitimize disastrous policies at home and abroad. There are thousands of scholars, religious leaders, scientists, engineers, airline pilots, firefighters and countless others who agree with him after studying the evidence.

Griffin names many of these experts in his conclusion. And they are not afraid of the absurd way the government and media accuse them of being "conspiracy theorists," since they know "as Lance deHaven-Smith explained in his book *Conspiracy Theory in America*, [that] the CIA started using 'conspiracy theory' as a pejorative term in 1964 to ridicule the growing belief, contrary to the Warren Report, that President Kennedy was killed by people within the U.S. government, including the CIA itself." Thoughtful people know, and the evidence has long proven, that the U.S. government is guilty of an extensive list of conspiracies, ranging from the alleged Gulf of Tonkin attack to its conspiracy to convince the American people that Saddam Hussein had weapons of mass destruction and extending back through many CIA-engineered coup d'états, the assassinations of JFK, Malcolm X, MLK, RFK, et al. The name calling has lost its sting when the documentary records confirm that the name callers are the conspirators.

So if you care about truth, your country, and the world; if you hate to be lied to; if you care about the victims of American violence everywhere—you should read *Bush and Cheney: How They Ruined America and the World*. It is a brave and brilliant book. Look at the evidence. Show others. Pass the book on. Give it as a gift.

And tip your hat to David Ray Griffin, a truth teller extraordinaire, who for nineteen years has been asking us to wake out of the hypnotic state of denial that has allowed the liars to bring the world to the edge of destruction. Griffin's persistence is the sign of hope we all need to join him in the fight against these unspeakable forces of evil.

A Genuine Actor: Francesco Serpico

"There are unconscious actors among them and involuntary actors; the genuine are always rare, especially genuine actors."
—**Friedrich Nietzsche,** ***Thus Spoke Zarathustra***

"Any artist who goes in for being famous in our society must know that it is not he who will become famous, but someone else under his name, someone who will eventually escape him and perhaps someday will kill the true artist in him."
—**Albert Camus, "Create Dangerously"**

"It ain't me you're lookin for, babe."
—**Bob Dylan, "It Ain't Me, Babe"**

The set was real but illusionary: A legendary old New England hotel dressed festively for Christmas and the holiday season. Norman Rockwell's magical realism. The lobby full with merriment, the cozy fire dancing to the sweet sound of violin and piano Christmas music mixed with a subtle alcoholic fragrance. Main Street USA. Snow on the street and the classic strains of "White Christmas" in the inner air. A mythic setting for meeting a legendary actor.

But as I entered the dimly lit set, the legend was nowhere to be seen. I approached the spot where the musicians were playing and didn't see him in the room opposite. Then, as I was greeting two actors with bit parts that I knew (unconscious actors, I should add), out of the shadows came a laughing Russian spy obviously dressed as a Russian spy, one red star on his hat, walking stick in hand. He and I were there to have a drink and enjoy the music that would allow us to talk privately without being overheard. A few hours earlier he had sent me a strange message from Epicurus: "It is impossible to lead a pleasant life without living wisely and well and justly, and it is impossible to live wisely and well and justly without living pleasantly ('justly' meaning to prevent a person from harming or being harmed by another)."

What did this cryptic message mean? The day before I had met a leading expert on the CIA on the same set and we had discussed the criminal activities of the Agency, how they dissembled and lied in their self-declared mission to defeat communism everywhere, even where it didn't exist. Those people were great at creating false myths, counter-myths, and Hollywood/media narratives to discombobulate a public already lost in an entertainment culture. Now I was meeting this crazy Russian whom I heard say to some passing actors that he was a communist, and then he said something in Latin that totally perplexed them, which made him laugh. A woman approached him and said she liked his hat. Again he replied in Latin with a Russian accent and her face dropped. Then we all laughed. She blushed, the scent of flirtation in the badinage. Was this guy serious or a comic having fun?

Off to the bar he and I went for some vino, wisecracks spewing from the mad Russian's mouth. Heads turned to watch our passage, for even on this movie set, his costume stood out.

As we settled in a corner with our drinks, a joyous warmth enveloped us. Play-acting was fun. Francesco was good at it. Here in the Red Lion Inn in Stockbridge, Massachusetts, no one took him for the legendary New York City Detective, Frank Serpico, shot in the face for being a whistleblower before that word became commonplace, and made mythic through the 1973 movie, *Serpico*. To the people surrounding us, he was just an amusing guy in an interesting hat, a man having fun with a buddy.

At a round table in front of the chairs we were sitting in, a group of six middle-aged adults sat playing cards. They were not conversing. Frank mentioned that they reminded him of those pictures of dogs playing cards. He got up and asked them if they were playing for high stakes. They laughingly said no, just for amusement. And what game were they playing? I asked. A children's game, the woman said. It was a perfect scene from a spoof, and Frank whispered to me, "The masses are deluded with TV, Hollywood, and children's games. Let's bark."

"Become who you are," advised Nietzsche.

Frank had done that, had always done it, despite decades of having to escape the mythic masked man Hollywood had made of him when Al Pacino played him in 1973, creating the legendary persona behind which the real person is expected to disappear, held hostage by the mask. While all persons are, by definition, masked, the word person being derived from the Latin, *persona*, meaning mask, there are those who are nothing but masks—hollow inside. Empty. No one home. Unconscious and involuntary actors living out a script written by someone else. Not Frank Serpico. He has consistently been an unmasker, a truth-teller exposing the fraud that is so endemic in this society of illusions and delusions where lying is the norm.

Frank has always understood masks. When he was an undercover cop, he used his play-acting skills to save his life. In the documentary film, *Frank Serpico,* directed by Antonino D'Ambrosio, he says he told himself: "You're going on the stage tonight. The audience is out there. I told myself I was an actor and I had to sell my role. I got my training in the streets of New York where I played many roles from a doctor to a derelict and how well I played those roles, my life depended on it." His acting skills were his protection, but these acts were performed in the service of protecting the citizens he had vowed to protect. Genuine acts.

Shakespeare was right, of course, "all the world's a stage," though I would disagree with the bard that we are "merely" players. It does often seem that way, but seeming is the essence of the actor's show and tell. But who are we behind the masks? Who is it uttering those words coming through the masks' mouth holes (the *per-sona,* Latin, to sound through). In Frank's case, the real man is not hard to find. Never was. From a young age he was incorruptible. When he became a cop and took his oath, he was the same honest guy, though not fully aware of the dishonesty that pervades society at all levels.

When this honest cop was lying in a pool of his own blood on the night of February 3, 1971, having been shot in the face in a set-up carried out by fellow cops, Frank Serpico heard a voice that said, "It's all a lie." In that moment as he fought for his life, he realized a truth he had previously sensed but never fully grasped in its awful reality. His honesty, his refusal to be a corrupt cop like so many others, his allegiance to the sacred oath he took when he became a police officer, was returned with a violent snarl by the liars he walked among. And in that moment, he was determined to live and return their lies with more truth, which he did in his subsequent eloquent testimony to the Knapp Commission that was investigating police corruption in the New York Police Department because of him.

But then came the rest of his life, not a small thing. Lionized and damned as a "rat" by many cops, recreated through the superb actor's mask of Al Pacino in the film Serpico, his legend was created by the celebrity machine. His truth was turned into a Hollywood myth; a true American hero became a cool movie star. But unlike a movie actor or entertainer, he was still Frankie the honest boy who became an honest cop, and he wanted to become who he was, not an actor playing someone else.

Police work was his "calling," he told me. That is a word with deep religious roots. A vocation (Latin, *vocare, to call*). The mythographer Joseph Campbell has written eloquently of "the call" in *The Hero with a Thousand Faces*. When one is called by this mysterious voice that many call God, this call to adventure and authenticity—the hero's way, he terms it—one is faced with a choice whether to accept or refuse. Campbell writes:

> [It] signifies that destiny has summoned the hero and transferred his spiritual center of gravity from within the pale of his society to a zone unknown. This fateful region of both treasure and danger may be variously represented: as a distant land, a forest, a kingdom underground, beneath the waves, or above the sky, a secret

island, lofty mountaintop, or profound dream state; but it is always a place of strangely fluid and polymorphous beings, unimaginable torments, superhuman deeds, and impossible delight.

From the start of his police work, Frank sensed he was moving in "a zone unknown" and danger lurked along the way, but he had accepted the call. Like the heroes in all the authentic myths, he could not be sure where it was all leading. He came to realize that it led to the depths of hell, the frightening underworld through which the hero must transit or perish. The dark night of the soul. A near death experience at the hands of the monsters. Unimaginable torments.

But dawn broke slowly, the same rosy-fingered dawn that greeted Odysseus as he contemplated the next step on his journey "home" from the war zone. So Frank left home, set sail for Europe, and although a wounded warrior, he took up the rest of his life. "Some may say I'm full of it," he said to me, "but my life has been like a serendipitous dream, one scene after another." This may surprise those who think of him only as Frank Serpico, the heroic and honest cop. But that was a role he played, something he did, not who he was. He has led a colorful, exciting, and adventurous life, but not because of the movie and book about his cop's life. His name Frank, after all, means a free man, and Frank is the epitome of a free-spirited soul, always trying to escape others' definitions of him. Sitting with our wine amid the music, he said:

> I wanted to be who I was before the shooting. Back then I knew more people and they knew me. Friends. Afterwards they made me into their own image. They were looking for perfection, but I wasn't perfect. So I became more guarded and felt I was living under a microscope. Even among friends, if we were playing a game in which you could make up things, like a word game, and pretend just for fun, and I did it like them, they would look at me as if I couldn't, that if I did, I was betraying myself as the honest cop. I had become the

legendary honest cop to them, not Frank, a guy who had lived up to his oath to be an honest cop, but who was also a regular person, not a celebrity. So I've had to deal with people being drawn to me because they think I'm a celebrity. I'm not an actor. I'm the real thing.

I was drawn to him because I sensed he was a *compañero*, similar to old, authentic friends I had grown up with in the Bronx. Guys with consciences, not crooks. Friends who could laugh and joke around. From our first meeting we connected: each of us dressed in individual camouflage—he, the bearded, aging Village hippie, concealing a conscience-stricken Italian-American kid from Brooklyn; me, sporting the look of an Irish-American something from the Bronx, concealing a conscience-stricken radical thinker and writer. Birds of a feather under different plumage, costumes concealing our true identities. Real play acting.

And then there was that Catholic thing. Both of us were products of New York Catholic families and schools. Thus conscience does not necessarily make cowards of us all. It also calls to us be honest, brave, and frank, despite the corruption of religious institutions. Nietzsche again: "'Christianity' has become something fundamentally different from what its founder did and desired. . . . What did Christ deny? Everything that is today called Christian." Frank hated school, and when he attended St. Francis Prep he was beaten by a religious Brother. Then, when this teacher died and was being waked, Frank looked at him in the coffin and found himself, to his own amazement, crying for the man. "That's how deep it goes into you," he said to me, "you end up crying for your tormentor." And while I understood his point of criticism that a corrupt society reaches into the cradle to poison us from the start, I thought there was more to it, some deep human empathy in that boy's soul. In the man's. Like Nietzsche, I sense in Frank a Romantic at heart. He once wrote a poem in which he said:

> *I was taught religion and all about race*
> *I was taught so well I felt out of place*

*But now I am a man and have no one to blame
So I must forget words like guilty, stupid, and shame.*

*And with the help of my soul I'll remember the way
And get back where I was on that very first day.*

Then he added in prose: "The God I believe in is not just my God, but the God of all beings no matter what language they speak.... I have no use for man-made religion.... They profane the name of Christ but none follow in his footsteps save a few perhaps like St Francis and even Vincent Van Gogh."

The few: St. Francis and Van Gogh. Telling choices. The wounded artist with a primal sympathy for the poor and the saint who drew animals to him out of love for all beings. St. Francis Prep, where Frank was first wounded by a sadist, a sign of things to come. And later, the lover of nature who lives in the country and feeds birds that eat out of his hands. The man who has written a beautiful essay about Henry David Thoreau. And the artist/genuine actor who writes, plays musical instruments, has acted in theatre, is producing a film about former Attorney General Ramsey Clark, another maverick who has also come in for severe criticism.

"What has been your reaction over the years to having been harshly criticized as a 'rat' by so many N.Y. cops?" I asked him.

"I took it as a joke," he said. "I am a rat. It's my Chinese zodiac sign."

But turning more serious, he added, "I never broke bread with these people, so I never could rat on them. I was never a part of them. In fact, when I was asked to wear a wire to record guys I worked with, I said absolutely not. I wasn't out to catch individuals, but to warn of corruption throughout the system, from bottom to top in the Police Department. It's the system I wanted to change, so in no way was I ever a rat."

"What sustained you all these years? Was it faith, love, family—what?

" It was wine, women, and song," he replied with a smile, as he held up his glass for a toast.

As we were walking through the crowded lobby, a woman was rocking in a rocking chair. Frank burst into song about a rocking chair to amuse me; then told me he was once sitting outside a café and someone approached him to act in a production of William Saroyan's *The Time of Your Life*. He said to the guy, "But I'm not an actor." "But you look the part of the Arab in the play," was the reply. So he took the part of the unnamed Arab and got to recite the most famous lines: "No foundation all the way down the line. No foundation all the way down the line." A refrain that echoes Frank's take on American society today. "It's all a lie" or "No foundation all the way down the line"—little difference.

Until we see through the charade of social life and realize the masked performers are not just the politicians and celebrities, not only the professional actors and the corporate media performers, but us, we won't grasp the problem. Lying is the leading cause of living death in the United States. We live in a society built of lies; lying and dishonesty are the norm. They are built into the fabric of all our institutions.

Later he quoted for me the preface to that play, words dear to his heart:

> In the time of your life, live—so that in that good time there shall be no ugliness or death for yourself or any life your life touches. Seek goodness everywhere, and when it is found, bring it out of its hiding place and let it be free and unashamed. Place in matter and flesh the least of the values, for these are the things that hold death and must pass away. Discover in all things that which shines and is beyond corruption. Encourage virtue in whatever heart it may have been driven into secrecy and sorrow by the shame and terror of the world. Ignore the obvious, for it is unworthy of the clear eye and kindly heart. Be the inferior of no man, or of any man be superior. Remember that every man is a variation of yourself. No man's guilt is not yours, nor is any man's innocence a thing apart. Despise evil and ungodliness, but not men of ungodliness or evil. These, understand. Have no

shame in being kindly and gentle but if the time comes in the time of your life to kill, kill and have no regret. In the time of your life, live—so that in the wondrous time you shall not add to the misery and sorrow of the world, but shall smile to the infinite delight and mystery of it.

And so I came to understand those words of Epicurus that this Thoreau-like bon-vivant had sent me. A pleasant life must be a just life, and if one is wise, and if one prevents people from harming or being harmed by others, one has chosen wisely and well. That is the way of the genuine actor. As Nietzsche meant it, a genuine actor is an original, one whose entire life is a work of art in which one begets oneself, or becomes who one is, as the Latin root of genuine (*gignere,* to give birth, to beget) implies. In a world of phony actors, Frank Serpico the real man, stands out.

He stood out long ago when he so courageously came forward to light a lamp of truth on the systemic corruption within the NYPD, and despite paying a severe price in suffering that almost cost him his life, he continues to speak out. Having spent a decade in exile in Europe where he entered into deep self-reflection ("There's nothing outside that isn't inside," he says), he returned "home" still passionately committed to shining a light on all that is evil but taken for normality that harms people physically and spiritually.

To this day his conscience gives him no rest. He is still fighting by lending his name and presence to cases of police corruption, injustice, racism, the silencing of dissidents, etc. He does not live in the past. A while ago he protested, along with some NYC cops, the deplorable treatment of the football player, Colin Kaepernick, by the National Football League. Just recently he spoke out for justice in the egregious 2004 police fatal shooting of Michael Bell, Jr. in the family driveway in Kenosha, Wisconsin. Supporting a video being distributed to 10,000 registered voters in a quest to get a public inquest, Frank wrote:

> This video equals the cell phone footage that captured the shooting of Walter Scott in South Carolina. Such

compelling and condemning evidence of a cover-up and abuse can no longer be ignored. For the sake of justice in American policing, Attorney General Brad Schimel and DA Michael Graveley must reopen this investigation if society's trust in their police is ever to be restored.

But before anyone gets caught up in hero worship of the genuine hero that Francesco is (not the pseudo-hero deceptively created by the celebrity and propaganda apparatus), his parting words are worth remembering. In this corrupt society, you had best not get ensnared in mythic fantasies about heroes coming to the rescue. It ain't him, babe, it ain't him you're looking for.

When you see injustice and corruption, when you open your eyes and see lying and deceit everywhere, you must be your own hero; you must be courageous and act. "Take care of it yourself," he says.

Or in the words of Nietzsche's *Zarathustra*, a book that serendipitously fell into his hands when he was alone in a friend's humble chalet in the Swiss Alps and shocked him with its relevance to his own experience: "'This is my way, where is yours?' thus I answered those who asked me 'the way.' For *the* way, that does not exist."

The Satanic Nature of the Atomic Bombings of Hiroshima and Nagasaki

> *"Ahab is forever Ahab, man. This whole act's immutably decreed. 'Twas rehearsed by thee and me billion years before this ocean rolled. Fool! I am the Fates' lieutenant; I act under orders."*
>
> —**Herman Melville,** *Moby Dick*

> *"The greatest evil is not now done in those sordid 'dens of crime' that Dickens loved to paint . . . . But it is conceived and ordered (moved, seconded, carried, and minuted) in clean, carpeted, warmed, and well-lighted offices, by quiet men with white collars and cut fingernails and smooth-shaven cheeks who do not need to raise their voice."*
>
> —**C. S. Lewis, author's preface, 1962,** *The Screwtape Letters*

American history can only accurately be described as the story of demonic possession, however you choose to understand that phrase. Maybe radical "evil" will suffice. But right from the start the American colonizers were involved in massive killing because they considered themselves divinely blessed and guided, a chosen people whose mission would come to be called "manifest destiny." Nothing stood in the way of this divine calling, which involved the need to enslave and kill millions and millions of innocent people that continues down to today. "Others" have always been expendable since they have stood in the way of the imperial march ordained by the American god. This includes all the wars waged based on lies and false flag operations. It is not a secret, although most Americans, if they are aware of it, prefer to see it as a series of aberrations carried out by "bad apples." Or something in the past.

Our best writers and prophets have told us the truth: Thoreau, Twain, William James, MLK, Fr. Daniel Berrigan, et al.: as a nation we are killers of the innocent. We are conscienceless. We are brutal. We are in the grip of evil forces.

The English writer D. H. Lawrence said it perfectly in 1923, "The American soul is hard, isolate, stoic and a killer. It has never yet melted." It still hasn't.

When on August 6 and 9, 1945 the American government killed 200-300 thousand innocent Japanese civilians with atomic bombs in Hiroshima and Nagasaki, it did so intentionally. It was an act of sinister state terrorism, unprecedented by the nature of the weapons but not by the slaughter. The American terror bombings of Japanese cities that preceded the atomic bombings of Hiroshima and Nagasaki—led by the infamous Major General Curtis LeMay—were also intentionally aimed at Japanese civilians and killed hundreds of thousands of them.

Is there an American artist's painting of Tokyo destroyed by the firebombing to go next to Picasso's much-celebrated Guernica, where estimates of the dead range between a comparatively mere 800 and 1,600? In Tokyo alone more than 100, 000 Japanese civilians were burnt to death by cluster bombs of napalm. All this killing was intentional. I repeat: Intentional. Is that not radical evil? Demonic? Only five Japanese cities were spared such bombing.

The atomic bombings were an intentional holocaust, not to end the war, which was already won, as the historical record amply demonstrates, but to send a message to the Soviet Union that we could do to them what we did to the residents of Japan. President Truman made certain that the Japanese willingness to surrender in May 1945 was made unacceptable because he and his Secretary-of-State James Byrnes wanted to use the atomic bombs—"as quickly as possible to 'show results'" in Byrnes' words—*to send a message* to the Soviet Union. So "the Good War" was ended in the Pacific with the "good guys" killing hundreds of thousands of Japanese civilians to make a point to the "bad guys," who have been demonized ever since. Russia phobia is nothing new.

Satan always wears the Other's face.

Many Baby Boomers like to say they grew up with the bomb. They are lucky. They grew up. They got to be scared. They got to hide under their desks and wax nostalgic about it.

The children of Hiroshima and Nagasaki who died under our bombs on August 6 and 9, 1945 didn't get to grow up. They couldn't hide. They just went under. To be accurate: we blew them to bits. Or they were left to suffer terribly for decades in pain and then die. But that it was necessary to save American lives is the lie. It's always about American lives, as if the owners of the country and the perpetrators of the deeds actually cared about them. But to tender hearts and innocent minds, it's a magic incantation. Poor us!

Fat Man, Little Boy—how the words echo down the years to the now fat Americans who grew up in the 1950s and who think like little boys and girls about their country's demonic nature. Such innocence—it is wonderful! We are different now. "We are great because we are good," that's what Hillary Clinton told us. The Libyans can attest to that. We are exceptional, special. The next election will prove we can defeat Mr. Pumpkin Head and restore America to its "core values."

Perhaps you think I am cynical. But understanding true evil is not child's play. It seems beyond the grasp of most Americans who need their illusions. Evil is real. There is simply no way to understand the savage nature of American history without seeing its demonic nature. How else can we redeem ourselves at this late date, possessed as we are by delusions of our own God-blessed goodness?

But average Americans play at innocence. They excite themselves at the thought that with the next election the nation will be "restored" to the right course. Of course there never was a right course, unless might makes right, which has always been the way of America's rulers. Today Trump is viewed by so many as an aberration. He is far from it. He's straight out of a Twain short story. He's Vaudeville. He's Melville's confidence man. He's us. Did it ever occur to those who are fixated on him that if those who own and run the country wanted him gone, he'd be gone in an instant? He can tweet and tweet idiotically, endlessly send out messages that he will contradict the next day, but as long as he protects the super-rich, accepts Israel's control of him, and allows the CIA-military-industrial complex to do its worldwide killing and looting of the treasury, he will be allowed to entertain and excite the public—to get them worked up in a lather in pseudo-debates. And to make this more entertaining, he will be opposed by the "sane" Democratic opposition, whose intentions are as benign as an assassin's smile.

Look back as far as you can to past U.S. presidents, the figureheads who "act under orders" (whose orders?), as did Ahab in his lust to kill the "evil" great white whale, and what do you see? You see servile killers in the grip of a sinister power. You see hyenas with polished faces. You see pasteboard masks. On the one occasion when one of these presidents dared to follow his conscience and rejected the devil's pact that is the presidency's killer-in-chief role, he—JFK—had his brains blown out in public view. An evil empire thrives on shedding blood, and it enforces its will through demonic messages. Resist and there will be blood on the streets, blood on the tracks, blood in your face.

But to even begin to hope to change the future, a confrontation with our demonic past (and present) is first necessary, a descent into the dark truth that is terrifying in its implications. False innocence must be abandoned. Carl Jung, in "On the Psychology of the Unconscious," addressed this with the words:

> It is a frightening thought that man also has a shadow side to him, consisting not just of little weaknesses— and foibles, but of a positively demonic dynamism. The individual seldom knows anything of this; to him, as an individual, it is incredible that he should ever in any circumstances go beyond himself. But let these harmless creatures form a mass, and there emerges a raging monster; and each individual is only one tiny cell in

the monster's body, so that for better or worse he must accompany it on its bloody rampages and even assist it to the utmost. Having a dark suspicion of these grim possibilities, man turns a blind eye to the shadow-side of human nature. Blindly he strives against the salutary dogma of original sin, which is yet so prodigiously true. Yes, he even hesitates to admit the conflict of which he is so painfully aware.

How can one describe men who would intentionally slaughter so many innocent people? American history is rife with such examples up to the present day. Iraq, Afghanistan, Libya, Syria, etc.—the list is very long. Savage wars carried out by men and women who own and run the country, and who try to buy the souls of regular people to abet their pact with the devil, to acquiesce to their ongoing wicked deeds. Such monstrous evil was never more evident than on August 6 and 9, 1945.

Unless we enter into deep contemplation of the evil that was released into the world with those bombings of Hiroshima and Nagasaki, we are lost in a living hell without escape. And we will pay. Nemesis always demands retribution. We have gradually been accepting rule by those for whom the killing of innocents is child's play, and we have been masquerading as innocent and good children for whom the truth is too much to bear.

"Indeed, the safest road to Hell is the gradual one," Screwtape the devil tells his nephew, Wormwood, a devil in training, "the gentle slope, soft underfoot, without sudden turnings, without milestones, without signposts."

That's the road we've been traveling.

The Spirit of Existential Rebellion

In the wake of World War II and the complete shattering of any illusion about the human capacity for evil, there arose in Western Europe, particularly in France and Germany, a "philosophy" called existentialism. More an attitude towards life rather than a formal philosophy, and with its roots going back at least as far as Kierkegaard and Nietzsche in the 19th century, existentialism emphasized individual freedom, authenticity, personal responsibility, and the need to confront the unimaginable horrors of World War II and the absurd situation in which human beings had created nuclear weapons that could obliterate the planet in a flash, as the United States had demonstrated by incinerating Hiroshima and Nagasaki. How to respond to the birth of global state nuclear terrorism became a task for the existential imagination.

The traditional belief that an all-powerful God could bring the world to an end had now been replaced by the idolatry of nuclear madmen who had hubristically violated the limits that the Greeks had long ago warned us not to exceed by making themselves into gods. When Robert Oppenheimer, known as the "father" of the atomic bomb, saw the first detonation of a nuclear weapon on July 16, 1945, he aptly quoted the Bhagavd-Gita: "Now I am become death, the destroyer of worlds." Having unleashed the Furies, these false gods have created a world in which the droning sound of nuclear intercontinental missiles haunts the secret nightmares of the world. We have been living with this unspeakable and unspoken truth for more than seventy years.

Opposition to the nuclear standoff and its accompanying proxy wars has waxed and waned over the years. Dissident minorities and sometimes many millions across the globe have mobilized to oppose not only nuclear weapons but the war makers who have waged continuous wars of aggression throughout the world and have created the national-security warfare state, seemingly intent on world destruction.

However, today the sound of silence fills the empty streets, as passivity has overtaken those who oppose the growing nuclear threat and the ongoing U.S.-led wars throughout the world. The spirit of resistance has gone to sleep. The German writer Karl Kraus understood this in the days of Hitler's rise during the 1930s when he said, "The real end of the world is the destruction of the spirit; the other kind depends on the insignificant attempt to see whether after such destruction the world can go on."

We need to somehow resurrect the spirit of resistance that will bring together millions of people across the world who oppose the death dealers. I think it is time to recall the power and possibility implicit in the spirit of existential thought.

The existential emphasis on individual responsibility and authentic truth telling in the works of various writers, including Jean Paul Sartre, Simone de Beauvoir, Gabriel Marcel, and Albert Camus (who didn't consider himself an existentialist but whose work emphasized many of the same themes), inspired large numbers of people in the late '50s into the mid-to-late '60s, including the international anti-nuclear movement and young American anti-war activists. Contrary to popular understanding, existentialism is not about navel gazing and hopelessness, but is about responding freely and authentically to the situations people find themselves in, which today, is the end-time, that is, a time when the fate of the world lies in the hands of nuclear madmen.

But by the end of the 1960s this existential spirit of rebellion started to dissipate. Academic gibberish replaced this rebellious spirit with the introduction of ideas such as post structuralism, leading eventually to postmodernist nonsense that not only refuted the need for personal responsibility, but eliminated the person altogether. By 1999 a leading exponent of postmodern rhetoric, Jean Baudrillard, was dismissing everything the existentialists emphasized. He said, "No one needs this kind of 'existential garb' any more. Who cares about freedom, bad faith, and authenticity today?"

If such words were just the ranting of an intellectual lost in a fantasy world of abstractions, that would be one thing. But they are a form of propaganda echoed throughout western societies, particularly the United States, through the repeated emphases over the decades that people are not free but are the products of biological brain processes, Darwinist evolution, etc. Deterministic memes have become dominant in cultural mind control. Such postmodern abstractions have denied everything that makes possible the fight against nuclear annihilation and the warfare states' domination of Western Europe and NATO, led by the United States.

The self is an illusion. Freedom is an illusion. Responsibility is an illusion. Guilt is an illusion. Everything is an illusion. A kaleidoscopic mad world in which no one exists and nothing really matters. This deterministic and nihilistic message has become the main current in western cultural propaganda since the late 1960s and has reached a crescendo in the present day. It is responsible for the growth of passivity and denial that dominates contemporary public consciousness. It underlies the refusal of so many otherwise intelligent people to engage themselves in the search for truth that would lead to their joining forces with others to create a massive anti-war movement.

While many people think of existentialism as only an atheistic approach to existence, this is incorrect. There are atheist and agnostic existentialists, yes, but existentialism's core emphases have deep roots in the various religious traditions, such as Judaism, Christianity, and Islam. That is because freedom, authenticity, truth telling, and social responsibility, while often buried within the institutional structures of these faiths, lie at their core. So if we are going to resurrect the spirit of rebellion necessary to transform today's world, we need to renew the virtues that all these emphasize.

A first step in this process is to ask with D. H. Lawrence the question, "How great a liar am I?"

In *Lightning East To West*, James Douglass made an intriguing suggestion when he said:

The exact opposite of the H bomb's destructive purpose, but psychic equivalent of its energy, is the Kingdom of Reality which would be the final victory of Truth in history—a force of truth and love powerful enough to fuse billions of individual psyches into a global realization of essential oneness. There is no reason why the same psyche which, when turned outward, was able to create the condition for a self-acting force of over 100 million degrees of heat, thus realizing an inconceivable thermonuclear fusion, cannot someday turn sufficiently inward to create the condition for an equally inconceivable (but nature balancing) fusion in its own psychic or spiritual reality. An end-time can also be a beginning. Gandhi said: "When the practice of the law becomes universal, God will reign on the earth as God does in heaven. Earth and heaven are in us. We know the earth, and we are strangers to the heaven within us."

While Gandhi's words are couched in religious language, their meaning can resonate with secular-minded people as well. These words speak to the power implicit in the human spirit as a whole. That power begins and builds when people of all persuasions are convinced that they must freely pursue the truth at all costs.

In these very dark times—these end-times created by nuclear weapons—seeing the truth is dependent on the will to truth, and the will to truth only arises when people believe they are free to alter the circumstances in which they find themselves. This belief in freedom is at the core of all existential thought and is why we need to resurrect it today.

Hovering in Cyberspace

We live in a fabricated reality where the visible world became nearly meaningless once the screen world became people's "window on the world." An electronic nothingness replaced reality as people gleefully embraced digital wraparound apparitions. These days people still move about in the physical world but live in the electronic one. The result is mass hallucination.

This is the fundamental seismic shift of our era. There is a lot of bitching and joking about it, but when all is said and done, it is accepted as inevitable. Digital devices are embraced as phantom lovers. Technological "advances" are accepted as human destiny. We now inhabit a technological nightmare (that seems like a paradise to so many) in which technology and technique—the standardized means for realizing a predetermined end most efficiently—dominate the world. In such a world, not only does the end justify the means, but to consider such a moral issue is beside the point. We are speeding ahead to nowhere in the most "efficient" way possible. No questioning allowed! Unless you wish to ask your phone.

These days there is much political talk and commentary about fascism, tyranny, a police state, etc., while the totalitarianism of technocracy and technology continues apace. It is not just the ecological (in the human/natural sense) impact of digital technology where one change generates many others in an endless spiral, but the fact that technical efficiency dominates all aspects of life and, as Jacques Ellul wrote long ago, "transforms everything it touches into a machine," including humans. For every problem caused by technology, there is always a technological "solution" that creates further technological problems, ad infinitum. The goal is always to find the most efficient (power) technique to apply as rapidly as possible to all human problems.

Writing nearly fifty years ago in *Medical Nemesis*, Ivan Illich explained how in medical care the human touch was being replaced by this technical mindset. He said:

> In all countries, doctors work increasingly with two groups of addicts: those for whom they prescribe drugs, and those who suffer from their consequences. The richer the community, the larger the percentage of patients who belong to both.... In such a society, people come to believe that in health care, as in all fields of endeavor, technology can be used to change the human condition according to almost any design.

We are of course living with the ongoing results of such medical technical efficiency. The USA is a country where many people are drugged, since the human problems of living are considered to have only technological solutions, whether those remedies are effective or anodyne. The "accidents" and risks built into the technological fixes are never considered since the ideological grip of the religion of technology is all-encompassing and infallible. We are caught in its web.

Marshall McLuhan, the media guru of the 1960s—whether he was applauding or bemoaning the fact—was right when he claimed that the medium is the message.

Cell phones, being the current omnipresent form of the electronification of life, are today's message, a sign that one is always in touch with the void. To be without this small machine is to be rendered an idiot in the ancient Greek sense of the word—a private person. Translation: one who is out of it, detached, at least temporarily, from the screens that separate us from reality, from the incessant noise and pinging messages that destroy reflection and create reflex reactions.

The price is very, very high.

One price, perhaps the most important, is the fragmentation of consciousness, which prevents people from grasping the present from within—which, as Frederic Jameson has noted, is so crucial and yet one of the mind's most problematic tasks—because so many suffer from digital dementia as their attention hops from input to output in a never-ending flow of mediated, disembodied data. As a result, a vicious circle has been created that prevents people from the crucial epistemological task of grasping the double-bind that is the ultimate propaganda. Data is Dada by another name, and we are in Dada land, pissing, not into Marcel Duchamp's ridiculous work of Dada "art," a urinal, but into the wind. And data piled on data equals a heap of data without knowledge or understanding. There is no time or space for grasping context or to connect the dots. It is a pointillist painting in the form of inert facts that few can understand or even realize that they don't.

I am typing these words on a Hermes 3000 manual typewriter, a beautiful piece of technology whose sound and movement creates a rhythmic sanctuary where my hands, head, and heart work in unison. It allows me to think slowly, to make mistakes that will necessitate retyping, to do second and third rereadings and revisions, to roll the paper out of the machine and sit quietly as I review it. My eyes rest on the paper, not a blue-lit screen.

Technology as such is not the problem, for my typewriter is a very useful and endurable machine, a useful technology that has enhanced life. It does not break or need to be replaced every few years, as computers do. It does not contain coltan, tantalum, or other minerals mined in the Democratic Republic of Congo, Rwanda, and other places by poor people working under oppressive conditions created by international consumer greed that is devouring the world. It does not allow anyone to spy on me as I type. I am alone and unplugged, disconnected, off-line and out of line, a sine qua non for thinking, and thinking about deep matters. The typewriter is mine, and mine alone, unlike the connected digital devices that have destroyed aloneness, for to be alone is to contemplate one's fate and that of all humanity. It is to confront essential things and not feel the loneliness induced and exacerbated by the illusion of always being in touch.

But while this typing machine allows me to write in peace, I am in no way suggesting that I have escaped the technological condition that we all find ourselves in. There are little ways to step outside the closing circle, but even then, one is still in it. I will eventually have to take my paper and type it into a computer document if I wish to publish it in the form you will be reading it. There is no other way. The technocrats have decreed it so. We are all, as George Orwell once wrote in a different context and meaning, "inside the whale," the whale in this case being a high-tech digital world controlled by technocrats, and we have only small ways to shield ourselves from it. Sitting in a quiet room, working on a typewriter, taking a walk in the woods without a cell phone, or not owning a cell phone, are but small individual acts that have no effect on the structural realty of what Neil Postman calls technopoly in his masterful book, *Technopoly: The Surrender of Culture to Technology*. And even in the woods one may look up to admire a tree only to find that it is a cell phone tower.

Humans have always created and used technology, but for a very long time that technology was subject to cultural and religious rules that circumscribed limits to its use. Today there are no limits, no rules to constrain it. The prohibition to prohibit is our motto. In our acceptance of technical efficiency, we have handed over our freedom and lost control of the means to ends we can't fathom but unconsciously fear. Where are we heading? Many probably wonder, as they check the latest news ping, no doubt about something to fear, as a thousand pieces of "news" flash through their devices without pause, like wisps of fleeting dreams one vaguely remembers but cannot pin down or understand. Incoherence is the result. Speed is king.

Of course, this kaleidoscopic flood of data confuses people who desire some coherence and explanation. This is provided by what Jacques Ellul, in *Presence in the Modern World,* calls "the explanatory myth." He writes:

> This brings us to the other pole of our bizarre intellectual situation today: the explanatory myth. In addition to its political and its mystical and spiritual function, the

explanatory myth is the veritable spinal column of our whole intellectual system . . . . Given that appearances produce confusion and coherence is needed, a new appearance unifies them all in the viewer's mind and enables everything to be explained. This appearance has a spiritual root and is accepted only by completely blind credulity. It becomes the intellectual key for opening all secrets, interpreting every fact, and recognizing oneself in the whirl of phenomena . . . this myth . . . [is] their one stable point of thought and consciousness . . . enables everyone to avoid the trouble of thinking for themselves, the worry of doubt, the questioning, the uncertainty of understanding, and the torture of a bad conscience. What prodigious savings of time and means, which can be put usefully to work manufacturing some more missiles . . . [they] have a good conscience because they have an answer for everything; and whatever happens and whatever they do, they can rely on the explanation that myth provides. This process places them within the most complete unreality possible. They live in a permanent dream, but a realistic dream, constructed from the countless facts and theories that they believe in with all the power of "mass persons" who cannot detach themselves from the mass without dying.

Today that myth is the religion of technology.

So if you have any questions you want answered, you can ask your phone.

Ask your phone why we are living with endless wars on the edge of using our most astounding technological invention: nuclear weapons.

Ask your computer why "nice" Americans will sit behind computer screens and send missiles to kill people half-way around the world with whom they are told they are at war.

Ask your smart device why so many have become little Eichmanns, carrying out their dutiful little tasks at Raytheon,

Lockheed Martin, and all the other war manufacturers, or not caring what stocks they own.

Ask your phone what really happened to the Ukrainian International Airlines Flight 752 in Iran. See if your phone will say anything about cyber warfare, electronic jamming, or why the plane's transponder was turned off preventing a signal to be sent indicating it was a civilian aircraft.

Ask who is behind the push to deploy 5 G wireless technology.

Ask that smart phone who is providing the non-answers.

Ask and it won't be given to you; seek and you will not find. The true answers to your questions will remain hidden. This is the technological society, set up and controlled by the rulers. It is a scam.

Google it!

God may respond.

Snow, Death, and the Bewildered Herd

> *"Few people at this hour—and I refer to the time before the breaking out of this most grim war, which is coming to birth so strangely, as if it did not want to be born—few, I say, these days still enjoy that tranquility which permits one to choose the truth, to abstract one in reflection. Almost all the world is in tumult, is beside itself, and when man is beside himself he loses his most essential attribute: the possibility of meditating, or withdrawing into himself to come to terms with himself and define what it is he believes and what it is that he does not believe; what he truly esteems and what he truly detests. Being beside himself bemuses him, blinds him, forces him to act mechanically in a frenetic somnambulism."*
>
> — José Ortega y Gasset, "The Self and the Other"

As I write these words, the house is being buried in a snowstorm. Heavy flakes fall slowly and silently as a contemplative peace muffles the frenetic agitation and speed of a world gone mad. A beautiful gift like this has no price, though there are those who would like to set one, as they do on everything. In my mind's eye I see Boris Pasternak's Yurii Zhivago, sitting in the penumbra of an oil lamp in the snowy night stillness of Varykino, scratching out his poems in a state of inspired possession. Outside the wolves howl. Inside the bedroom, his star-crossed lover, Lara, and her daughter sleep peacefully. The wolves are always howling.

Then my mind's lamp flickers, and Ignacio Silone's rebel character, Pietro Spina (from the novel *Bread and Wine*) appears.

He is deep into heavy snow as he flees the Italian fascists by hiking into the mountains. There, too, howl the wolves, the omnipresent wolves, as the solitary rebel—the man who said "No"—slowly trudges in a meditative silence, disguised as a priest.

Images like these, apparitions of literary characters who never existed outside the imagination, might at first seem eccentric. But they appear to me because they are, like the silent snow that falls outside, evocative reminders of our need to stop the howling media streams long enough to set our minds on essential truths, to think and meditate on our fates—the fate of the earth and our individual fates. To resist the forces of death we need to concentrate, and that requires slow silence in solitude. That is why the world's archetypal arch-enemy, Mr. Death himself, aka Satan, aka Screwtape, advises his disciple Wormwood in C. S. Lewis's *The Screwtape Letters* to befuddle people against the aberration of logic by keeping them distracted with contradictory, non-stop news reports. He tells him that "Your business is to fix his attention on the stream. Teach him to call it 'real life' and don't let him ask what he means by 'real.'"

It is a commonplace to say that we are being buried in continuous and never-ending information. Yet it is true. We are being snowed by this torrent of indigestible "news," and it's not new, just vastly increased in the last twenty-five years or so.

Albert Camus once said that "at any street corner the feeling of absurdity can strike any man in the face." While that is still true today, I would add that the feeling of an agitated and distracted bewilderment is everywhere to be seen as multitudes scan their idiot boxes for the latest revelations. Beeping and peeping, they momentarily quell their nervous anxieties by being informed and simulating proximity through the ether. Permanently busy in their mediated "reality," they watch as streaming data are instantly succeeded by streaming data in acts of digital dementia. For Camus the absurd was a starting point for a freer world of rebellion. For Walter Lippman, the influential journalist and adviser to presidents and potentates, "the bewildered herd"—his name for regular people, the 99%—disorientation was a beginning and a desired end. His elites, the 1%, would bewilder the herd in order to control them. His wish has come true.

A surfeit of information, fundamental to modern propaganda, prevents people from forming considered judgments. It paralyzes them. Jacques Ellul writes in *Propaganda*:

> Continuous propaganda exceeds the individual's capacity for attention or adaptations. This trait of continuity explains why propaganda can indulge in sudden twists and turns. It is always surprising that the content of propaganda can be so inconsistent that it can approve today what it condemned yesterday.

Coherence and unity in claims aren't necessary; contradictions work just as well. And the more the better: more contradictions, more consistency, more complementarity—just make it *more*. The system demands *more*. The informed citizen craves *more*; craves it faster and faster as the data become dada, an absurdist joke on logical thinking.

Wherever you go in the United States these days, you sense a generalized panic and an inability to slow down and focus. Depression, anxiety, hopelessness fill the air. Most people sense that something is seriously wrong, but don't know exactly what. So they rage and rant and scurry along in a frenzy. It seems so huge, so everything, so indescribable. Minds like pointilliste canvases with thousands of data dots and no connections.

In the mid-1990s, when the electronic world of computers and the internet were being shoved down our throats by a consortium of national security state and computer company operatives (gladly swallowed then by many and now resulting in today's total surveillance state), I became a member of The Lead Pencil Club founded by Bill Henderson (The Pushcart Press) in honor of Thoreau's father's pencil factory and meant as a whimsical protest: "a pothole on the information superhighway." There were perhaps 37 1/3 members worldwide, no membership roll, and no dues—just a commitment to use pencils to write and think slowly.

"Why should we live with such hurry and waste of life?" Thoreau asked. "We are determined to be starved before we are hungry."

So I am writing these words with a pencil, an object, to paraphrase Walter Benjamin, which haunts our present electronic world by being a ruin of the past. It is not a question of nostalgia, for we are not returning to our lost homes, despite a repressed urge for simpler times. But the pencil is an object that stands as a warning of the technological hubris that has pushed our home on earth to the brink of nuclear extinction and made mush of people's minds for grasping the reasons why.

I think of John Berger, the great writer on art and life, as I write, erase, cross out, rewrite—roll the words over and look at them, consider them. Berger who wrote: "Writing is an off-shoot of something deeper"; that "most mainstream political discourse today is composed of words that, separated from any creature of language, are inert.... dead 'word-mongering' [that] wipes out memory and breeds a ruthless complacency."

The pencil is not a fetish; it is a reminder to make haste slowly, to hear and feel my thinking on the paper, to honor the sacredness of what Berger calls the "confabulation" between words and their meaning. I smell the pencil's wood, the tree of life, its slow ascent, rooted in the earth, the earth our home, our beginning and our end.

Imagining our ends, while always hard, has become much harder in modern times in western industrialized nations, especially the United States that rains death down on the rest of the world while pretending it is immortal and invulnerable to the nuclear weapons it brandishes. Yet the need to do so has become more important. When in 1939 Ortega y Gasset warned in the epigraph of a most grim war coming to birth so strangely, as people acted "mechanically in a frenetic somnambulism," he was writing before nuclear weapons, the ultimate technology. If today we cannot imagine our individual deaths, how can we imagine the death of the earth? In a 1944 newspaper column George Orwell made an astute observation: "I would say that the decay of the belief in personal immortality has been as important as the rise of machine civilization." He connected this growing disbelief to the modern cult of power worship. "I do not want the belief in life after death to return," he added, "and in any case it is not likely to return. What I do point out is that its disappearance has left a big hole, and that we ought to take notice of that fact."

I think that one reason we have not taken notice of this fact of the presence of a huge absence (not to say whether this disbelief is "true") is the internet of speed, celebrated and foreseen by the grandmaster of electronic wizardry and obscurantic celebrator of retribalized man, Marshall McLuhan, who called the electronic media our gods whom we must serve and who argued that the extensions of human faculties through media would bring about abstract persons who would wear their brains outside their skulls and who would need an external conscience. Shall we say robots on fast forward?

Once the human body is reduced to a machine and human intercourse accepted as a "mediated reality" through so-called smart devices, we know—or should—that we are in big trouble. John Ralston Saul, a keen observer of the way we live now, mimics George Carlin by saying, "If Marx were functioning today, he would have been hard put to avoid saying that imaginary sex is the opiate of the people."

Saul is also one of the few thinkers to follow-up on Orwell's point. "Inexplicable violence is almost always the sign of deep fears being released and there can be no deeper fear than mortality unchained. With the disappearance of faith and the evaporation of all magic from the image, man's fear of mortality has been freed to roam in a manner not seen for two millennia." Blind reason, amoral and in the service of expertise and power, has replaced a holistic approach to understanding that includes at its heart art, language, "spirit, appetite, faith and emotion, but also intuition, will and, most important, experience." People, he argues, run around today in an inner panic as if they are searching for a lost forgotten truth.

Zygmunt Bauman, the brilliant sociological thinker, is another observer who has noticed the big hole that is staring us in the face. "The devaluation of immortality," he writes, "cannot but augur a cultural upheaval, arguably the most decisive turning point in human cultural history." He too connects our refusal in the West to contemplate this fact to the constant busyness and perpetual rushed sense of emergency engendered by the electronic media with its streaming information. To this end, he quotes Nicole Aubert:

> Permanent busyness, with one emergency following another, gives the security of a full life or a "successful career," sole proofs of self-assertion in a world from which all references to the "beyond" are absent, and where existence, with its finitude, is the only certainty. . . . When they take action people think short-term—of things to be done immediately or in the very near future. . . . All too often, action is only an escape from the self, a remedy from the anguish.

McLuhan's abstract persons, who rush through the grey magic of electronic lives where flesh and blood don't exist, not only drown in excessive data that they can't understand, but drift through a world of ghostly images where "selves" with nothing at the core flit to and fro. Style, no substance. Perspective, no person. Life, having passed from humans to things and the images of things, reduced and reified. Nothing is clear, the images come and go, fact and fiction blend, myth and history coalesce, time and space collapse in a collage of confusion, surfaces appear as depths, the person becomes a perspective, a perspective becomes a mirror, a mirror reflects an image, and the individual is left dazed and lost, wondering what world he is in and what personality he should don. In McLuhan's electronic paradise that is ours, people don't live or die, people just float through the ether and pass away, as do the victims of America's non-stop wars of aggression simply evaporate as statistics that float down the stream, while the delusional believe the world will bloodlessly evaporate in a nuclear war that they can't imagine coming and won't see when gone. Who in this flow can hear the words of Federico Garcia Lorca:

"Beneath all the totals, a river of warm blood/A river that goes singing/past the bedrooms...."?

> If you shower the public with the thousands of items that occur in the course of a day or a week, the average person, even if he tries hard, will simply retain thousands of items which mean nothing to him. He would need a remarkable memory to tie some event to another that happened three weeks or three months ago.... To obtain a rounded picture one would have to do research, but the average person has neither the desire or time for it. As a result, he finds himself in a kind of kaleidoscope in which thousands of unconnected images follow each other rapidly.... To the average man who tries to keep informed, a world emerges that is astonishingly incoherent, absurd, and irrational, which changes rapidly and constantly for reasons he cannot understand.

Jacques Ellul wrote that in 1965. Lucid summations are surely needed now.

Here's one from Roberto Calasso from *The Forty-Nine Steps*: "The new society is an agnostic theocracy based on nihilism."

Anyone who sits silently and does a modicum of research while honestly contemplating the current world situation will have no trouble in noticing that there is one country in the world—the USA—that has used nuclear weapons, is modernizing its vast obscene arsenal, and has announced that it will use it as a first strike weapon. A quick glance at a map will reveal the positioning of U.S. NATO troops and weapons right up to Russia's borders and the aggressive movement of U.S. forces close to China. Hiroshima and Nagasaki make no difference. The fate of the earth makes no difference. Nothing makes a difference. Obama started this aggressiveness, but will this change under Trump? That's very unlikely. We are talking about puppets for the potentates. It's easy to note that the U.S. has 1,000,000 troops stationed in 175 countries because they advertise that during college basketball games, and of course you know of all the countries upon which the U.S. is raining down death and destruction in the name of peace and freedom. That's all you need to know. Meditate on that and that hole that has opened up in western culture, and perhaps in your heart.

"If you are acquainted with the principle," wrote Thoreau, "what do you care for myriad instances and applications?" Simplify, simplify, simplify.

But you may prefer complexity, following the stream.

The snow is still falling, night has descended, and the roads are impassable. The beautiful snow has stopped us in our tracks. Tomorrow we can resume our frantic movements, but for now we must simply stay put and wonder.

Eugene Ionesco, known for his absurdist plays, including *Rhinoceros*, puts it thus:

> In all the cities of the world, it is the same. The universal and modern man is the man in a rush (i.e. a rhinoceros), a man who has no time, who is a prisoner of necessity, who cannot understand that a thing might be without usefulness; nor does he understand that, at bottom, it is the useful that may be a useless and back-breaking burden. If one does not understand the usefulness of the useless and the uselessness of the useful, one cannot understand art. And a country where art is not understood is a country of slaves and robots.

Ionesco emphasized the literal insanity of everyday life, comparing people to rhinoceroses that think and act with a herd mentality because they are afraid of the solitude and slowness necessary for lucid thought. They rush at everything with their horns. Behind this lies the fear of freedom, whose inner core is the fear of death. Doing nothing means being nothing, so being busy means being someone. And today being busy means being "plugged into the stream" of information meant to confound, which it does.

I return to the artist Pasternak, since the snowy night can't keep me away. Or has he returned to me? I hear Yurii Zhivago's uncle Nikolai speaking:

Only individuals seek the truth, and they shun those whose sole concern is not the truth. How many things in the world deserve our loyalty? Very few indeed. I think one should be loyal to immortality, which is another word for life, a stronger word for it.... What you don't understand is that it is possible to be an atheist, it is possible to not know whether God exists, or why, and yet believe that man does not live in a state of nature but in history.... Now what is history? It is the centuries of systematic explorations of the riddle of death, with a view to overcoming death. That's why people discover mathematical infinity and electromagnetic waves, that's why they write symphonies. Now, you can't advance in this direction without a certain faith. You can't make such discoveries without spiritual equipment. And the basic elements of this equipment are in the Gospels. What are they? To begin with, love of one's neighbor, which is the supreme form of vital energy. Once it fills the heart of man it has to overflow and spend itself. And then the two basic ideals of modern man—without them he is unthinkable—the idea of free personality and the idea of life as sacrifice. Mind you, all of this is still extraordinarily new.... Man does not die in a ditch like a dog—but at home in history, while the work toward the conquest of death is in full swing; he dies sharing in this work. Ouf! I got quite worked up, didn't I? But I might as well be talking to a blank wall.

I look outside and see the snow has stopped. It is time to sleep. Early tomorrow the plows will grind up the roads and the rush will ensue. Usefulness will flow.

But for now the night is beautiful and slow. A work of art.

Playing on the Devil's Chessboard: Allen Dulles and the CIA

David Talbot's book, *The Devil's Chessboard: Allen Dulles, the CIA, and the Rise of America's Secret Government,* is a bold and profoundly important book, not only for the portrait of the evil spymaster Allen Dulles, but even more so for its examination of the legacy he spawned—the creation of a cabal hidden behind the public face of the United States government that secretly runs the country today on behalf of wealthy elites. The psychopathic Allen Dulles was the enforcer for this group, called "the power elite" by C. Wright Mills in the 1950s. In recent years, especially since September 11, 2001, as its power has expanded, it has been given different names—the deep state, the national security state, deep politics, etc.—but that has not diminished its power one jot. Like a patient who goes to a doctor seeking a label for vague yet disturbing symptoms, people may feel relief from the naming, but the dis-ease continues until the root cause is eliminated. Aye, there's the rub!

Dulles is dead, but the structure he created lives on and flourishes under new operatives.

Because of his intrepid examination of these forces, David Talbot can expect to be ignored and attacked by disinformation specialists of various stripes, who will use specious reasoning, lies, and any small weaknesses in his style or sourcing to dismiss the essential truths of his well-documented and beautifully written thesis. First ignore, and if that doesn't work, then attack, is the modus operandi of these propagandists who populate the mainstream media, the people Dulles had in his pocket and whom Talbot excoriates throughout the book.

When an author has the guts to accuse America's longest-reigning CIA Director of "a reign of treason," he can expect blowback from media and academic spokesmen of the deep-state.

Talbot is a gifted writer whose narrative style quickly engrosses the reader. Two chapters into *The Devil's Chessboard*, one can't help being nauseated by his account of Allen Dulles's blood-chilling betrayal of large numbers of European Jews targeted by Hitler. "Dulles," Talbot writes, "was more in step with many Nazi leaders than he was with President Roosevelt." Together with his brother John Foster Dulles, who would become Secretary of State under Eisenhower, Allen Dulles had long-standing business ties to German industrial giants such as I G Farben (manufacturers of Zyklon B used in the gas chambers) and Krupp steel. Their law firm, Sullivan and Cromwell, "was at the center of an intricate network of banks, investment firms, and industrial conglomerates that rebuilt Germany after World War I." Slow to publicly break with Hitler and his allies, the Dulles brothers, especially Allen, reserved a place in his heart and a place at the table for his Nazi friends. When he was recruited into the Office of Strategic Services (OSS) in 1941 and slipped into neutral Switzerland in late 1942, he was there not so much to support Roosevelt's war efforts as to protect the interests of his law firm's German clients. In doing so, he betrayed personal friends and anonymous Jews to Hitler's killers in a heartless manner hard to fathom. Whenever Dulles had a chance to publicize the plight of the Jews, he buried the reports. For example, when a German cable reported that 120,000 Hungarian Jews, including children, were to be taken for work in the "labor services"—a euphemism for a trip to Auschwitz—"Dulles's communiques to OSS headquarters used the same banal language as the Nazis, referring blandly to the 'conscription' of Hungary's Jews." While noting that academic researchers decades later remain hesitant to condemn Dulles for this, Talbot will have none of it. It is for good reason that he entitles his book *The Devil's Chessboard*. He thinks Dulles was satanic.

In addition to his chilling indifference to the slaughter of the Jews, Dulles worked overtime to undermine FDR's adamant insistence that he would accept nothing less than an "unconditional surrender" and that Nazi war criminals would face justice. Dulles worked his wiles at saving many Nazi war criminals and returning them to power in post-war West-Germany. Among them was Reinhard Gehlen, Hitler's notorious chief of intelligence. In a talk to the Council of Foreign Relations on December 3, 1945, as the first Nuremburg trial was underway, Dulles told the meeting, "Most men of the caliber required to [run the new Germany] suffer a political taint. We have already found out that you can't run the railroads without taking in some [Nazi] party members." Couching this in anti-Soviet rhetoric for an audience of like-minded power brokers, many of whom were no doubt as ant-Semitic as he was, Dulles made sure it happened. He worked hard to save the neck of Himmler's former chief of staff and commander of the security forces in Italy, SS general Karl Wolff. Called the "Bureaucrat of Death," this killer was one of many Dulles saved under his separate peace pact, Operation Sunrise, a traitorous circumvention of Roosevelt's insistence on justice. SS colonel Eugen Dollman was another. In this operation, he worked closely with James Jesus Angleton, the future CIA head of counterintelligence who saw Dulles as his maestro. Working together they helped many notorious Nazi war criminals escape to the United States, Latin America, and other countries via the "Nazi ratlines."

In Part II of the book, Talbot buttresses these historical and well-sourced facts with a detour into Dulles's personal life and relationships. It is not a reassuring portrait. We learn that his wife Clover and one of his mistresses, Mary Bancroft, called him "the Shark." (Bancroft was the best friend of Ruth Paine's mother-in-law; it was at Ruth Paine's house that Marina and Lee Harvey Oswald lived at the time of JFK's assassination.) Bancroft refers to "those cold blue eyes of his" and his "peculiar mirthless laugh." Carl Jung, who treated both women, said Dulles was "quite a tough nut." Talbot notes that there was "an impenetrable blankness that made him hard to read." This description approximates Jung's take on Hitler that Talbot juxtaposes on the same page—that

Hitler seemed like "a mask, like a robot, or a mask of a robot." Mary Bancroft recalled that the emotionally dead Dulles's favorite word was "useful." People were only good to him if they were useful. His daughter Joan told Talbot that her father was "clearly not interested in us." A grinning Dulles once told Mary that his feigned bonhomie, his avuncular demeanor, and trusting attitude toward people were an act. He said, "I like to watch the little mice sniffing at the cheese just before they venture into the little trap. I like to see their expressions when it snaps shut, breaking their little necks."

After his WW II work assisting Nazis, Dulles turned his attention to stirring the cauldron in Eastern Europe. This time he betrayed many thousands to Stalin's thugs in a make-believe plot called Operation Splinter Factor that was meant to panic Stalin. It achieved its goal and once again the victims were "useful" to him. His ideological obsession in countering the Soviet Union in the Cold War knew no bounds. Talbot reports that private citizen Dulles funded espionage activities with treasure looted from Jewish families; that he set up, together with Frank Wisner and others, his own espionage unit deep within the State Department—the Office of Policy Coordination; that he was instrumental in the rise of Richard Nixon to political prominence. Throughout the late 1940s and early 1950s he was hard at work constructing the infrastructure of the CIA and a powerful secret government that would outlast him.

Once he finagled his way into the position of CIA Director under Eisenhower, "the CIA would become a vast kingdom, the most powerful and least supervised agency in government.... More in keeping with an expanding empire than with a vibrant democracy." Talbot closely chronicles the rise of Senator Joseph McCarthy, the bullying Red hunter, and Dulles's dirty battles with him. Secret dossiers, sexual blackmail, every trick imaginable—these were the methods Dulles used in his winning battle with McCarthy. This victory gave him cachet with Washington liberals, who celebrated Dulles's CIA as a safe place for the liberal intelligentsia. This was a fateful turn of events; "it established a dangerous precedent," Talbot notes, for Dulles now had a freer hand to grow the CIA and expand its secret powers with liberal support against the "real" communist threat, not the hyped-up sort McCarthy stood for.

"In truth," he writes, "the CIA became an effective killing machine under Dulles." Assassination had always been one of his favorite methods, and now it had found an institutional home. Today it is also at home in the White House, whether under Obama or Trump, a development well-documented, and a sign of Dulles's expanded and enduring influence.

Talbot has two excellent sections on what Dulles felt were two of his greatest successes: the CIA led 1953 coup in Iran and the 1954 coup in Guatemala, both of which ousted democratically elected leaders and installed dictators for the benefit of multinational corporations' foreign investments. Hundreds of thousands of innocent people were eventually killed and tortured as a result, and we are dealing with the consequences today.

Throughout his narrative Talbot mentions many of Dulles's protégés who will figure prominently in future events, including assassinations of American and foreign leaders: Howard Hunt, James Angleton, David Atlee Philips, Richard Helms, William Harvey, David Morales, to name but a few. As one reads through his excellent chronicle of the CIA's coups, its MKULTRA mind control project, its cultural engineering that captivated artists and intellectuals, one can't help feeling that Dulles's machinations are leading to a defining culmination.

Enter Senator John F. Kennedy and an explosive speech he delivered on the Senate floor on July 2, 1957. Talbot correctly notes this speech's significance when he writes, "Breaking from the Cold War orthodoxy that prevailed in the Democratic as well as Republican parties, JFK suggested that Soviet expansionism was not the only enemy of world freedom; so, too, were the forces of western imperialism that crushed the legitimate aspirations of people throughout the Third World."

This speech set the stage for the CIA's future war with Kennedy that ended in his assassination on November 22, 1963. JFK was challenging the entire worldview of the Eisenhower / Dulles / Republican/ Democratic establishment. He had crossed the Rubicon. Talbot updates it aptly: "Even today, no nationally prominent leader in the United States today would dare question the imperialistic policies that have led our country into one military nightmare after another." If one could imagine a leader doing so, and that politician was then elected president, what would be his fate? Talbot's implication is sobering, and again recalls those prominent leaders who dared to question the imperialist agenda—JFK, Malcolm X, Martin Luther King, and Robert Kennedy.

In the last section of the book Talbot covers a lot of familiar territory regarding the Bay of Pigs, Dulles's firing by Kennedy, and Kennedy's assassination. He accurately claims that the Bay of Pigs was a setup of Kennedy by Dulles that "was meant to fail" so as to force Kennedy to launch a full-scale invasion of Cuba. "The wily CIA chief set a trap for Kennedy, allowing the president to believe that his 'immaculate invasion' could succeed, even though Dulles knew that only U.S. soldiers and planes could ensure that." What he doesn't mention, but would buttress his argument further, is that classified documents uncovered in 2000 revealed that the CIA had discovered that the Soviets had learned of the date of the invasion more than a week in advance, had informed Castro, but never told Kennedy. This treasonous withholding was not lost on Kennedy who knew that "Dulles had lied to his face in the Oval Office about the chances for the operation's success." When JFK refused the bait and courageously avoided the trap Dulles had set for him—"to break his little neck"—Dulles and his followers were enraged. "That little Kennedy . . . he thought he was a god," Dulles let slip in 1965 on a stroll with the writer Willie Morris.

Talbot's section on the attempted coup d'état against French President Charles de Gaulle is terrific. This CIA backed event, launched in the same month as the Bay of Pigs, was also clearly meant to embarrass Kennedy and to send the message that it was the CIA, not Kennedy, who was in charge. The July 1962 assassination attempt on de Gaulle emphasized the message: those who dare to recognize the independence of Third World countries, as JFK had proposed in 1957 and de Gaulle was in the process of doing with Algeria, would be eliminated.

Talbot convincingly shows that although he was out as CIA Director, Dulles was still very much in power, avidly conferring and plotting with his CIA acolytes, his moles in the Kennedy administration, and his military allies led by the Joint Chief's chairman Lemnitzer, who hated Kennedy. He writes:

> Like the Time-Life building in Manhattan, Dulles's brick house on Q Street was a boiling center of anti-Kennedy opposition. The actively "retired" spymaster maintained a busy appointments calendar, meeting not only with CIA old boys like Frank Wisner and Charles Cabell [the brother of the mayor of Dallas on the day Kennedy was murdered], but with a steady stream of top-rank, active-duty agency officials such as Angleton, Helms, Cord Meyer, and Desmond Fitzgerald. More surprisingly, Dulles also conferred with mid-level officials and operational officers such as Howard Hunt, James Hunt (a key deputy of Angleton, and no relation to Howard), and Thomas Karamessines (Helm's right-hand man).

In October 1963 Dulles gave a speech ridiculing the Kennedy administration's "yearning to be loved" by the rest of the world. His best-selling book, *The Craft of Intelligence*, also appeared that fall and was sycophantically praised by his media allies at *The New York Times* and *Washington Post*, papers that would then give their seal of approval to the Warren Commission report that Dulles would control and which has been called the Dulles Commission. Talbot correctly notes throughout the book that Dulles always had the backing of powerful mainstream media such as *The New York Times, The Washington Post, Time-Life*, etc. Their owners and executives were a key part of his network of friends and insiders who worked in tandem to support their mutual interests at home and abroad.

He has a revelatory section on Dulles's retreat on the weekend of JFK's assassination to the top-secret "Farm," a CIA command facility, officially known as Camp Peary. From Friday, November

22, the day of the assassination, through Sunday, the 24th, the day Ruby shot Oswald, Dulles hunkered down at this training center for assassins, as described by former CIA agents Philip Agee and Victor Marchetti. It was also a "black site" where extreme interrogation methods were used on suspected enemies. What he was doing there is unknown, though highly suspicious.

The weakest part of Talbot's final section, where he marshals plenty of circumstantial evidence that strongly suggests but doesn't prove Dulles's part in the assassination, is his analysis of Ruth and Michael Paine. Talbot interviewed them in their retirement community and came away a bit starry-eyed. Ruth Paine was the Dallas housewife who had befriended Marina Oswald and taken her—and Lee Harvey on weekends—to live with her. She was the key witness for the Warren Commission. It was at her home where incriminating evidence against Oswald was found. The Paines' connection to the CIA, Dulles's network, and other CIA operations, confirmed by excellent researchers in great detail, escapes him, although he does note their connection to Mary Bancroft, Dulles's former mistress. Of the Paines he writes, "In their immaculate innocence, the Paines played right into the hands of those who were manipulating Oswald." I'm afraid Talbot is the innocent here. The Paines are very important figures in the assassination and seeing them clearly would add to his powerful thesis. Perhaps he was tired at this point in his pursuit of the satanic Dulles.

He does raise three interesting issues in his last hundred or so pages. (I should note that *The Devil's Chessboard* is a very long—661 pages—and heavily documented book.) They are: the aforementioned account of Dulles at "the Farm," the connections to the attempted coup and assassination against de Gaulle, and the very real possibility of CIA operative William Harvey being involved in the killing of Kennedy. Otherwise, there is not much new about the assassination, though he does do an excellent job of marshalling the available recent research on the subject and sprinkling his text with intriguing suggestions.

One of the most interesting new details he offers is from a book by de Gaulle's information minister Alain Peyrefitte,

C'etait de Gaulle, which was never translated into English. In it the French president, just home from JFK's funeral, confides to Peyrefitte that he knew that the CIA was behind the assassination.

> What happened to Kennedy is what nearly happened to me. His story is the same as mine. . . . The security forces were in cahoots with the extremists. . . . But you'll see. All of them together will observe the law of silence. They will close ranks. They'll do everything to stifle any scandal. They will throw Noah's cloak over these shameful deeds. In order not to lose face in front of the whole world. In order to not risk unleashing riots in the United States. In order to preserve the union and to avoid a new civil war. In order to not ask themselves questions. They don't want to know. They don't want to find out. They won't allow themselves to find out.

Thus the "unspeakable," although an open secret, was born. But JFK's assassination isn't a mystery. As Dr. Martin Schotz said twenty years ago, "Any citizen who is willing to look can see clearly who killed President Kennedy and why." The basic facts are long known that he was killed by a CIA led operation to eliminate him for his intention to end the Vietnam War, for his support of Third-World independence, for his opposition to the military-corporate-industrial complex, and for his efforts to end the Cold War. Talbot knows all this. He knows that JFK's American University address of June 11, 1963 sealed his fate. He knows and says that Robert Kennedy was also killed as a result of a conspiracy, and he needed to be stopped before he became president and reopened the investigation into the killing of his brother. Talbot's valiant effort to put faces on the conspirators is laudatory. But while being also highly suggestive, it may not be necessary.

The Devil's Chessboard is a very important book. David Talbot has exposed the face of evil incarnate in Allen Dulles, the hit-man for the power elite. He has documented the rise of the secret state that holds the ignorant in its grip today, is waging war around the globe, and spying on the American people. He has warned us that evil often wears the mask of civility and high society. Satan, he suggests, wears many masks, and he continues to move the pawns with a smile.

"Dead for nearly half a century," he concludes, "Dulles's shadow still darkens the land." And although he is reticent to name today's names who carry on his legacy, and refers to them as "faceless security bureaucrats," they do have faces, and names, as Allen Dulles did—so it's time to call them out and name them. Otherwise we are playing Dulles's mind-control games, and we will have to wait another fifty years to read a comparably excellent study showing future readers who Dulles's clones are today.

Like Arthur Schlesinger, Kennedy's craven assistant, who, when asked to watch the Zapruder film's infamous frame 313 kill shot, turned his head and walked away saying, "I can't look and won't look," we will become accomplices by neglect in the ongoing hijacking of the country by the secret state.

David Talbot is a true patriot for giving us this extraordinary book.

Love is Lovelier the Third Time Around, Isn't It?

I sure as hell hope so. I've been going through a rough patch these last few years. My search for true love has been disastrous. I suppose this is not unusual, but for it to be concentrated in just a few years has made me quite desperate. I am thinking about embarking on my third serious relationship in three years, including one marriage and a divorce. But I am hopeful now since . . . well, let me first give you the sad background of how I got to this point, and then maybe you can give me your advice, which I imagine is based on deep experience and good luck.

I've never written to Miss Lonelyhearts, but I am really desperate and don't want to enter into another dreadful relationship, one that could compromise me in more ways than one. I'd never recover.

And I know the world is full of serious issues that make my story seem so trivial, and I guess it is, but I'm feeling so down I just have to tell somebody.

A few years ago, when I woke up one morning and looked in the mirror, I said to my image, "Man, you are a pathetic sad sack." Hearing that, one of us thought there must be a way to get okay with his self, all things being equal and everything being relative. I remembered seeing a book in a used book store with the title, *I'm OK—You're OK*, and thinking I wasn't really OK, I was depressed and had a hard time concentrating on anything except my face in the mirror and the sorry state of my life. All the men I knew seemed so down too, so waddya call it, so fucked up or so fucked down. I never could understand which is the right way to say it. Is there a right way or can you say it any way you want? Up down—just fucked, or maybe not. These other guys were dragging too, but I needed to focus on little old me. I was definitely not OK.

So I got in my truck and cruised around, listening to some stupid news show on the radio when I heard a report that startled me and gave me a great idea. I drove to the Dollar Store to get a wedding card to send to myself. This report I heard said the latest cool thing was to marry yourself—they called it sologamy, I think the guy said. It made you feel good about yourself. OK, I think the guy said. They interviewed this woman who had just married herself and boy was she flying high and enthusing about the great feeling it gave her. She said she had realized she had fallen out of love with herself and marrying herself was like the second time around. It really stirred my blood and got me thinking what I could do for myself. I started humming that old song, you know, "Love is lovelier, the second time around. . . ."

Like I said, so many of the guys I saw around seemed so down, in the bar they sat over their beers with their shoulders slumped and in the supermarkets I saw the old guys looking so hangdog as they pushed those shopping carts after the women who had notes in hand and little calculators as they took charge of the food buying. Those women seemed OK at least. The men always seemed to be one or two steps back and the women talking and smiling all the time. I even noticed that when I passed an exercise studio the women came out in those yoga outfits looking so OK and up for things but the guys I knew who went to the gym looked all tied in knots after heaving the weights like they were performing some grim duty that would keep them above water for a while. The women seemed like they had gotten religion and were saved.

Then I stopped in the local coffee shop to get a pick up and think about this marrying myself thing. That's when I lucked out for sure. Or is it lucked in? Like I said, these sayings confuse me, I never know what's correct or not, out or in, up or down. Are there some rules to all this or can you just wing it? I get really confused. Anyway, there was a bunch of newspapers lying around and I glanced at a *New York Times* on the table. There was this weird article that jumped out at me about transracialism and transgenderism and this big debate about these big words and a philosopher who claims if you can self-identify as a different sex, or is it gender, I can never get them straight, you should also be able to self-identify as a different race. It was a long article with a lot of people arguing back and forth and I couldn't concentrate on it all, but I got the gist of the professor's point and thought this might be for me, it might help me get OK, which was my goal. As I said, I saw all those women up and smiling all the time and the guys down and hang dogged and I always noticed that Magic Johnson the hoops star of old is always smiling on the tube and I've always wondered why that was.

So to get to my point, I made a decision then and there. I gave it a shot and married myself on June 9th since they say June is the best marrying month, and I decided to follow the philosopher's suggestion and self-identify as a black woman as well. I figured it couldn't hurt and might help. The guy was a philosopher after all, and aren't philosophers supposed to know a lot? That woman part was just for the day of course, and I planned on going back to being me a man the next day, me married to I. I was just hoping the woman switch would be a happy trick, and the day after, when I looked in the mirror, I'd hear that smiling face say, "Man, You're OK, I'm OK."

Of course, I invited no one to the wedding, for I knew they'd understand how intimate the ceremony was.

That was two years ago.

The relationship didn't work out, actually it was a disaster, and so I eventually filed for a divorce. It was no one's fault really, but we were emotionally devastated nevertheless. At least we had no children. Sologamy didn't seem to suit us. We had acted impetuously. As I said, I had gotten the idea after hearing an NPR radio report about a woman who fell in love with herself and said that after she tied the knot, she had never been happier. I was an American and felt happiness was my right, too.

The world was getting me down at the time with all the political news about the Russians coming and insinuating themselves between me and you and all good Americans who had just wanted to elect Hillary Clinton and be happy. And as I was thinking about this happy married couple—the woman and herself, not Bill and Hillary—I chanced upon that *New York Times* article in the coffee shop that convinced me to take the plunge. So I self-identified as I and me, a couple, and we said I do and I do too, in a private ceremony. I had really wanted to be happy like that woman and to forget all the stuff about Trump being in bed with the Russians, and the Russians trying to get into our heads and voting booths, maybe even our beds where they would whisper lies about capitalism being immoral and other sweet nothings meant to confuse us about our identities and what was right and wrong. I had figured going to bed with myself might help me forget.

But it didn't work out as we expected. Six months into the marriage, on New Year's Eve, we had a little party and had a few anime hologram friends over. As usual, we had talked about the past year and old times and old friends and sang a few lines of Auld Lang Syne as we toasted left hand to right with some nice Prosecco with pomegranate juice since we heard that was the drink all the smart set used to celebrate their clever happiness. But then we got to arguing, and between you and me, it wasn't pretty. Our hologram friends were mortified. It was a scene straight out of *Who's Afraid of Virginia Woolf?* The Prosecco had gone to our head, so we didn't remember all the scathing interchanges, but I do know our anime friends said not a word and that I said to me at one-point words that seemed to echo Martha and George's from the play.

> MARTHA: Truth or Illusion, George; you don't know the difference.
> GEORGE: No, but we must carry on as if we did.
> MARTHA: Amen.

So then, on the day after, we carried on "as if." Amen, indeed! And though our head hurt a bit, we talked over coffee and decided to split up, amicably of course. It was a new year, and like most people, we wanted to make a fresh start. I wished me the best and knew me reciprocated. We went separate ways but it was very lonely. Facebook friends helped somewhat, but they were no substitute for the intimacy of our time together. I didn't know who would then help me make it through the night? And what about poor I? Forgive me, but I was so confused and had a hell of a headache.

Although I wanted 2019 to be a happy year, I knew 2019 would be a long night from hell politically and culturally, with fake news everywhere and our Russian enemies infiltrating our minds at every turn with backstopping and sheep dipping their spies throughout the media and academia. I was so lonely trying to make sense of it all. Without my me-spouse, I knew it could only get worse. Even CNN's Anderson Cooper's New Year's Eve words of comfort to the lonely from Times Square didn't help much. Like Fox News's "Fox and Friends," Anderson is always there with a helping hand, and when I and me were arguing, I could always go to my true friends in the media for a dose of truth and sustenance. They knew all about the Russian threat.

But while I was grateful for their comfort in those confusing times, I needed more. With apologies to Kris Kristofferson, I thought loving me would be easier than anything I'd ever do again. I needed easy, real easy, easier even than when I would say something and me would disagree but we would let it slide for the sake of our relationship. It was easier that way. But our relationship was probably doomed from the start.

But thank God for technology and CNN that had alerted me to a new technological possibility with a report about a Japanese man, Akihito Kondo, a school administrator, who fell in love years ago with Miku, a cyber-celebrity hologram. He had finally taken the plunge and married Miku in a lovely ceremony in front of thirty-nine people. Kondo seemed radiantly happy and not at all confused.

Such a possibility was right in front of my nose all along: my anime hologram friends who watched me and I get drunk that New Year's Eve. One of them—Meto—was cute as a button and was always looking to snuggle and comfort others. So, after divorcing myself, I proposed to her and after a dignified waiting period, maybe an hour or so, she said yes. But we didn't get officially married, just lived together, since I was scarred from the ordeal of being married to me.

For this past year, I carried on as if loving her was easier than anything I'd ever done before. Boy, was I wrong. It wasn't that she got headaches or said she was very stressed and overworked whenever I was in a loving mood. She was always willing but never really there, if you know what I mean. I'm a Bud Light guy, but Meto's lightness just didn't cut it. At least when I and me were married we had a body.

So here we are in late February 2020 and I am thinking of risking all for love once more. If I do, and this doesn't work out, I'm going to fold my cards and walk away, but a friend who is big into technology and who has tried this method assures me it is foolproof. I trust her, even though she is a little way-out-there with her electronic obsessions, always buying the latest cell phone and other gadgets that she says make her life so much better, even though she is tattooed everywhere and thinks of herself as a free spirit. I don't get it.

I'm more old-school, although I did fall for Meto in one of my weaker moments. I use little technology: don't use a smart phone, don't text, listen to music on CDs, never listened to a book on tape, etc.—I essentially live in an alternative reality from so many people in this digital age. But I have become a desperado for love. I drive an old Toyota pickup truck and sometimes think I am that guy from *The Bridges of Madison County* who had luck with the farmer's wife, except I've had no luck.

Truth or illusion? Let us carry on as if we knew. I have no idea. I know there are very few farms around here anymore, and those that exist are run by rich people for rich people and for expensive restaurants that advertise farm-to-table food and locally raised organic meat and everything that makes the wealthy diners feel OK and think they will live forever. I don't feel OK. I feel forlorn, fucked-up, even though I'm not sure if that is the right way to put it. Forlorn? What's that? I understand fucked-up, don't you? But forlorn?

Anyway, here's what I'm thinking. My friend told me I should look into a sexbot. That's a robot that you can have sex with and people are marrying these days. She says they are increasingly life-like, far realer than a hologram. She said she felt one and it felt just like a human body. And now that they are powered by very sophisticated artificial intelligence (AI), you can get one that is far more than a sex doll but has real feelings and emotions and you can have a genuine relationship with. I told her I've seen them, but she misunderstood. I meant the entertainment/media/Hollywood industry that is full of them, Barbies and Kens, lookalikes parading across screens everywhere. She laughed and said, "But the sexbots are intelligent, and if you want to feel OK, don't you want an intelligent woman?"

I saw her point, and said I did, but not too intelligent since I'm not very smart myself and most of my relationships, including with myself and Meto, didn't work out because I didn't understand a lot of what they said to me. As I told you, I'm just a regular Joe, driving my pickup truck, drinking Bud Light, and looking to feel OK. I just feel like crap and have to do something. She got this article on her phone to show me where a professor of robotics at a college in Iowa said that "Because they would be programmable, sexbots would meet each individual user's needs." He's a professor, she said, he must know. What could I say? I had a lot of unmet needs, and I'm in no position to question this professor who is an expert on robots.

What do you think? Should I take the plunge? I just want to feel OK for once.

To make matter worse, just this morning I saw headlines that Russia is at it again, meddling to fix the 2020 election for Trump. Or is it Sanders? I guess those Russians are really good at the cyberwarfare stuff and have many experts in artificial intelligence, but what about human intelligence—make up your mind, Russians, is it Trump or Sanders?

I had this really scary thought. What if I get a sex robot and she is named Svetlana, made in Moscow?

I'll really be screwed then.

Help!

I need somebody, not just anybody.

Help me if you can, I'm feeling down.

Ghostly Voices Dancing in the Rain

> *"In the other room Rateau was looking at the canvas, completely blank, in the center of which Jonas had merely written in very small letters a word that could be made out, but without any certainty as to whether it should be read solitary or solidary."*
>
> —Albert Camus, "The Artist at Work"

A solitary, early Sunday morning walk in the rain. As I like it, my only walking companion was the soothing sound of rain in the trees and on the lake. From the shallow water at the lake's swampy edge, a blue heron, perched on one leg, froze my gaze as I stopped and stared. As I turned to walk on, it rose with blue beating wings and soared up through the raindrops, alighting high above out on a limb. The road was flooding as I walked, water streaming down the hill, creating eddies as it met the water backing up from the over-filled lake. The eddies formed whirling patterns, artistic visions running counter to the main current.

My mind swirled with thoughts as I walked and talked to all my ghosts, dead and living, who accompany me everywhere, but whose presence is so palpable in the rain. Their voices seemed to descend with the drops, bouncing off the water and echoing in my mind.

I heard my mother say to me, "Eddy, you were always a contrarian. I worry about you." Yes, I answered, I am, but you named me, and Eddy is the correct spelling. I'm an eddy, a whirlpool, a contrarian, one who runs counter to the mainstream. But, dear mother, the mainstream is flowing fast toward destruction, carrying everyone and everything with it. We have to reverse course and resist. Please, mother, worry only if I wasn't walking against the wind.

Through the weeping trees I heard Thomas Merton, the Trappist monk, whisper:

> I told you that someday they will sell us the rain. Everyone and everything is for sale. "They" are the people who don't understand that rain is a free and useless festival, and because it is a gift, they wish to control it. The weather modifiers and geo-engineers are working overtime now. Together with the nuclear madmen, they will rain poisonous death upon us all unless we stop them. Remember: to be a contemplative is to be an outlaw. Don't divorce resistance from contemplation; they are married for life. Joy and suffering are their children.

I didn't reply, just kept walking, sloshing and slamming through the puddles. Merton has an eerie way of insinuating himself into odd private moments, and I didn't want an extended conversation. I just wanted to enjoy the rain.

The sloshing brought voices from my children's young years, the exultation as we romped streaming-wet through the wild beating storm, singing at the top of our voices, "If all the raindrops were lemon drops and gum drops/Oh what a rain it would be/I would stand outside with my mouth open wide/ Ah ah ah ah . . ." I opened my mouth wide, tongue out, and tilted my head back. Ah, the sweet taste of love and joy. I heard my children scream ecstatically, "Yippee!" and whirl and twirl with mouths agape.

On I walked, listening and watching. The rain fell harder, so hard it was difficult to see and all other sounds were completely obliterated. Bubbling up from somewhere came the rhythm of Jacques Prévert's poem, "Barbara":

> *Remember Barbara*
> *It rained all day on Brest that day*
> *And you walked smiling*

> *Flushed enraptured streaming wet*
> *In the rain*
> . . .
>
> *What shitstupidity the war*
> *Now what's become of you*

And here I was walking and wondering in the rain about Barbara and her lover and all the dead and lost in Brest in the "Good War" and whether we will have a sequel or has it already started. I called out to Barbara, but only the wild rain hammered its reply: resist resist resist the warmakers.

The soaking I was getting refreshed me, but now the beating of the rain and the ghostly voices seemed to ping-pong my mind between joy and sorrow, solitude and solidarity, resistance and contemplation, enjoyment and commitment. Did I have the right to enjoy the rain when thousands were dead in South Asian flooding and Houston was under water?

Then my old lugubrious friend Fred surprised me with something he said to me years ago:

> We do not belong to those who have ideas only among books, when stimulated by books. It is our habit to think outdoors—walking, leaping, climbing, dancing, preferably on lonely mountains or near the sea where even the trails become thoughtful. Our first questions about the value of a book, of a human being, or a musical composition are: Can they walk? Even more, can they dance?

Surprised me because Nietzsche wasn't exactly a barrel of laughs and I couldn't imagine him moon-walking with Michael Jackson. Anyway, I was walking, and why was he bothering me about books? I was alone in the rain, trying to enjoy myself.

Then Willie Yeats popped out of the lapping lake, book in hand, and blocked my path. Standing ghostlike in the mist, the crazy Irishman read these words from a poem I had tried to remember to forget:

> *Seventy years have I lived*
> *No ragged beggar-man*
> *Seventy years have I lived,*
> *Seventy years man and boy,*
> *And never have I danced for joy.*

My ghosts were getting on my nerves and Yeats depressed me, so I pushed through him and moved on. Just then, in this melancholy pensive mood, I was startled, not by a voice but by the sight of a mother raccoon, bedraggled by the heavy rain, scurrying past me with a sidelong glance, her baby hanging from her mouth, as she took her kit to a higher, drier home up the hill. My heart quivered. I remembered having read in a book that raccoons take their young out in their mouths for what are called "adventures," and perhaps this mother had been doing that when the rains came down. It was a beautiful sight, and my mother's voice came back to me: "Beauty is as Beauty does." Action, not words. And yet . . . Weren't words actions? Or were they useless. What, I wondered, was art for?

So I too turned and headed home, my ghostly voices melding into a chorus of song that I can't fully explain, nor do I want to. Like that blue heron, they were balancing on one leg out on a limb, and I was happy. The rain was still beautiful, and I rejoiced in its baptism, but I knew with Bob Dylan that "a hard rain's a-gonna fall" and that there are children to be saved from those intent on raining destruction on their heads. But on my way back, I was still going to kick up the puddles and join Gene Kelly in singing in the rain. And no Puritan cop, haunted by the fear that someone somewhere was happily enjoying himself, however briefly, was going to stop me, even if one stopped Kelly.

Camus was right: the solitary artist works in solidarity with everyone, when he tells the truth.

And to think I thought I walked alone.

The Silent Cries of Hiding Children: Half a Century after MLK's Riverside Church Speech

> *"In the cellar, darkness prevails day and night, and even when we are carrying a lighted candle, we see shadows dancing on the dark walls."*
> —Gaston Bachelard, *The Poetics of Space*

> *"I found myself in full accord when I read its opening lines: 'A time comes when silence is betrayal.'"*
> —Martin Luther King, "Beyond Vietnam," April 4, 1967

Come, let's play hide-and-seek, America's favorite game.

As we all know, children love to play hide-and-seek, but they don't like to have to hide and be sought. It's the playing that they like; it allows them to control the terrifying IT, real and imagined, that seeks to find and destroy them, body and soul. In the game, even if whoever is IT catches you before you can reach the safety of home, there is always the next game and the opportunity to switch roles. In kids' games you can always go home again.

But in the world where adults make the rules and pretend the emperor's nakedness is a beautiful robe, children often have no second chances. And when they do, they must deal with the wounds that result from the adults' treachery that often cripples them for life.

Reading about all the terrified children who were hiding in the cellar of a building in Mosul, Iraq, and were killed by America's flying monsters, got me thinking about the day and night terrors of child victims everywhere. While doing so, a student of mine at the college where I teach, a woman of extraordinary sensitivity to the world's suffering, shared with me a poem she wrote about domestic abuse:

Fear Remembered

At the top of the stairs,
A little girl waits in her dark room.
Facing the wall, afraid to go to sleep.
Blankets pulled up tight,
She holds her breath.
Breathless as she hears the stairs creak,
Slow steps, heavy tread.
No ordinary monster this.
The father-tormentor coming in the night,
Will take his pound of innocent flesh.
She lives in a house of fear and betrayal.
Where are the ones to love and trust?
Who will protect her from her "loved ones"?
Theses monsters don't hide under the bed,
Or in dark closets.
They live everyday lives.
Going to work.
Keeping house.
Appearing normal to outsiders.
Keeping their dark secrets.
A child unwillingly locked in a conspiracy of
* silence,*
She goes off to school each day.
At the top of the stairs,
A little girl waits in her dark room.
Facing the wall, afraid to go to sleep.
Blankets pulled up tight.

Breathless, she hears the creak of the stairs.
She waits for the shadow in the doorway.

The anonymous author, a middle-aged woman, is at least still alive, despite so many years of pain and shame. The children in Mosul, and in all the other places where children are slaughtered, will not be writing any poems. Having hidden, they were found and dispatched by faceless and "innocent" killers to another home from which none return. As Army Chief of Staff General Mark Milley put it last year, "On the future battlefield, if you stay in one place for longer than two or three hours, you will be dead." That future is now.

In the American myth, our killers are always "innocent," and, as Bob Dylan put it, "the executioner's face is always well hidden." If pushed by the obvious as in Iraq, Syria, Afghanistan, etc., Pentagon spokesmen say we'll look into it, we might have played a role, and even if we played a role, the enemy was using these children, we were provoked, we'll get to the bottom of it, we surely meant well, we regret any loss of life, but our investigation will take weeks, etc. The same bullshit they've been repeating for decades. When the weeks have gone by, any American who knows of or even cares about the atrocity will have forgotten about it and the media accomplices will have moved on to something else. The so-called investigation will result in a pile of lies that no one will read, even if they could find it. The myth of American innocent good intentions will carry on. Kurt Vonnegut was right: "So it goes."

"The essence of the lie implies in fact that the liar actually is in complete possession of the truth which he is hiding," wrote Jean-Paul Sartre in *Existential Psychoanalysis*.

Knowing this, and reading the poem, I wanted to vomit. And I felt the urge to strangle the father who raped his young daughter as recounted in the poem and the people who killed these children in Mosul. I also knew that such a sentiment was wrong and lay at the heart of these evil acts. I thought of the words of my hero, Dr. Martin Luther King, on compassion and non-violence; how it was the only way to break the circle of violence. Yet my rage stuck in my throat and I had a hard time swallowing the fact that Americans are capable of such deeds and skilled at hiding such truths from themselves. Or worse—that they didn't care.

But then I realized I was an American, and despite our myth of innocence that has long dominated public consciousness, killing children is an American tradition.

On April 4, 1967—at Riverside Church in New York City, Dr. King stood in the pulpit and thundered out his warning. Speaking of Vietnamese children, he said:

> They know they must move on or be destroyed by our bombs. So they go, primarily women and children and the aged. . . . So far we may have killed a million of them, mostly children . . . . thousands of the children, homeless, without clothes, running in packs on the streets like animals.

"Surely this madness must cease," he pleaded. "We must stop now." But of course we didn't stop. The government that continued to rain bombs and napalm down on the Vietnamese, the Laotians, and then the Cambodians, stopped MLK a year to the day later in Memphis and then Robert Kennedy two months later in Los Angeles. Nixon declared himself the peace candidate, proceeded to secretly sabotage Johnson's peace endeavors, and then savagely waged the war for six more years, killing millions more. For his reward, the American people reelected him.

No, "these monsters don't hide under the bed/or in dark closets/they live everyday lives."

Jump to May 12, 1996. Lesley Stahl, on CBS's 60 Minutes, asked Bill Clinton's Secretary of State Madeleine Albright if the death of over 500,000 Iraqi children was worth the price of Clinton's Iraq sanctions. To which Albright coolly replied, "I think this is a very hard choice, but the price—we think the price is worth it."

A few months later the American people overwhelmingly reelected Clinton and the killing of the Iraqis continued apace. Hey, he played the sax. Cool.

"Liberals," conservatives. Democrats or Republicans—it makes no difference. Nixon, Reagan, Bush, Clinton, Bush, Obama, Trump—all killers who are embodiments of the myth of American innocence as the American people play dumb, hiding their heads in the sand as if the world can't see their asses in the air. Desperate for false hope and phony innocence, they argue over the merits of their favorite killers to justify their complicity in a tradition of war-making where children's deaths matter no more than Frank Perdue's dead chickens.

Seeking the "hidden" truth takes little searching; it is our open dirty secret. We are not innocent. The myth must be destroyed. The world's children shouldn't have to hide from our predators, electronic and human. To continue to make them do so is to incur a heavy debt of guilt that will continue to mark us as silent accomplices in evil.

Martin King bravely raised his voice and paid with his life. If we want to honor him as we say we do, we should heed his words:

> A true revolution of values will lay hand on the world order and say of war, "This way of settling differences is not just." This business of burning human beings with napalm, of filling our nation's homes with orphans and widows, of injecting poisonous drugs of hate into the veins of peoples normally humane, of sending men home from dark and bloody battlefields physically handicapped and psychologically deranged, cannot be reconciled with wisdom, justice, and love. A nation that continues year after year to spend more money on military defense than on programs of social uplift is approaching spiritual death.

More than fifty years have elapsed since that warning. The world's children keep hiding from our killing machines, and Americans still turn deaf ears to their cries. Now we may be spiritually dead. It seems that way.

Hiding in a North Vietnamese bomb shelter in 1969 while he cradled a little boy in his arms, Fr. Daniel Berrigan S.J., anti-war rebel priest and poet, wrote the following lines as American bombs sought to kill him and all those he sheltered with.

> *In my arms, fathered*
> *In a moment's grace, the messiah*
> *Of all my tears, I bore reborn*
> *A Hiroshima child from hell.*
> *Can we, the dead, awaken from our acquiescence?*

The Cell Phone and the Virgin: A Montreal Odyssey

"And the sun pours down like honey
on our lady of the harbor
And she shows you where to look
among the garbage and the flowers
There are heroes in the seaweed,
there are children in the morning
They are leaning out for love and
they will lean that way forever
While Suzanne holds her mirror"

—**Leonard Cohen, "Suzanne"**

"Before this historical chasm, a mind like that of Adams felt itself helpless; he turned from the Virgin to the Dynamo as though he were a Branly coherer. On one side, at the Louvre and at Chartres, as he knew by the record of work actually done and still before his eyes, was the highest energy ever known to man, the creator of four-fifths of his noblest art, exercising vastly more attraction over the human mind than all the steam-engines and dynamos ever dreamed of; and yet this energy was unknown to the American mind. An American Virgin would never dare command; an American Venus would never dare exist."

—**Henry Adams, "The Dynamo and the Virgin" (1900)**
in ***The Education of Henry Adams***

> "The voices blend and fuse in clouded silence;
> silence that is infinite of space:
> and swiftly, silently the sound is wafted over regions
> of cycles of cycles of generations that have lived."
>
> —James Joyce, *Ulysses*

The first thing I noticed as I walked around downtown Montreal was the grotesque new architecture that was destroying the charming and humane ambience the city once embodied and that allowed for human thoughts and feelings. I had not been in the city for many years but remembered a more human scale that had entranced me. I wondered if my memory were playing tricks on me but realized it was not. Everywhere I looked, massive glass-skinned towers stood over the streets, sentinels for the financial, insurance, and real estate speculators, a post-modern world of abstractions. Looking deep into the construction sites that were everywhere, I marveled at the modern feats of engineering that would raise more glass cathedrals to the heavens. The power of modern technology astounded me. The City of Saints had turned into the city of money, even while the streets maintained their saintly names—Rue Saint Paul, Saint Catherine Street, etc.—and the beautiful churches held their ground despite dwindling worshippers.

I stood in front of Notre-Dame-de-Bon-Secours Chapel, looking up at the Virgin glimmering in the afternoon sun. The old port. The sailor's church. Like Henry Adams, I thought of the powerful force of the Virgin throughout history. Her protection across life's tempestuous seas. And Leonard Cohen, the Montrealer, who as a young man would come to this chapel and sit in meditation and write his beautiful song, "Suzanne," invoking "our lady of the harbor." Leonard, who would stand in awe of the woman as protectress, as mother, as lover, as muse: As in "Night Comes On":

> *I said, Mother I'm frightened*
> *The thunder and the lightning*
> *I'll never come through this alone*

She said, I'll be with you
My shawl wrapped around you
My hand on your head when you go

I understood the fear, the protective power, and the creative inspiration of the Blessed Mother down through the ages. I recalled the Miraculous Medal (the Medal of Our Lady of Graces) I wore as a teenager. Like so much, it had disappeared, and I didn't know where it went. Who had abandoned whom? While all around me tourists were using cell phones to capture the image of the Virgin's chapel, as if they could bottle the spirit and be on their way. I wondered if God had a cell phone; how far did wireless communications extend? I marveled at the way the owners of these devices—which seemed to be everyone but me—took for granted the power of the new technology that had "conquered time and space" and redesigned the world and their minds. Everywhere they went, they held these little rectangles in front of their faces, repetitively trying in vain to capture something they were not sure of, including their own images. Their connection to these little boxes seemed anatomical, and the power they contained almost divine. I could hear the clashing of an unspoken war between the spirit and the machine as I observed my surroundings.

More than a century before at the Great Exposition in Paris, Henry Adams had also stood and wondered; he, about the Branly coherer, the first radio wave detector used widely for radio communications. The first wireless. Being an American, Adams was sure that technology and gadgets would take preference over the Virgin when help was needed. After all these years, I was also sure that if most people wanted help, they would turn to their phones, the little divine protectors and preservers they carried everywhere. Notre-Dame-de Bon Secours (Our Lady of Good Help) was only for sailors of old, men afraid of drowning, but sophisticated moderns did not think like the shipwrecked—those whom Ortega y Gasset said were the lost ones, who have recognized that to live is to be lost, and realizing that, "will look round for something to which to cling, and discover that tragic, ruthless glance, absolutely sincere, because it is a question of his [their] salvation" will lead them not to embrace a machine, but the spirit of all life. Leonard Cohen sang to me as I stood there musing:

> *And Jesus was a sailor when he walked upon the water*
> *And he spent a long time watching from his lonely wooden tower*
> *And when he knew for certain only drowning men could see him*
> *He said all men will be sailors then until the sea shall free them*
> *But he himself was broken, long before the sky would open*
> *Forsaken, almost human, he sank beneath your wisdom like a stone*

But no one else heard the singer, for what are a dead poet's words remembered by heart worth in an age when one can "google it"? Just standing, looking, and listening seemed so out of date, like the Virgin looking down upon the tourists as they scurried next store to the Bonsecours Market, a large commercial hall where, rather than receive the good help of spiritual sustenance, they could buy apparel and accessories in the church of commerce. Tourists swam safely through the place, seeking help and salvation in a buyer's paradise, the current wisdom.

So I turned and walked away, climbing the crosstown streets that would take me to the neighborhood around McGill University. In *The Word* bookstore, I spent an hour looking through the used books and talking with the owner, Adrian. Here I felt at home, greeted as I was by a black and white framed photo of Leonard Cohen that welcomes all poets and dreamers who frequent this intimate storefront housed in an unprepossessing nineteenth century brick building. I overheard a woman ask Adrian for directions, and his reply gave me reason to hope. Adrian said to the woman, "Well, you can always get lost and see what you find. That may be more interesting." And I chuckled. But the woman wanted the straight way, the road more traveled, nothing serendipitous;

getting lost was not on her agenda. And after a few minutes, she went outside the store to wait for her companion who was still looking at the books. The woman was studying something on her cell. I imagined it was the bars.

The way the bookstore was arranged seemed to mirror my mind, a mind that seemed out of tune with the times. For my mind moved from one category of thought to another, as the books on the shelves moved from art to poetry to philosophy without signs signifying a change. They flowed into each other. I knew, of course, that all thought was one continuous stream fed by tributaries, and even many of the tributaries couldn't be found since they ran underground. It was only the modern mind that wished to categorize and control, the instrumental reasoning mind that had come to dominate the Western world and had proclaimed that humans, albeit biological, were machines, that wished for signs declaring separable categories of life and thought. I knew that the best writers in the books that surrounded me wrote so many of their truest words when they thought they were writing something else. This inadvertent way of living seemed to make the woman looking for directions nervous.

I often got lost, for I didn't have a smart phone to give me directions. A colleague I had met for lunch laughed when I told him that. These phones are really indispensable, he had said; you really should get one. And then he showed me photographs he had stored on the machine. He had hundreds. Its power was awe inspiring, a small device that allowed world-wide communication in a flash anywhere you were. You could capture the past with it; travel the world in an ethereal instant without moving; never be out of "touch" without being touched. It made me wonder: Where does true power lie? Was I out of touch? What did I want to touch?

On I walked through the City of Saints, passing McGill University, where I noticed the innocent appearance of students walking to and fro. I wondered what it must be like to be beginning one's studies. Did they learn anything about what had gone on at their university in times past? Did they learn about the deep currents that informed history, the true nature of current affairs, or were their professors spouting superficial nonsense that kept them safely ensconced in cushy positions? From my own experience in academia, I knew that the university had been co-opted by the state and now functioned as an appendage of the war makers. Liberal arts now meant neo-liberalism and political correctness and dissent meant dismissal. And so I realized that only those students who might browse through used bookstores like *The Word* might serendipitously discover the truth about their world. Most would be brainwashed. But they won't know it.

I had no phone, but I could hear the screams and groans coming from McGill's Allen Memorial Institute; could hear the people screaming no, no, no from Dr. Donald Ewen Cameron's "Sleep Room," as he fed hallucinogens and electrical shocks to "patients," the victims of his notorious CIA MKUltra mind control experiments in which he wiped the brain clean of so-called negative thoughts and replaced them with "good ones." I was not dreaming. I heard Val Orlikow screaming, as the good doctor, the President of the American and Canadian Psychiatric Associations, made her mind a blank slate by erasing any memory of her husband and reducing her to toddler status. She thought she was being treated for post-partum depression. The sounds of torture rattled my mind, the sounds of human desperation and the sounds of Cameron's taped messages fed to almost comatose patients in what he called "psychic driving." The prototypical experiments for the age of digital dementia. Black sites. I saw Cameron smile, his legacy as a pioneer of "psychic driving" that has become a stable technique in torture around the world secure.

I felt immensely sad as I saw a young college student cross in front of me. She seemed to be in a trance and almost bumped into me. She was beautiful, and her ears were plugged with ear buds, and when I turned to see her walk away, I noticed her backpack had a small pink teddy bear hanging from it, bringing to mind again the concluding lines to Cohen's "Suzanne":

> *And you want to travel with her, and you want to travel blind*
> *And you know that you can trust her*
> *For she's touched your perfect body with her mind*

Walking brought memories, associations, reveries, and thoughts. Drugs and technology could erase them. I realized that there was as much worth forgetting as remembering, as both were arts that opposed the sick science and technology that had overtaken so much of society. But what to remember and what to forget? Was that student trying to remember or forget something with that teddy bear that hung as a talisman? Were those earbuds drowning out memories or dangerous thoughts? Who had touched her mind? Thoreau had said it's very hard to forget what's worse than useless to remember. And I realized that I had honed my own forgettery to rid my mind of all the useless data the corporate mass media were pumping out, data used to create chaos and confusion, when much was so obvious if one was just willing to admit the truth. If I had a cell phone, I mused, I might never have to remember or forget. The secret to communication might be solved. Maybe someday I could be downloaded or uploaded into a phone, whichever it is, and all my problems would be solved.

"Come here, I want to see you," Alexander Graham Bell said to Watson in the first telephone call. Watson remembered it differently. He recalled Bell saying, "Come here I want you." So much wanting and forgetting and remembering made my head spin. So much desire for the presence of the absent other. But whom to call? How? Or was it the absence of the present other? Could one turn and say, "What is it you want?"

My wife and I then kept walking toward the Montreal Museum of Fine Arts where there was an exhibit of Picasso's use of African art and artifacts: "From Africa to the Americas: Face-To-Face Picasso, Past and Present." Picasso, a believer in magic and the occult, was notoriously opposed to reason and logic and understanding. He once said that "people who try to explain pictures are usually barking up the wrong tree." My wife and I had once attended a gala opening of a large Picasso retrospective at the Museum of Modern Art in New York. The galleries were filled with celebrities, their masks intact, oohing and ahhing at the art work. At the time I wondered what they would say if I asked them how they understood this or that piece. Did they just stand or understand? Would they say, "What a genius; he had the magic touch?"

I had admired a goat sculpture that spoke to me. I can't remember what the goat said, but I remembered wondering if I was the goat surrounded by brilliant minds who could decipher hidden meanings lost on me. Now I wondered what Picasso might communicate to me with his African inspired works. Should I try to understand them, or was that too plebian? Was there some esoteric trick to it all? Could Picasso shed light on the enigma that perplexed Adams and me? Or was there nothing to understand? Was it all just a mystery beyond comprehension? Beyond explanation? Beyond communication? Was it simply art appreciation or magic?

I hoped that maybe before my odyssey around Montreal was over, I would discover the answer to the dilemma that perplexed me: Was it in the cell phone or the Virgin that true power lay? Digital or sacred force? Adams never truly resolved it; maybe I could. Or had a century and more made it more difficult? Impossible?

I knew that from photography and the phonograph to the computerized cell phone, memory had achieved a strange jailbreak from the body that made writing seem like a crude form by comparison. Could visual art reveal the truth? Picasso? McGill's Dr. Cameron and his CIA accomplices had mastered the black arts of disassociating the personality (as Picasso had done with art), of erasing memories and implanting new ones, of using drugs, technology and the occult to materialize the psychic and control volition and memory—they were masters of the electronic mind-body interface and worldview warfare that their Nazi friends had bequeathed to them. They had taken the lessons of black magic and the machine god adored by the fascist Marinetti and his "Futurism" art movement, with its superstitious occult roots hidden behind its pseudo-scientific mumbo jumbo, and made it their own. They had conjured up a satanic brew of technology and hallucinatory drugs and rituals to promote the idea that the supernatural machine ruled mankind and they controlled the machine, and no one could defeat them. They considered themselves the spearhead of the new colonial imperial powers, who colonized the minds of the masses.

It seemed to me that at some unconscious level all the people I saw with cell phones had been disassociated but didn't know it. They were victims of the latest version of MKUltra on a vast scale. They had been invaded by "special forces."

Here I was on a simple few days' vacation, and my mind was whirling with all these perplexing thoughts. I needed to communicate, and I wondered who would hear me if he cried out, if I spoke to the air. Rilke's words came to me:

> *Who, if I cried out, would hear me among the*
> *Angelic Orders?*
> *. . .*
>
> *Every Angel is terror.*
> *And so I hold myself back and swallow the cry*
> *of a darkened sobbing.*

But I held my tears and walked on, resolved to solve the enigma before the day was up.

When we arrived at the museum, I was again struck by the thought that museums were very strange places. I always felt as though I were entering a graveyard, where art was isolated from the living. This funereal quality was amplified by the required silence, as if one were in the presence of ghosts or gods who required adoration. Museums seemed to me to be temples of the rich where the art was their war booty on display, the victims of their conquests antiseptically absent. I felt half-dead when in them.

This particular exhibit came to be because the European colonial powers had looted their colonies for art and artifacts that they brought back to their home countries and locked up in museums and in the homes of the rich. The spoils of war. It happened that in 1907 Pablo Picasso visited a dusty museum in Paris, the Muse d'Ethnographie du Trocadéro, where he was startled by the African art and artifacts he saw there. He later said:

> The greatest artistic emotion I have felt was when I was suddenly struck by the sublime beauty of the sculptures carved by anonymous artists in Africa. Passionately religious, yet rigorously logical, these works are the most powerful and most beautiful things ever produced by the human imagination.

Then he proceeded to again appropriate the appropriated art, and now some of the results lined the walls of the Montreal Museum of Fine Arts. I couldn't help noticing Picasso's doubling down on rigorous logic in his opportunistic "borrowing." But the "passionately religious" nature of the artist's work that graced the gallery escaped me, unless the museum had become the new cathedral. This seemed quite probable. I doubted that Picasso shared Adams' lofty assessment of Chartres Cathedral, since Picasso considered African sculpture "the most beautiful things produced by the human imagination," and his attitude toward the "religious" was colored by its foreign and exotic qualities, elements absent from the familiar European Christian or Islamic heritage of his Spanish homeland, or from France and Europe as a whole.

Picasso did most of this African-inspired work between 1906 and 1909, before turning to what has been called his Cubist period, which only lasted until the "War to End All Wars" ended the lives of over 20 million people, while wounding even more. Like Picasso's African and Cubist work, the war surely offered a different perspective. It was all so logical and technological, the height of modern efficiency, yet seemed conjured up from the darkest pit of hell. It gave one a different understanding of time and space, and relativized plenty of bromides. I remembered reading with sardonic amusement the words of Freud, who was so disappointed by the great white man's betrayal of his highest "ideals" by waging the First World War:

> We had expected the great world-dominating nations of white race upon whom the leadership of the human species has fallen, who were known to have world-wide interests as their concern, to whose creative powers were

due not only our technical advances towards the control of nature but the artistic and scientific standards of civilization—we had expected these people to succeed in discovering another way of settling misunderstandings and conflicts of interest.

This memory of the great white father's racist thoughts so discombobulated my mind that for a few minutes I had to find a seat and close my eyes in meditation. I remembered that Freud, the atheist, had his consulting room filled with hundreds of ancient figurines of gods and goddesses that created the effect of an eerie sacred chamber where religious rites were performed. Like a temple or a museum, he meant this room to suggest that this art and these artifacts from other times and places and the land of memory could effect magical cures on those who came for the cure of their souls. For a minute I thought I was in Freud's consulting room and was free-associating. Then I opened my eyes to see Picasso's mask staring down at me. It jolted me to my feet!

I mused about these connections as I read the anthropological wall plaques explaining how, over a century or more, "the decolonization of the colonial gaze" has been taking place. I thought this very good, and was looking forward to the parallel exhibit—"Here We Are Here: Black Canadian Contemporary Art"—that was meant to exhibit this change. I wondered if the artists who created this new art of the decolonized gaze grasped the nature of the new colonialism, if they knew of the United States Africa Command (AFRICOM) and NATO countries' military ongoing penetration of the African continent, of the World Bank and the International Monetary Fund's control, of the NGOs' work with the CIA and USAID and the foundations that served as masks to hide the true nature of continued Western control without the use of the term "colonies." Taking control of the gaze was but a first step.

My primary odyssey, however, was to try to unmask the true font of power in the contemporary world. The world had suffered a series of radical breaks with historical continuity and loss of identity with place, starting shortly after Adams was born in the mid-nineteenth century. Space and time had been contracted by the new technology. Adams had contemplated the dynamo. The computerized cell phone was its current symbol, and its evil twin the concentrated power of nuclear weapons. The modern mind had suffered severe dislocation and confusion. All the ruins, antiques, and artifacts of the past that were collected and commodified over the last 150 years could no more restore lost identities than could the prolific growth in museums in the same period. The museums were the mausoleums of societies dying from within.

As I walked around the exhibit, I realized that Picasso, for all his obvious talent, especially visible in the works that comprised this show, had no solution. He was rather a symptom of the depth of the problem, the neurotic symptom that allowed for an ersatz solution, which was, of course, no solution. Like a neurotic who goes for help with his symptoms that have squeezed the life out of him but help him hide from his true problems, Picasso's masks, distortions, and play-acting art were impotent. Seemingly potent and wildly celebrated, they hid the "extinction of living inner religiousness," as Spengler put it, that was disappearing from so much of the world, particularly Europe and the United States, the countries that have embraced militarism and war-making as their nihilistic modi operandi. Even the women that populate so much of Picasso's work—"For me there are only two kinds of women," he said, "goddesses and doormats"—these women of all shapes and poses, do not offer us a true clue to the power of the Virgin Adams was contemplating alongside the dynamo.

As an only brother with seven sisters, I had grown up among women. I learned that they, like me, were complex, surely neither goddesses nor doormats. One of my sisters had been an artist of rare power. She wished to live as a liberated woman before society sanctioned this. Her art couldn't save her. She died by her own hand, terribly torn between a depraved and distorted religious orthodoxy and dreams of spiritual and artistic freedom. She seemed to me to be a genuine symbol of the nature of modern life, where people yo-yoed back and forth between equally false solutions without grasping the larger cultural and social forces at work. I sensed her tragedy was the tragedy of so much of history, where a reactionary cycle seemed to operate. Technology, colonialism, industrialization, the relativization of thought and religion preceded Picasso's grasping of African art and what was perceived as its magical qualities. France for years had been abuzz with the occult, esoterica, magic, trances, etc. Madame Blavatsky and her ilk were celebrated as liberators. Then came the Cubist revolution that ended in France in 1914. The war that brought such vast physical suffering and death ushered in a death in the soul, what John Berger called "inverted suffering," that created vast confusion in people's minds as they became lost within themselves trying to comprehend the absurdities that ensued and what it all could possibly mean. Logic had been turned on its head where it remains, but technology has triumphed. Or so it thinks.

I was exhausted. I grasped Adams' disillusionment. For years I had diligently studied and written about the three political assassinations that had marked my life: JFK, MLK, and RFK. Doing so had become a spiritual necessity for me. I knew why and how they were killed. I knew the culprit: the CIA, the masters of the dark arts. And I knew that the killers had used all the tricks and masks in the magician's playbook to confuse and confound the American public. They had used technology and drugs and art and artists and writers and culture and the mass media to sow bewilderment, to disassociate the minds of average people already confused by the unraveling of history and identity that started in Adams' day. It had been a long century and a long day.

I wished to report my findings, and thought of ending with the following paragraph, that while true, was not a very definitive ending, surely not an answer to the enigma that the day's wandering had brought me:

> America has always taken tragedy lightly. Too busy to stop the activity of their twenty-million-horse-power society, Americans ignore tragic motives that would have overshadowed the Middle Ages; and the world learns to regard assassinations as a form of hysteria, and death as neurosis, to be treated by a rest cure. Three hideous political murders, that would have fattened the

Eumenides with horror, have thrown scarcely a shadow on the White House.

No doubt it would have made an eloquent conclusion, but since these were Adams' words, written in 1902, I thought best of it. The words are still true, and sent a shiver down my spine when I remembered them. But I knew they would not satisfy my restless, conspiratorial mind or anyone who might read it. I reminded myself that all my study had led me to the conclusion that life and history are far more obvious than the world prefers to believe.

The problem is that people prefer unbelief to belief, mirages to water.

"The world is becoming a giant military base," wrote the great Latin American writer, Eduardo Galeano, "and that base is becoming a mental hospital the size of the world. Inside the nuthouse, which ones are crazy?"

I was standing in the middle of the gallery lost in thought. An attendant came up to me and tapped me on the shoulder. "Sir," he said, "it's closing time."

So out of the museum my wife and I walked. We found a little French restaurant where we ate a delicious meal accompanied by fragrant wine. All my dilemmas disappeared for the nonce. I forgot the purpose of my long odyssey around town. While walking back to our hotel under a resplendent full moon, I was at peace. The world was beautiful, as I knew it was. As we prepared for sleep, I promised myself I would dream the answer to my quest and in the morning would visit our lady of the harbor and tell her my dream.

Morning came with no breakthrough. But I had promised the lady a last visit, at least to apologize and to ask forgiveness for my ignorance. I walked to Notre-Dame-de-Bon-Secours. I glanced at my watch and realized I had first arrived here exactly twenty-four hours before. I was back where I started. I had gone in a circle and had no great insight to show for it. I glanced up to Our Lady a bit ashamed and entered the chapel. It was empty and silent. I sat in a pew half-way down and let the silence envelop me as I meditated. I listened. Would she speak to me? Minutes passed, when I was startled by the sound of the door behind me opening. I heard footsteps as someone walked down the aisle. It felt like an intrusion, and I was irritated. A man slipped into the aisle next to me. It was the dead Leonard Cohen. He gave me a wry smile. He didn't look any different. He said nothing and looked straight ahead. Then he started singing his angelic song, and I knew I had arrived at an answer beyond explanation, one that went so deep it didn't need one. The power of song; that was it. I had long felt but never expressed that nothing moved and unsettled me more than songs, and so I had both fled and embraced them in an alternating cycle of futility down my days. Now my tears were tears of joy that overwhelmed me as I listened to Leonard sing "Suzanne."

I wish to share with you such beauty, and I wonder what Henry Adams would think. No doubt our lady of the harbor, Notre Dame, was enchanted.

Ladies and Gentlemen, take a few minutes to listen to Leonard Cohen, alive and well, singing *Suzanne*.

SLOW SUICIDE AND THE ABANDONMENT OF THE WORLD

"The condition of alienation, of being asleep, of being unconscious, of being out of one's mind, is the condition of the normal man. Society highly values its normal man. It educates children to lose themselves and to become absurd, and thus to be normal. Normal men have killed perhaps 100,000,000 of their fellow normal men in the last fifty years. Our behavior is a function of our experience. We act the way we see things. If our experience is destroyed, our behavior will be destructive. If our experience is destroyed, we have lost our own selves."

—**R.D. Laing,** *The Politics of Experience,* **1967**

"The artist is the man who refuses initiation through education into the existing order, remains faithful to his own childhood being, and thus becomes 'a human being in the spirit of all times, an artist.'"

—**Norman O. Brown,** *Life Against Death*

Most suicides die of natural causes, slowly and in silence.

But we hear a lot about the small number of suicides, by comparison, who kill themselves quickly by their own hands. Of course their sudden deaths elicit shock and sadness since their deaths, usually so unexpected even when not, allow for no return. Such sudden once-and-for-all endings are even more jarring in a high-tech world where people are subconsciously habituated to thinking that everything can be played back, repeated, and re-wound, even lives.

If the suicides are celebrities, the mass media can obsess over why they did it. How shocking! Wasn't she at the peak of her career? Didn't he seem happy? And then the speculative stories will appear about the reasons for the rise or fall of suicide rates, only to disappear as quickly as the celebrities are dropped by the media and forgotten by the public.

The suicides of ordinary people will be mourned privately by their loved ones in their individual ways and in the silent recesses of their hearts. A hush will fall over their departures that will often be viewed as accidental.

And the world will roll on as the earth absorbs the bodies and the blood. "Where's it all going all this spilled blood," writes the poet Jacques Prévert. "Murder's blood . . . war's blood . . . blood of suicides . . . the earth that turns and turns with its great streams of blood."

Of such suicides Albert Camus said, "Dying voluntarily implies you have recognized, even instinctively, the ridiculous character of that habit [of living], the absence of any profound reason for living, the insane character of that daily agitation, and the uselessness of suffering." He called this feeling the absurd, and said it was widespread and involved the feeling of being an alien or stranger in a world that couldn't be explained and didn't make sense. Assuming this experience of the absurd, Camus wished to explore whether suicide was a solution to it. He concluded that it wasn't.

Like Camus, I am interested in asking what is the meaning of life. "How to answer it?" he asked in *The Myth of Sisyphus*. He added that "the meaning of life is the most urgent of questions." But I don't want to explore his line of reasoning to his conclusions, whether to agree or disagree. I wish, rather, to explore the reasons why so many people choose to commit slow suicide by immersing themselves in the herd mentality and following a way of life that leads to inauthenticity and despair; why so many people so easily and early give up their dreams of a life of freedom for a proverbial mess of pottage, which these days can be translated to mean a consumer's life, one focused on staying safe by embracing conventional bromides and making sure never to openly question a system based on systemic violence in all its forms; why, despite all evidence to the contrary, so many people embrace getting and spending and the accumulation of wealth in the pursuit of a chimerical "happiness" that leaves them depressed and conscience deadened. Why so many people do not rebel but scramble for a seat on this ship of fools.

What can we say about the vast numbers of people who commit suicide slowly, by a series of acts and inactions whose impacts last a long lifetime and render them among the living dead, those masses whom Thoreau so famously said "lead lives of quiet desperation"? Is the meaning of life for them simply the habits they fell into at the start of life before they thought or wondered what's it all about? Or did they embrace the habit after shrinking back in fear from the disturbing revelations thinking brought them? Did they ever seriously question their place in the lethal fraud that is organized society, what Tolstoy called the Social Lie? Why do so many people kill their authentic selves and their consciences that could awaken them to break through the social habits of thought, speech, and action that lead them to live "jiffy lube" lives, periodically oiled and greased to roll smoothly down the conventional highway of getting and spending, refusing to resist the murderous actions of their government?

An unconscious despair rumbles beneath the frenetic surface of American society today. An unspoken nothingness. I think the Italian writer Robert Calasso says it well: "The new society is an agnostic theocracy based on nihilism." It's as though we are floating on nothing, sustained by nothing, in love with nothing—all the while embracing any thing that a materialistic, capitalist consumer culture can throw at us. We are living in an empire of illusions, propagandized and self-deluded. Most people will tell you they are stressed and depressed, but will often add—"who wouldn't be with the state of the world"—ignoring their complicity in that, having chosen compromised, conventional lives devoid of the spirit of rebellion.

I keep meeting people who, when I ask them how they are, will respond by saying, "I'm hanging in there."

Don't common sayings intimate unconscious truths? Hang—among its possible derivatives is the word "habit" and the meaning of "coming to a standstill." Stuck in one's habits, dangling over nothing, up in the air, going nowhere, and hanging by a string. Slow suicides. The Beatles sang it melodically: "He's a real nowhere man/Sitting in his nowhere land/Making all his nowhere plans for nobody/Doesn't have a point of view/Knows not where he's going to/Isn't he a bit like you and me." It's a far cry from having "the world on a string," as Harold Arlen wrote many years before.

Maybe if we listen to how people talk or what popular culture throws up, we will learn more through creative associations than through all the theories the experts have to offer.

There have been many learned tomes over the years trying to explain the act of suicide, an early and very famous one being Emile Durkheim's groundbreaking sociological analysis *Suicide* (1897). In thousands of books and articles other thinkers have approached the subject from various perspectives—psychological, philosophical, biological, etc. They contain much truth and a vast amount of data that appeal to the rational mind seeking general explanations. But in the end, general explanations are exactly that—general—while a mystery usually haunts the living whose loved ones have killed themselves.

But what about the slow suicides, those D. H. Lawrence called the living dead (don't let "the living dead eat you up"), those who have departed the real world for a conscienceless complacency from which they can cast aspersions on those whose rebellious spirits give them little rest. Where are the expert disquisitions about them?

We've had more than a century of pseudo-scientific studies of suicide and the world has gotten much worse. More than a century of psychotherapy and people have grown progressively more depressed. Large and increasing numbers are drugged to the teeth with pharmaceutical drugs and television and the internet and cell phones and shopping and endless talk about food and diets and sports and nothing. Talk to talk, surface to surface. Pundits pontificate daily in streams of endless bullshit for which they are paid enormous sums as they smile with their fake whiter-than-white teeth flashing from their makeup masks. People actually listen to these fools to "inform" themselves. They even watch television news and think they know what is happening in the world. We are drowning in a "universe of disembodied data," as playwright John Steppling has so aptly phrased it. People obsessively hover over their cell phones, searching for the key that will unlock the cells they have locked themselves in. Post literacy, mediated reality, and digital dementia have become the norm. Minds are packaged and commodified to the point of madness.

Not stark-raving screaming madness, just a slow, whimpering acceptance of an insane society whose very fabric is toxic and which continues its purportedly God-ordained mission of spreading death and destruction around the world in the name of freedom and democracy. A nice madness, you could say, a pleasant, depressed and repressed madness. A madness in which people might say with T. S. Eliot's "J. Alfred Prufrock" (if they still read or could remember): "I have measured out my life with coffee spoons . . . . And I have seen the eternal Footman hold my coat, / and snicker, / And in short, I was afraid."

But why are so many so afraid? Everyone has fears, but so many normal people seem extremely fearful, so fearful they choose to blend into the social woodwork so they don't stand out as dissenters or oddballs. They kill their authentic selves; become conscience-less. And they do this in a society where their leaders are hell-bent on destroying the world and who justify their nuclear madness at every turn. Perhaps you think I exaggerate, but I feel that madness is much more the norm today than when Laing penned his epigraphic comment. Laing was right that this goes back to our experience. When genuine experience is denied or mystified (it's now disappeared into digital reality), real people disappear. Laing wrote:

> In order to rationalize our industrial-military complex, we have to destroy our capacity to see clearly any more what is in front of, and to imagine what is beyond, our noses. Long before a thermonuclear war can come

about, we have had to lay waste our sanity. We begin with the children. It is imperative to catch them in time. Without the most thorough and rapid brainwashing their dirty minds would see through our dirty tricks. Children are not yet fools, but we shall turn them into imbeciles like ourselves, with high I. Q.'s if possible. From the moment of birth, when the Stone Age baby confronts the twentieth century mother, the baby is subjected to these forces of violence, called love, as its mother and father, as their parents and their parents before them, have been. These forces are mainly concerned with destroying most of its potentialities, and on the whole this enterprise is successful. By the time the new human is fifteen or so, we are left with a being like ourselves, a half-crazed creature more or less adjusted to a mad world. This is normality in our present age. Love and violence, properly speaking, are polar opposites. Love lets the other be, but with affection and concern. Violence attempts to constrain the other's freedom, to force him to act in the way we desire, but with ultimate lack of concern, with indifference to the other's own existence or destiny. We are effectively destroying ourselves by violence masquerading as love.... We live equally out of our bodies and out of our minds.

So yes, I do think most people are victims. No one chooses their parents, or to be born into poverty, or to be discriminated against for one's race, etc. No one chooses to have their genuine experience poisoned from childhood. No one chooses to be born into a mad society. This is all true. Some are luckier than others. Suicides, fast and slow, are victims. But not just victims. This is not about blame, but understanding. For those who commit to lives of slow suicide, to the crushing of their true selves and their consciences in the face of a rapacious and murderous society, there is always the chance they can break with the norm and go sane. Redemption is always possible. But it primarily involves overcoming the fear of death, a fear that manifests itself in the extreme need to preserve one's life, one's so-called social identity, and sense of self by embracing social conventions, no matter how insane they may be and whether or not they bring satisfaction or fulfillment. Whether or not they give life a meaning that goes deep.

For those who have taken their lives and are no longer among us, hope is gone. But we can learn from their tragedies if we are truthful. For them the fear of life was primary, and death seemed like an escape from that fear. Life was too much for them. Why? We must ask. So they chose a life-in-death approach through fast suicide. Everyone is joined to them in that fear, just as everyone is joined by the fear of death. It is a question of which dominates, and when, and how much courage we can muster to live daringly. The fear of death leads one to constrict one's life in the safe surroundings of conventional society in the illusion that such false security will save one in the end. Death overcomes them before it takes them. This is what I call slow suicide.

But in the end as in the beginning and throughout our lives, there is really no escape. The more alive we are, the closer death feels because really living involves risks and living outside the cocoon of the social lie. Mr. Pumpkin Head might seize you, whether he is conceived as your boss, an accident, disease, social ostracism, or some government assassin. But the deader we feel, the more obscured and distant death seems because we feel safe. Pick your poison.

But perhaps there is no need to choose our poison if we can regain our genuine experience that parents and society, for different reasons, conspire to deny us. Could the meaning of our lives be found, not in statements or beliefs, but in true experience? Most people think of experience as inner or outer. This is not true. It is a form of conventional brainwashing that makes us schizoid. It is the essence of the neuro-biological materialism that reduces humans to unfree automatons. Proffered as the wisdom of the super intelligent, it is sheer stupidity.

All experience is in-between, not the most eloquent of phrasing, I admit, but accurate. Laing, a psychiatrist, puts it in the same way as do the mystics and those who embrace the Tao. He says:

The relation of my experience to behavior is not that of inner to outer. My experience is not inside my head. My experience of this room is outside in this room. To say that my experience is intrapsychic is to presuppose that there is a psyche that my experience is in. My psyche is my experience, my experience is my psyche.

Reverie, imagination, prayer, dream, etc. are as much outer as inner, they are modalities of experience that exist in-between. We live in-between, and if we could experience that, we would realize the meaning of life and our connection to all living beings, including those our government massacres daily, and we would awaken our consciences to our complicity in the killing. We would realize that the victims of the American killing machine are human beings like us; are us, and we, them. We would rebel.

Thoreau said a life without principle was not worth living. Yet for so many of the slow suicides they only had principals in high school. Such word confusion is understandable when illiteracy is the order of the day and spelling passé. Has anyone when in high school ever had Thoreau's admonition drummed into his head: "The ways by which you may get money almost without exception lead downward. To have done anything by which you earned money merely is to have been truly idle or worse." Of course not, since getting a "good" living is never thought to involve living in an honest, inviting, and honorable way. It is considered a means to an end, the end being a consumer's paradise. "As for the means of living," Thoreau added, "it is wonderful how indifferent men of all classes are about it, even reformers, so called—whether they inherit, or earn, or steal it."

Is it any wonder so many people end up committing slow suicide?

WHEN WARRIORS BECOME SAINTS

As I sit on the small balcony on the top floor of an old house in the working-class neighborhood of Alfama in Lisbon, Portugal, it is early evening, the time for wine and voices wafting on the fragrant breeze through the twisting cobble-stoned streets. The National Pantheon (Panteao Nacional) stares me in the face. I stare back, and then look up to the heavens and to the cross that is silhouetted against the blue sky. It crowns the Pantheon's massive dome. On its façade stand three statues, only one of which I can see clearly. She is Santa Engracia, a Christian martyr from before the period when the Roman Emperor Constantine legalized and legitimatized Christianity, transforming the cross into a sword. It was her church before the state found it acceptable to convert it into a space to glorify its secular saints and its military and political prowess.

Rome never dies. It falls in different guises, then is resurrected by the human urge to dominate others. The savage complicity between church and state perdures through the ages.

Wherever you go, the monuments and statues glorifying humanity's violent history are always presented as a form of liberation. Tourist attractions. Generals, princes, and kings atop horses, brandishing swords and guns, "grace" squares and monuments, looking down on the common folk to remind them of whom they should look up, or look out. Yet even when they do show obeisance to their "masters" who rule them from the heights, the commoners are left out of the spoils of empire, and if they object, they are taken out without hesitation.

On a clothesline outside the windows of the house across the street where a woman peeks out, the pants and underwear humbly sway to a different tune, a sad Fado moan that seems to ask: What has happened? Has it always been like this?

I am tempted to tell the underwear it has but realize its job is to cover-up, not expose the truth.

Rilke, a German poet of most delicate sensibilities, asked from one of his castle abodes provided by one of his many rich lady friends:

> *Who, if I cried out, would hear me*
> *Among the angels' hierarchies?*
> *And even if one of them*
> *Pressed me against his heart*
> *I would be consumed in that*
> *overwhelming existence.*

But down below, the omnipresent graffiti on the walls is a bit less circumspect. It shouts: Fuck the elites!

The old poor murmur their prayers and the angry young spray their rage on every canvas they can find. Both seek hope outside the museums and mausoleums erected by the wealthy to glorify themselves.

And fate answers: It's the same old story, a fight for love and glory. Those seeking glory, the rich elites, the powerful with the guns in all the countries across the planet, with a few exceptions, smash the lovers and the humble people as they struggle to keep faith and hope alive. Who will free them?

Who among the elites will hold the arm of the old Portuguese woman on the one crutch as she teeters on her struggle up the steep hill to the little grocery store? "Orbrigada—Deus te abinçoe" is her response to a stranger, whose heart aches.

Here in Lisbon there is a famous tourist attraction, Castelo De S. Jorge, a massive hilltop castle and fortress overlooking the city. Built by the Moors in the eleventh century, it was conquered by Dom Afonso Henriques, who became the first king of Portugal, and began what is so nobly described as "its golden age as a home for the royalty." Royals are always noble, and castles and mythic saint/soldiers like St. George are their intimate friends. It is a marriage made in hell.

The Spaniard, Ignatius of Loyola, was a soldier seriously wounded in war at the age of thirty. He subsequently underwent a religious conversion. He founded the Jesuit order eighteen years later and was sainted in 1556, sixty-six years after his death. Having been educated by the Jesuits, I vividly recall the motto of my Jesuit high school that adorns the school seal, *Deo et Patriae*, a not so subtle reminder of how my priorities should be linked. I have failed that test, just as I failed a freshman mathematics exam, probably because I couldn't figure out what two plus two equaled, since I was reading Dostoevsky's *Notes from Underground* at the time and might have thought it was five because I believed I was free and not what Ignatius urged Jesuits to be—"as if a dead body" in obedience to the Pope.

The so-called rational ones have brought the earth to the point of extinction with their instrumental rationality and their diseased souls. We are living in the Crystal Palace that Dostoevsky so mocked long before the crystal turned digital. One plus zero may equal one in such a glass house, but such counting will not protect us from the whirlwind we have conjured from the smart man's equation of $E=mc^2$.

Only a spiritual equivalent will save us, as James Douglass has so eloquently argued in his slim but powerful book, *Lightning East to West: Jesus, Gandhi, and the Nuclear Age*, where, taking up Gandhi's suggestion, he argues that there is a spiritual equivalent to Einstein's law of physical change that we must discover that will allow for a radical transformation of society and the world. Douglass's country is the world.

I, however, am reminded of a very different Jesuit-trained American (one among many), who has passed the American indoctrination exam "admirably" and who has worked assiduously for God and country and followed that American motto of "In God We Trust" when he recently led the CIA in its holy wars under President Barack Obama, the Nobel Peace Prize winner—John

Brennan. Was his excuse that he was just following orders, "as if a dead body"?

I think the dead children in Afghanistan, Libya, Syria, Yemen and so many other places he helped to destroy would not buy that excuse. Yet Fordham University thought to honor him. Is this what the Jesuit motto means: *Ad maiorem Dei gloriam inque hominum salutem* (for the greater glory of God and the salvation of humanity)?

Has Fordham never heard of the Nuremberg Trials?

In the men's room of St. George's Castle, there is a wall dispenser selling M&Ms. Imperialism and colonialism take many forms.

It is hard to say what's new since humanity's savage history just rolls along. The technology changes, but people do not. Spray paint is about 75 years old, about the same age as nuclear weapons, both products of WW II. One leads to "Fuck the elites," while the other says, "We are the elites and see what we can do to the Japanese."

War spurs technological development like nothing else, and as the brilliant French social thinker Paul Virilio has shown with his war model, "history progresses at the speed of its weapons systems." Modern societies, with increased technological speed, the administration of fear (terror), and digital gadgetry, are engaged in a battle for people's minds through technological perception management. Virilio makes it clear, following on the work of his fellow countryman Jacques Ellul, that built into the technology is the "integral accident," by which he means that every new technology creates its own potential lethal "accident."

While most people welcome new technology because they have been conditioned to think only in scientific and positivistic terms, they fail to see the price to be paid. The nuclear bomb, nicknamed "The Gadget" by its one-dimensional, sick scientific inventors, is an accident waiting to happen, unless human madness again leads to its use before that.

Now we have what Virilio calls the "information bomb," the glut of information that overloads people's ability to concentrate or think clearly, but a boon to the elites who think they are in full control of people's minds and the technology they promote.

On the ramparts of Castelo de S. Jorge, the tourists snap photo after photo with their cell phones, failing to realize that these memories they are "shooting" from the heights where cannons once shot the infidels have imprisoned them in a dungeon of departed time as deep and dark as the one in the castle below their feet.

Visiting castles, like so many trips into the past, can awaken one to the truth of human history or put one to sleep. It is usually the latter.

The Spanish philosopher Ortega y Gassett, who lived here in Lisbon for a year after fleeing Franco's Spain, said it best: "The only genuine ideas are the ideas of the shipwrecked. All the rest is rhetoric, farce."

We are all shipwrecked now, not just the Portuguese sailors long lost at sea never to return home despite the lament of the Fado singers.

If we are to make this earth our home again, we had better learn to sing a different tune. If not, we will be eliminated by accident or intent, and no one will be singing for our return. It is a harsh truth, but quite simple.

In the Foz district of Porto, Portugal on the Atlantic, in the park and on the beaches, children play and laugh and the music of their voices rises into the air to remind me that they are our hope on this dark and tempestuous sea on which we are shipwrecked, hoping to find our way home.

Dostoevsky said it well: "The soul is healed by being with children."

Can we hear their voices, singing?

Bob Dylan: A Masked Man in Search of Redemption?

"He wears a mask and his face grows to fit it."
—**George Orwell, "Shooting an Elephant"**

    The lobby of the temple of time travel called the Triplex Cinema in Great Barrington, Massachusetts was suffused with a nostalgic vibe tinged with the whiff of encroaching death when I walked in for *The Rolling Thunder Revue: A Bob Dylan Story*. I had earlier asked the ticket girl if most of the tickets for the two sold-out preview shows were being purchased by old people; she told me no, that many younger people had also bought tickets. However, I didn't see any.

    All I saw were grey or white heads and beards, not with "Time Out of Mind," as Dylan titled his 1997 album, but with time on their minds, as they shuffled into the dark to see where their time had gone and perhaps, if they were not mystified by their fetishistic worship of Dylan, to meditate on who they had become and where they and he were heading in the days to come. I imagined most were aware that Dylan had said that he's been singing about death since he was twelve, and that his music is haunted by images of love and time lost as bells toll for those traveling the road of life in search of forgiveness for their transgressions.

    How, I wondered, would this Dylan documentary "story" fashioned by Martin Scorsese, whose own work is marked by themes of guilt and redemption, affect an audience that might never have taken the roads less traveled of their youthful dreams but "fell" into the conformist and oppressive American neo-liberal way of life? Would this film, in Dylan's words, get the audience wondering "if I ever became what you wanted me to be/Did I miss the mark or overstep the line/That only you could see?"

Would nostalgia for their youth be a liberating or mystifying force, now that forty plus years have transformed American society into a conservative, postmodern, shopper's paradise where commodity capitalism has reified all aspects of life, including art objects and artists such a Dylan, imbuing them with magical powers to redeem those who buy their products, which include songs and celebrity "auras"?

I assumed many of those around me had fetishized Barack Obama as a savior even while he was waging endless wars and killing American citizens, bailing out his Wall St. and bank supporters, and jailing more whistleblowers than any American president in history. I knew that Dylan had accepted the Presidential Medal of Freedom from this icon of rectitude, who had served to quell all thoughts of rebellion and whose war victims were not counted by those who bought his brand since God was on his side. Here in this darkened dream factory in a hyper-gentrified "liberal" town, my mind was knotted with thoughts and questions that perhaps the film would address.

The Man Who Isn't

I knew that no one would answer my questions, but I asked myself anyway. Moreover, I knew there is no Bob Dylan. He is a figment of the imagination—first his own and then the public's. Perhaps behind the character Bob Dylan there is a genuine actor, and I hoped to catch an unintended glimpse of him in the film, but I knew if he appeared it would be obliquely and through a gradual dazzling of truth, as Emily Dickinson would say. An unconscious disclosure. For if the real Bob Dylan took off his mask and stood up, his ardent fans would receive it as a slap in the face, and their illusions would transmogrify into delusions as the spell would be broken. To tell the truth directly is a dangerous undertaking in a country of lies.

Dylan, the spellbinder, has, through his public personae, hypnotized his followers with his tantalizing and wonderful music. "Not I, not I, but the wind that blows through me," wrote D.H. Lawrence in his poem, "Song of a Man Who Has Come Through." This sounds like Dylan's artistic credo. His masks (*personae* = to sound through) have served as his medium of exchange. He has been faithful to his tutelary spirit (if not to living people), what the Romans called one's genius that is gifted to one at birth and is one's personal spirit to which one must be faithful if one wishes to be born into true and creative life. If one sacrifices to one's genius, one will in return become a vehicle for the fertile creativity that the genius can bestow. A person is not a genius but a transmitter of its gifts.

Like Lawrence, Dylan has served as a vehicle for his genius. His many masks, unified by Bob Zimmerman under the pseudonym Bob Dylan, have served as ciphers for the transmission of his enigmatic and arresting art. But while the music dazzles, the "real" man behind the name can't stand up—or is it, won't?—because, as always, he's "invisible now" and "not there," as his songs have so long told us.

I wondered if my theater companions understood this, or perhaps didn't want to. Could that be because their own reality now, if viewed from then, is problematic to them? Do generations of his fans sense a vacancy at the heart of their self-identities—non-selves—as if they have been absent from their own lives while reveling in Dylan's kaleidoscopic cast of characters? Do Dylan's lyrics—"People don't live or die people just float"—resonate with them? Lacking Dylan's artistry, are many reluctant to ask why they are so intrigued by the legerdemain of a man who insists he is absent? Has a whole generation gone missing and been trying to find where they went?

I am only familiar with the musician who acts upon a special social stage, and I love his creations. Because Dylan the performer has the poet's touch, a hyperbolic sense of the fantastic, he draws me into his magical web in the pursuit of deeper truths. He is an artist at war with his art and perhaps his true self, and therefore forces me to venture into uncharted territory and ask uncomfortable questions. His songs demand that the listener's mind and spirit be moving as the spirit of creative inspiration moved him. A close listening to many of them will force one to jump from verse to verse—to shoot the gulf—since there are no bridges to cross, no connecting links.

A Magic Show

From the start, *The Rolling Thunder Revue*, a fused compilation of film from a tour throughout New England concocted by Dylan that took place in 1975–6 as a rollicking experiment in communal music making, announces that we are going to be played with and that Dylan and Scorsese are conjurers whose prestidigitations are going to dazzle us. The film is gripping and cinematically beautiful. The opening scene is taken from a very old film in which a woman is sitting in a chair and a man throws a cloth over her. When he pulls the cloth away, the woman has disappeared. Call it playful magic, call it fun, call it entertainment—we can't say we haven't been warned—but after decades of postmodern gibberish with the blending of fact and fiction, fake news, endless propaganda, and the fiction-of-nonfiction, one might reasonably expect something more straightforward in 2019.

I could understand it if it served some larger purpose, but as the film shows, it doesn't. Later in the film, Dylan says, as if he needed to pound the point home, "If someone's wearing a mask, he's gonna tell you the truth. If he's not wearing a mask, it's highly unlikely." This may be true for him as an artist, but as a general prescription for living, it is bullshit. Of course lies are commonplace, but isn't it best to strive for truth, and doesn't that involve shedding masks? Then again, what does he mean by a mask?

Society trains us all from an early age to lie and deceive and to be socially adjusted persons on the social stage, and since person means mask, do we need some white face paint to obviously mask ourselves to tell the truth? Why can't one take off the masks and be authentic? Why can't Dylan? In an interview in 1997 with the music critic Jon Parles, Dylan said while he is mortified to be on stage, it's the only place where he's happy. "It's the only place you can be who you want to be."

These are the sad words of a man living in a cage on a stage, and only he might know why. Yet we are left to guess why Dylan is unhappy off stage, but such guessing is the other side of the social game where gossip and pseudo-psychoanalysis sicken us all as we try to decipher the personal lives of the celebrities we worship. Maybe we should examine our own looking-glass selves.

The Mask Falls

Despite being a masked man, there are times in this fascinating film when the lion in Dylan breaks out of the cage, and while the face paint and costume remain, one can see and hear a sense of short-lived liberation in his performances. His performance of "A Hard Rain's A-Gonna Fall" is so true, so passionate, so real, so intense that his true face shines through in its genuine glory. The same for his performance of "Hurricane" and a few others. It's all in his face and body, his articulation and energy, his fiery eyes. The performances refute his claim that only a masked man can speak the truth. As Joan Baez mordantly says, "Everything is forgiven when he sings."

There is something elegiac about the film, for many of the people in it are now dead and their film presence—that eerie afterlife that technology confers—conveys the ephemerality of fame—and life. Allen Ginsberg and Sam Shepard are dead, and many of the others are in their twilight years. But to see them young and frisky and bouncing around on stage and off, giving off sexuality and joy in the music and the trip they're on, one can't help be gripped by the passing of time and the contrast between then and now when depression and its pharmaceutical fixes has so many in its grip. Dylan's craggy, lined face in interviews for the film belies the young man we see perform and laugh, and though he stills performs and is addicted to being on the road so often—quite a feat for a 79-year-old—the juxtapositions of the images underscore the power of Dylan's musical messages. "Once upon a time," Dylan croons these days, "somehow once upon a time/ never comes again."

When one puts the then and now into historical and social perspective—which is essential since works of art are rooted in time, place, economic and political realities—one is jolted further. It's almost as if this Rolling Thunder Revue tour was the last gasp for a dying political and artistic culture that represented some hope for change, however small, while also being a symptom of the encroaching theatricality of American life, what Neal Gabler aptly calls, *Life: The Movie: How Entertainment Conquered Reality*.

The Triumph of Techno-Entertainment

Trace, if you will, the transformation of the United States from 1975–6 until today. It's as if the theatricality of the tour was announcing the end of straightforward dissent and the ushering in of the endless postmodern gamesmanship that is still with us. Masks. Games. Generations disappearing into technological and consumer fantasies where making money, watching television, and entering the system that destroys one's soul became the norm, as the American empire ravaged the world and Baby Boomers found life in their cell phones and on yoga mats, as Herbert Marcuse and his compatriots of the Frankfurt School warned. The culture industry absorbed dissent and spat it back out as entertainment in the service of the maintenance and consolidation of the power of the ruling class. How to transform a depraved society when the culture industry has corrupted so many people at their cores is where we're at now. "The carpet too is moving under you," Dylan intoned in 1965, "It's all over now, Baby Blue."

I looked around the movie theater before the film began and the rows were lit up by old folks staring at their little lit-up rectangular talismans. It was enough to bring me to despair. I was reminded of being in the circus in Madison Square Garden as a child where the kids were swinging sticks with cords attached with lights at the end that lit up the place.

They say the circuses are all closing, but I think not. "It's not dark yet/but it's getting there."

In an exchange between Dylan and Sam Shepard, who was on the tour as some sort of writer, Dylan asks Sam how he writes all those plays, and Sam says he does so by "communing with the dead." *The Rolling Thunder Revue* is like that, a medium between a time when passion still lived, and today when death, dying, and nostalgia are the norm for so many whose passion has fled into things.

Capitalism has conquered consciences with commodities.

Home Before Dark?

Dylan had his fallow period after the late seventies. To his great credit, he found new life, starting in the late 1990s with his *Time Out Of Mind* album and continuing through his recordings of the great American songbook of love ballads, the terrain of Sinatra and Bennett. Listening to him sing these great songs he did not write, I find his masks have fallen away and that a sad, lonely man emerges. A man filled with regrets and melancholia. An old man lamenting in a movingly raspy voice lost loves and haunted by what was and what might have been. A death-haunted man voicing raw emotion that is palpable. An uncaged man.

So much about Bob Dylan is paradoxical, or is it contradictory? Hypocritical?

Friedrich Nietzsche, another man of many faces, who advised us to "become who you are," once wrote, "There are unconscious actors among them and involuntary actors; the genuine are always rare, especially genuine actors." I don't know if the man behind the name Bob Dylan is a "genuine actor" (genuine being cognate with genius, both suggesting the act of giving birth, creating), for I have never met him. I hope he has met himself. He hints that someone is missing, whether that is the fictional actor or the genuine one, is difficult to discern. Is he becoming who he is, or is he lost out on the road "with no direction home"? He is always on the go, leaving, moving, restless, always seeking a way back home through song, even when, or perhaps because, there are no directions.

The Rolling Thunder Revue is a nostalgic trip. No doubt, audiences of a certain age will experience it as such. Such an aching for home comes with a cost: the acute awareness that you can't go home again. When the nursing and funeral home beckon, however, one can perhaps take a chance on truth by examining one's conscience to ask if and why one may have betrayed one's better youthful self and settled for a life of comforting conformity and resigned acceptance of the "system" one once raged against.

Younger people, if they are patient and watch the entire film, will experience a profound aesthetic shock that may give them hope. To see through the camera's eye the youthful Dylan's face as he gives some of the most passionate performances of his life will thrill them so that a shiver will go down their spines and their hair will stand on end. "And this is what poetry does," writes Roberto Calasso in *Literature and the Gods*, "it makes us see what otherwise we wouldn't have seen, through a sound that was never heard before." To watch just a handful of these performances makes the film worthwhile.

Become Who You Are?

At one point, today's Dylan says that he has always been "searching for the Holy Grail." I suppose one could interpret that as meaning eternal youth, happiness, redemption, or some sort of immortality. He has surely created a capitalist's corporate empire, though that doesn't seem to satisfy him, as it never has genuine poets. But maybe to become very, very rich and famous has always been his goal, his immortality project, as it is for other tycoons. One can only guess. I prefer not to. But without question, Dylan has the poet's touch, a hyperbolic sense of the fantastic that draws you into his magical web in the pursuit of deeper truth. In ways, he's like the Latin American magical realist writers who move from fact to dream to the fantastic in a puff of wind.

He is our Emerson. His artistic philosophy has always been about movement in space and time through song. "An artist has got to be careful never to arrive at a place where he thinks he's at somewhere," he's said. "You always have to realize that you are constantly in a state of becoming and as long as you can stay in that realm, you'll be alright."

Sounds like living, right.

Sounds like Emerson, also. "Life only avails, not the having lived. Power ceases in the instant of repose; it resides in the moment of transition from a past to a new state, in the shooting of the gulf, in the darting to an aim. Thus one fact the world hates, that the soul becomes."

Like Emerson, Dylan creates a sense of restlessness in the listener that forces one to ask: Who am I? Am I? He has said "that a song is like a dream, and you try to make it come true." In a similar way, Scorsese has created a dream with this film. It takes us back and forth in time via an hallucinatory experience. A sort of documentary with a wink.

It is quite a story, powerful enough to bring one to ask: Who are we becoming in this American Dream? Will we keep sleeping through the nightmares we create and support, or will we return home with Dylan and embrace the radical truth he once gifted us with and dare to "tell it and speak it and think it and breathe it/ And reflect from the mountains so all souls can see it" that our country continues to kill and oppress people all around the world, even here at home.

Dylan emphatically answered that question with his midnight message to JFK's ghost in late March 2020, when he unexpectedly released a new song. He burst forth from behind his many masks and gifted the world with his incandescent song about the assassination of President Kennedy, with a title taken from *Hamlet*, from the mouth of the ghost of the dead King of Denmark—"Murder Most Foul." For those who have wondered over the years if Dylan had "sold out," here is the answer. For those who have wondered if he would go to his grave reciting the words of T.S. Eliot's J. Alfred Prufrock—"I am no Prince Hamlet nor was meant to be"— here is Hamlet's booming response. Not only does this song lay bare the truth of the most foundational event in modern American history, but it does so in such a powerfully poetic way and at such an opportune time that it should redeem Dylan in the eyes of those who ever doubted him.

I say "should," but while the song's release has garnered massive publicity from the mainstream media, it hasn't taken long for that media to bury the truth of his words about the assassination under a spectacle of verbiage meant to damn with faint praise. As the media in a celebrity culture of the spectacle tend to do, the emphasis on the song's pop cultural references is their focus, with platitudes about the assassination and "conspiracy theories," as well as various shameful and gratuitous digs at Dylan for being weird, obsessed, or old. As the song says, "they killed him once and they killed him twice," so now they can kill him a third time, and then a fourth ad infinitum. And now the messenger of the very bad news must be dispatched along with the dead president.

The media like their Hamlets impotent and enervated, but Dylan has come out roaring like a bull intent on avenging his dead president.

If you listen to Dylan's piercing voice and follow the lyrics closely, you might be startled to be told, not from someone who can be dismissed as some sort of disgruntled "conspiracy nut," but by the most famous musician in the world, that there was a government conspiracy to kill JFK, that Oswald didn't do it, and that the killers then went for the president's brothers.

> *Your brothers are comin', there'll be hell to pay*
> *Brothers? What brothers? What's this about hell?*
> *Tell them, "We're waiting, keep coming," we'll get*
>   *them as well*

This is an in-your-face tale, set to music with a barely tinkling piano, a violin, and a soupçon of percussion, whose lightest words, as Hamlet's father's ghost said to him:

> *Would harrow up thy soul, freeze thy young blood,*
> *Make thy two eyes like stars start from their*
>   *spheres,*
> *Thy knotty and combinèd locks to part,*

*And each particular hair to stand on end
Like quills upon the fretful porcupine.*

"Murder Most Foul" truly startles. It is a redemptive song. Dylan holds the mirror up for us. He unlocks the door to the painful and sickening truth. He shoves the listener in, and, as he writes in *Chronicles,* "your head has to go into a different place. Sometimes it takes a certain somebody to make you realize it."

Bob is our certain somebody. In these dark times, he has offered us his voice.

Sometimes a Pair of Pants Can Give You Vertigo

> *"Between the experience of living a normal life at this moment on the planet and the public narratives being offered to give a sense to that life, the empty space, the gap, is enormous. The desolation lies there, not in the facts."*
>
> —**John Berger, "A Man with Tousled Hair"**
> in ***The Shape of a Pocket***

A few days ago, as I stepped into my pants to start the day as is my habit, I happened to notice the label at the waist band. It read "Gap," and the sight of this word sent my mind spinning into a whirling contemplation of this void that lies at the center of life today, a subject that has disturbed me for a long time.

I had earlier that morning made the mistake of checking the news headlines on the computer. This too is a habit that I no doubt share with millions of other people. It is a dastardly habit no sane person should inflict on themselves. To rise from one's night dreams and step into a litany of hyperbolic headlines shouting doom and gloom at every turn is to inject oneself with a poisonous drug before the sap of life has a chance to rise in one's veins and one's imagination might give birth to new possibilities.

Standing in my pants, I felt as though I were hovering over Berger's enormous empty space, and if I didn't wake up, I would tumble endlessly away. Thoreau's words floated up: "To be awake is to be alive. I have never yet met a man who was quite awake. How could I have looked him in the face?"

So I stepped over the hole at my feet and tried to shake the monotonous clatter of the monstrous media's messages from my mind. In my vertiginous state I dared not look in a mirror. So many of the media's lying words that I had already ingested with coffee seemed to float around and within me in an unreality disconnected from the actual world, even the world they were ostensibly reporting on.

I too had written many words about the drastic condition of our world today, thinking somehow my words, different from the corporate media's, could move the world by pulling back the curtain that the powerful have created through clichés to conceal the sordid reality they have made of this beautiful earth. Yet the presentation of facts seemed to make no difference. Very little, if anything, made a difference. Most of those who read my words more or less already agreed with me. And many, even friends and family, just ignored them, anticipating that my words would disturb them. And the mainstream publications shunned them like the plague.

Between my desire for a changed world and the world that seemed to change only for the worse lay the desolation Berger identified.

Many people feel it, I know, especially dissidents who fight in various ways against the powerful. But we prefer not to go there, to see what it consists of and how we may transmute it into acts and words that might make a difference. We prefer to make believe we are making a difference by repeating ad nauseum the same prefabricated responses, usually directly political, to the atrocities committed daily. We are caught in what Czeslaw Milosz, writing in a different context, called "ontological anemia"—"among this illness's symptoms is the nothingness sucking from the center in." We try and try but seem to devour ourselves by repeating the same approaches, as if all the slaves know is what their masters have taught them. Milosz knew this because he was an artist and a spiritual seeker, not just a political analyst, and also had personal experience with the totalitarian mindset that is descending on the West.

The twists of history can make one's head spin.

Words and deeds are turned upside down on desolation row where, as Bob Dylan reminds us:

Between the windows of the sea where lovely
   mermaids flow
And nobody has to think too much about
   Desolation Row

Being online is being on Desolation Row, a digital line created to suck us into a drug habit from which we can't begin to imagine an exit. The dealers who created this electronic trap in the 1990s are in the process of closing the circle with their creation of a high-tech dystopia in which quaint ideas like freedom and nature are replaced by the electronic control of every aspect of life. The high-tech companies together with the national-security state are grinning with glee at our stupidity.

We need to think again. Imagine! Today we are caught in a void of clichés and in the clutches of rapacious elites. Only acts of creative imagination can free us from their clutches.

I look to my right and on a shelf I see a vividly painted Matryoshka doll. It startles me into the thought that like Matryoshka dolls, so many of our personal habits that deaden us to imagining a way across the gap to a better world are nestled within social habits of thought, speech, and action. We are so often encased like tiny cloned dolls in the social clichés that make us smaller versions of the powers that we say we oppose but which we mimic. We are carved and painted in their likeness, and caught in the habit of reacting to them in ways that reinforce their control.

We must disrupt our routines. We must find new ways, not to just respond, but to take the initiative. When we react according to habits, although we may not realize it, we are being controlled and not in control. Habits, like the word's etymology reveals, may reassure us that we have, hold or possess a position of strength from which we can move the world in our direction, but the only Archimedean lever and fulcrum capable of that is inspiration.

That involves a new way of seeing, not vertiginous but visionary, not electronic but natural.

For a start, I think I'll change my pants.

Kevin Love:
Making a Hole in Denial

"For behind the sense of insecurity in the face of danger, behind the sense of discouragement and depression, there always lurks the basic fear of death, a fear which undergoes most complex elaborations and manifests itself in many indirect ways. . . . No one is free of the fear of death."

—**Gregory Zilboorg, psychanalyst**

"An anxiety is a lack that causes pain; a game is a lack that causes pleasure."

—**John Fowles,** *The Aristos*

"What we play is life."

—**Louis Armstrong**

In a moving essay revealing his existential anxiety and panic attacks, "Everyone Is Going Through Something," National Basketball Association star Kevin Love has touched a nerve that underlies not just sports and male experience, but life itself. He is right to say, "This is an everyone thing." In doing so, he has performed a public service far beyond getting men and boys to open up about their fears and feelings. He has, as befits his surname, opened many people to a consideration of the marriage of love and death, and why all efforts to divorce them result in the diminishment of life's passion and intensity.

Commenting on the unavoidable but often denied link between love and death, the important American psychologist Rollo May said this in *Love and Will*:

> To love means to open ourselves to the negative as well as the positive—to grief, sorrow and disappointment as well as to joy, fulfillment, and an intensity of consciousness we did not know was possible before.

So it is fitting that in telling us of his conversations with a therapist, the one personal experience Kevin tells us about is the death of his Grandma Carol, who meant so much to him and was like another parent when he was growing up. Busy with his basketball career, he didn't see her when she was dying. "I felt terrible that I hadn't been in better touch with her in her last years," he writes. Deeply pained at losing her and guilty about his behavior, he shared this with no one, bottling it up as he had learned since boyhood (Be strong, be a man), and like the athlete that he is, perhaps thought that if he did not dwell on this loss, the next game would be a win and he could somehow move on. But this never works for long, as Love learned when panic burst into his consciousness and took him down during a game last November. "It came out of nowhere," he says, having learned, however, that nowhere is somewhere, even when a surprise.

Substitute sportswriter for athlete, as Richard Ford does in his dazzling novel, *The Sportswriter*, whose main character Frank Bascombe, a sportswriter haunted by the death of his young son from Reye's syndrome but trying to lose himself in the ordinariness of sports writing, says, "Since after all, it is one thing to write sports, but another thing entirely to live a life," and we have Love's cautionary tale.

For sports (shopping for women) is the perfect metaphor for the modern American male's flight from authenticity. As the etymology of the word sport attests (from old French, *desporter* to divert, literally "to carry away"), sports are a diversion from something. Let's call it "real life," the place from where, as Ernest Hemingway so aptly put it in the title to his short story, "The

Winner Takes Nothing." Trophies are handed out at post-season dinners, but as the American philosopher William James said, "The skull will grin in at the banquet."

Although sports can inspire one to think deeply, for most people, athletes and spectators alike, sports are a diversion from existential matters involving relationships, fears, deep feelings, life's meaning, love and loss, death, etc. While surely fun, entertaining, and lucrative for professionals, sports are also absurd since they involve movements through time and space toward unnecessary and fictitious goals where someone wins (lives) and someone losses (dies) in a game of unreality. In sports we play to overcome artificial and superfluous obstacles for fun and money—and for deeper reasons we may not realize.

Take golf, for example (my apologies to golfers). Why does anyone care who can hit a little white ball with a stick in the fewest strokes down stretches of green grass into a hole in the ground? Many do. They spend enormous amounts of time and money trekking after those little white balls. They care primarily because it's fun, and fun is good. Such fun is utterly meaningless in the larger scheme of things, but many find it relaxing from the "stress" of everyday life—a relaxing distraction. And of course distractions can be good in moderation. It is not sports that are the problem, but the obsession with them.

I knew a woman who felt her husband was overly obsessed with sports, and although she was wrong, she used to say to him, "With you it's balls, balls, balls." To which he would respond, also erroneously, "And with you it's malls, malls, malls." But their humorous exchange catches a widespread truth about men and women in American society where there are plenty of obsessively distracted people of both sexes.

Sports only matter because they don't. And it is in that gap between mattering and not where panic, anxiety, and depression can appear "out of nowhere." Another athlete, the Nobel Prize winning French author Albert Camus, a soccer goalie in his youth and a lifelong fan, phrased this experience differently when he said, "At any street corner the feeling of absurdity can strike any man in the face."

Athletes ride intense emotional roller coasters. You win, you lose, you're up, you're down—like "real life," just faster and with a much quicker turn-around time. While Kevin is right to say that "everyone is going through something that we can't see," athletes live at a different pace and intensity, and the resulting highs bring deep lows as well. One day you're dead; the next day you are resurrected, as long as there is another game or season. Some days you are in purgatory and wonder if all the aches and pains you endure are worth the cost.

This is true for the spectators also, absent the physical pains. Many fans are fanatics for a reason. The intensity of sports, its unpredictability, its "never over till it's over" drama makes it the perfect distraction from more important matters. It has an extraordinary power to energize and deflate, but all in a land of make-believe that often blinds its devotees from trying to understand "something that we can't see" in their own lives.

But a fan's life can last until actual death, while an athlete has a limited amount of time to perform. One day when your playing days are over your confrontation with "reality" happens, either consciously or out of the blue. For many former athletes, men particularly, because women have come late to the games, the rest of their lives are lived in a desperate reliving of the past among "the fraternity of missing men," as Don DeLillo says in his dazzling novel, *Underworld*. It is a place where "desperation" speaks.

A few years ago there was a short Grantland documentary, "The Finish Line," about Steve Nash. An uncanny professional basketball player, Nash was battling injuries and age, and the documentary shows him pondering whether or not to retire or continue his rehabilitation and attempt a comeback. In the opening scene Nash goes out with his dog into the shadowy pre-dawn where he muses on his dilemma. His words are hypnotic. "I feel," he said, "that there's something that I can't quite put my finger on that—I don't know—I feel that it's blocking me or I can see it out of the corner of my mind's eye, or it's like *this dark presence* .... is it the truth that I'm done?"

Hobbled by a nerve injury that severely limited his movement, he played a few more games and retired within a year. He had brought an infectious joy to his playing, but he left without fulfilling his dream of winning an NBA championship. Of his retirement he said, "It's bittersweet. I already miss the game deeply, but I'm also really excited to learn to do something else." Unlike many athletes, Nash was moving on; his "dark presence" wasn't a final death but a step on the road to a hard rebirth. It was a Dylanesque restless farewell: "And though the line is cut/It ain't quite the end/I'll just bid farewell till we meet again."

I think it safe to say that behind every panic attack, at the deepest level, lies what William James called "the worm at the core," by which he meant death, the fear of it, the anxiety it engenders that rumbles beneath the placid surface of everyday life and breaks the surface here and there when least expected. Sometimes it happens during "little deaths," what the French call *La petite mort* in reference to the sensation following sexual orgasm, but which happen throughout life in so many guises such as losing a game, missing a shot, or failing an exam. It can happen anywhere and anytime, even in moments of great success, such as hoisting a trophy above one's head after being named the Most Valuable Player.

A few years ago my friends and I were playing in basketball tournaments for men over fifty and we qualified for the Senior Olympics at the University of Pittsburgh. We acquired a sponsor, a local funeral home that made warm-up jerseys for us. Being used to dealing with bodies at rest, these comedians knew we were a bunch of aging hoopsters intent on keeping our bodies in motion for as long as we could. So they had shirts made with that up-beat and adolescent cliché printed on the front, "Basketball is Life." Lest we forgot, and being in the trade of taking bodies at rest to the underworld, on the back they had printed "Leave the Rest to Us: Flynn and Dagnoli Funeral Home."

Kevin Love's essay, "Everybody Is Going Through Something" is like that shirt. He reminds us that at the back of everyone's face there are matters that deserve scrutiny even when we can't see back there.

He deserves a Most Valuable Person award for making a hole in a denial that is an "everyone thing."

HILLARY CLINTON: THE HEARTLESS QUEEN

The 2016 Democratic Convention confetti raining down on smiling faces should not conceal the bloody truth that trails Hillary Clinton. As the balloons rise to celebrate her triumph, her victims continue to fall.

Following the bidding of her oligarchic backers in the hidden government, she has always been fervently eager to lend her immoral authority to the massacre of foreign peoples and the destruction of their central governments. Iraq, Syria, Afghanistan, Ukraine, Serbia, etc.—the list is as long as her moral turpitude is deep.

But as the Queen of Heartless is crowned and feted in the City of Brotherly Love, it is crucially important that we recall her role five years ago in the destruction of the African country that had the highest living standard on the continent, excellent health care, free education, good social services, etc.—Libya.

Now that Libya, according to plan, has descended into civil war and chaos (see Iraq, Syria, etc.) as a result of the 2011 "humanitarian intervention" instigated by Clinton and her ilk, it has disappeared from mainstream media propaganda. Out of sight, out of mind. It will reappear in the corporate press if the American/NATO aggressors decide to bomb the country again in alliance with their friend, the Egyptian dictator Abdel Fattah el-Sisi, probably in support of the CIA-affiliated General Khalifa Haftar, who is presently wreaking havoc in eastern Libya with western support, as leaked tapes have shown. The time for that renewed bombing may be fast approaching, though it might be delayed for political reasons until after the presidential election.

In the popular mind, Clinton is associated with the controversial events of September 2012 in Benghazi that resulted in the death of Ambassador Christopher Stevens and three other Americans. As the Secretary of State, she was no doubt aware of Stevens' work with the CIA organizing the transfer of the seized Gaddafi government weapons to Turkish ports. As the Italian historian Paolo Sensini writes in his eye-opening book, *Sowing Chaos: Libya in the Wake of Humanitarian Intervention*, "The arms were then transferred to the jihadi forces engaged in terrorist actions against the government of Syria under Bashar al-Assad." While bi-partisan outrage over the Americans' deaths was duly noted by the media and became a political football, the nature of Stevens' work under Clinton and Obama received no mainstream media coverage, and the illegal and immoral wars against the two countries continued apace.

But the Stevens issue pales in comparison to Clinton's larger role in waging war on a sovereign nation for propagandistic "humanitarian" reasons. As with Iraq (Hussein) and Syria (Assad), she was a central player in the lies told about Mu'ammar Gaddafi to justify a war of aggression. Each in his turn was declared to be the new Hitler. In Gaddafi's case, he was falsely accused of killing 10,000 people in Tripoli, having his soldiers use Viagra and rape as a matter of policy, and of being a bloody mad dictator intent on genocide. Rwanda and the Holocaust were elicited as warnings. President Obama justified the savage attack on Libya, fully supported by his Secretary of State Clinton, with the following lie: "We knew that if we wanted [*sic*] . . . if we waited one more day, Benghazi, a city nearly the size of Charlotte, could suffer a massacre that would have reverberated across the region and stained the conscience of the world." And he announced he was sending Clinton to London to meet with the Libyan "opposition"—aka terrorists.

The western media ran with these false accusations, as usual, as did Al Jazeera and Al Arabiya, prominent Arab media. Like Iraq, Syria, and Serbia, it was another war of aggression based on lies, and Clinton was a primary player.

She was fully aware of developments in Libya from the start; knew that the rebels were Islamic militants armed and trained by the U.S., Britain, France, Egypt, Saudi Arabia, and UAE; knew that they summarily executed anyone they considered their enemies; knew that this war of lies was aimed at preventing Gaddafi from fulfilling his goal of economic independence, not just for Libya, but for the entire continent of Africa by introducing the gold dinar into Africa as common currency; knew, in short, that Libya had to be raped, its Central Bank destroyed, for its exploitation by western globalists. Thus her boss, Obama, in August 2011, confiscated $30 billion from Libya's Central Bank that Gaddafi had planned to use for the establishment of the African IMF and African Central Bank. This is what Clinton termed "smart power at its best." Under the pretext of "humanitarian intervention," Clinton supported the killing of tens of thousands and the destruction of an independent country to serve her masters.

Paolo Sensini characterizes the Democratic presidential nominee perfectly:

> Mrs. Clinton's joyous exclamation on hearing the news of Gaddafi's death sums up the recklessness and irresponsibility of an entire political class—an unrepentant class that has wreaked havoc around the world on a truly unprecedented scale.

When she thought cameras and microphones were off and exclaimed, "We came, we saw, he died," she was speaking not just for herself but for the party and interests that she now represents.

"I'm with her," says Michelle Obama.

"I am proud to stand with her," says Bernie Sanders.

I wonder where the dead children of Libya stand.

Answering the Mysterious Call of an Artist's Spiritual Vocation

"Friend, hope for the Guest while you are alive."
—**Kabir, "To Be a Slave of Intensity"**

*Strange how a man
Can enter your life
Just like that: a knock
Out of nowhere
And you've slipped away
To a rendezvous with destiny
That always awaited you.*

—**EJC, "The Birth and Death of Trauma"**

Myths and popular tales, like life, are replete with accounts of those not answering the call, of locking the door to their hearts and shutting themselves up in sterile and safe lives where the rest of the world is not even an afterthought, where others suffer and die because of one's indifference. Answering can be very dangerous, for it can take you on a journey from which you may never return, surely, at least, not as the same person. Only the courageous heed the call.

When Carolyn Forché, a twenty-seven year old naïve academic poet living in the San Diego area, miraculously answered the call of a Salvadorian stranger named Leonel Gómez Vides, who showed up at her door out of the blue, to go to El Salvador, a country she knew very little about but to which he said war was coming and her poet's eye was needed, she acted intuitively and bravely from her deep soul's murmurings and said yes, not knowing why or where she was heading except into the unknown.

This memoir, a souvenir of hope and terror and a call to resistance, a poet's lucid dreaming between childhood and an adult awakening, invites the reader to examine one's life and conscience through language that emulates our living experience as it strains toward meaning through a wandering dialectical consciousness that weaves the past present with the present past and lucid dreaming with the waking state. One experiences this book as one does life, not, as the French existentialist Gabriel Marcel, has said, "as a problem to be solved but a mystery to be lived." It is impossible to adequately "review" a book that breathes. One can only conspire with it to uncover the conspiracy of silence that is American government propaganda.

For at the heart of this mystery are facts, which Forché describes in graphic detail, the truth of how the United States government has long been doing the devil's murderous work in El Salvador, throughout Latin America and the world, as current events confirm. Forché asks us to enter into her memories not to wax nostalgic, but to awaken to the truth of today. The truth that little has changed and the past was prologue. The U.S. is still "Murder Incorporated," and Americans must see this clearly, and resist.

Carolyn's "Yes" to the enigmatic stranger Leonel, so I sense from her reveries, was the fruit of a seed of faith planted when she was a child of ten or so in Michigan. "The girl I once was, who had been a Catholic, woke for the bells of the Angelus at six in the morning, *Angelus Domini*. I sang to myself as I walked to morning Mass under a canopy of maples, through a wetland of swamp cabbage and red-winged blackbirds, the quiet, low Mass where it was possible to pray in peace, with the Latin liturgy a murmur in the air. . . . I felt at peace in the church, on the padded kneeler near the stained-glass windows depicting the seven sorrows along the west wall, the seven joys along the east. . . . When I knelt beside them, the floor, the pews, and my own body were quilted in colored light." But she tells Leonel that she has "fallen" because she no longer attends Mass.

Leonel, a "non-believer" who says "I believe with my life, how I live," tells her about Padre Rutilio Grande, a Jesuit priest who was murdered with an old man and a boy by the U.S. trained and supported Salvadorian death-squads. "God that Padre Grande taught was not up in the sky lying in some damn cloud hammock. This was a God who expected us to be brothers and sisters and to make of earth a just place."

This was her introduction to a new theology, a way of connecting her spiritual core from a conservative Catholic childhood piety to the liberation theology that created Christian base communities of the poor and persecuted in El Salvador and other Latin American countries. Dissident Christianity. True Christianity. When she went to El Salvador soon thereafter, not only did the poet leave the quiet of her study where her work might have revolved around herself, but the little girl left the church building to discover, as a changed woman, Christ among the poor and persecuted in the living world.

One night she meets a man in the shadows of such a Christian base community where a few of its members had been killed and dismembered by the government death squads. His pseudonym is Inocencio. "You can say Chencho," he tells her. At first he thinks she is a nun ("although, as a girl, I considered that vocation"), because she smokes, and some of the foreign nuns smoke and don't dress in traditional habits. He asks her why she is there and she says, "You know, I'm not sure." She then explains how an unnamed person invited her to come to see the truth for herself because war was coming, and when she returned to the United States to "explain the reasons for the war to the North Americans, because my friend tells me that this will be important, that the real reasons be known, so that the people of the United States understand."

Chencho is a catechist who secretly moves under darkness of night from one small Christian base community to another, encouraging the *campesinos* to keep the faith because God is with them, *la gente, los pobres*, the people, the poor. He says to Carolyn:

> Listen to me, *hermana*. We are brothers and sisters in Christ, and Christ is moving through the world now, through us. He is acting through us in the struggle against injustice, poverty, and oppression. To be with God now is to choose the fate of the poor, to be with them, to see through their eyes and feel through their hearts, and if this means torture and death, we accept. We are already in the grave.

Later, Leonel takes her to visit a friend who is in a prison from hell where men are tortured in padlocked wooden boxes the size of washing machines. Afterwards she vomits. Then they go to visit a dirt-poor young mother giving birth in a *casita* in which there was nothing, "really nothing: a candle, a plastic basin, a ladle hanging against the wall, and, in the candlelight, the shadow of a wooden chair dancing on the wall."

> I followed him [Leonel] through the darkness into a passage, then through a door lit by a candle and, by the light of it, saw people gathered and one of them, someone, took me by the hand and drew me into the circle surrounding a young woman who was lying on her side on a blanket on the floor, her head propped in her hand. There was a cardboard box beside her, and in the box, a newborn girl with her hair still wet, lying in a towel. Leonel was looking at me from across the room. "She was born about a half hour ago," a young man beside me whispered. "She's early. We're going to name her Alma. *Bellisima!*"

Then it is on through night to meet with four young impoverished men who read their "political" poems for her, written under pseudonyms for fear for their lives, poems they hope might stir the hearts of people in the United States.

That night I knew something had changed for me, and that I wasn't going to get tired or need a shower or want to call something off so I could rest, and I hoped that if I forgot this I would somehow remember Alma in the cardboard box in the barrio, and the mimeographed poems.... The woman who went into the prison in Ahuachapán left herself behind in a barrio called La Fosa, the grave.

The naïve young poet is buried and the political poet of witness is born. It is impossible not to be deeply moved and nourished by such a birth. Who, I wonder, are the "fallen" ones? What is writing for? What good are poets? Why say yes to a stranger's request when it is so much easier to not answer the knock on the door? So much easier to barricade ourselves behind walls of denial and say "me first." So much easier to ignore the truth that this book reveals: that the United States is the greatest purveyor of violence in the world and our society rests on keeping the poor poor and under the vicious thumbs of the rich.

The world is filled with writers who bear witness only to their imprisonment in their own egos. When Carolyn Forché said yes to Leonel and then returned from El Salvador to write "political" poems such as "The Colonel," she was attacked by writers wishing a poet would stay in her box and not disturb their universe. That she was not like them angered these J. Alfred Prufrocks who were not going to come back from the dead to tell us all as she has, poets who had time on their hands to neurotically contemplate their navels with their fellow Americans:

> *Time for you and time for me,*
> *And time yet for a hundred indecisions,*
> *And for a hundred visions and revisions,*
> *Before the taking of a toast and tea.*

Having heard Leonel's descriptions of "the silence of misery endured" and the American supported death-squads massacring impoverished Salvadorians, she tells us:

I knew that if I didn't accept his invitation, I could never live as if I would have been willing to do something, should an opportunity have presented itself. I could never say to myself: If only I'd had the chance. This was, I knew, my chance.

Wasn't such a daring decision by this "fallen" poet the quintessence of the creative act, exactly what inspired artists do when they see the act of writing as an adventure into the unknown where startling truths wait to reveal themselves to the unsuspecting author? A journey fraught with danger and delight, perhaps delightful danger or dangerous delight, but always ready to surprise with hidden truths that might unlock the prison gates that enclose the world in suffering and pain? Does not the artist proceed into this alien territory armed only with a fierce faith in the power of truth to reveal its face and so strengthen us? Doesn't a poet trust in a power greater than herself and know what she wishes to say only in the act of saying it? Isn't real writing a transmission between the creative spirit and the world of flesh and blood, the living and the dead, a visionary opening into the future where freedom beckons?

Carolyn somehow knew this then and now, and her memoir is the result, a haunting trip into the past to liberate the present. "The strange, mysterious, perhaps dangerous, perhaps redeeming comfort that there is in writing," wrote Kafka in his diary. Perhaps there are certain writings that cannot be adequately reviewed but must be experienced. *What You Have Heard Is True: A Memoir of Witness and Resistance* is such a book. How do you review a prayer and a mystery? You must enter them if you are willing.

Carolyn, drawing on the uncanny spirit of her mystical, Gypsy-spirited Czechoslovak grandmother Anna ("I will get Anna out of you if it's the last thing I do" her mother told her, to no avail), chose to develop her "legitimate strangeness," as the French poet René Char urged, heeding his words that "what comes into the world to disturb nothing merits neither attention or patience." Disturbed and perplexed by the stranger's tales and her former husband's experiences in Vietnam and the United States' savage war there, as well as by her mystical Catholic childhood's faith and its tug of conscience, she joins the mysterious Leonel in El Salvador.

To those ensconced in instrumental rationality, her decision seems insane. However, instrumental rationality is insane, and it has taken us to the brink of nuclear extinction. It is to the poet's truth we should turn. The data driven instrumental rationalists have given us WW I, II, Auschwitz, Vietnam, the CIA, death squads, Iraq, Syria, etc.—should I give you numbers, list it all, do the logic? When has such logic convinced the disbelievers? Logicians don't trust the soul's promptings and, like Carolyn, take a chance, take a leap of faith. They do calculations, follow computer models, and dare not enter the world outside if they are told there is a 60% chance of rain. And if they are told the sun will shine and all will be well with the world, but a hard rain does fall and the poet shouts there is blood on our hands, they act shocked. Always shocked at the truth that was there from the start. If only we had known.

Is it any wonder so many Americans are depressed?

The German holocaust atrocities haunted Carolyn, a child of Czechoslovakian ancestry, and she grew up suffering from periodic depressions that would lift once she felt the urge to do something about the injustices she saw. The urge to act for others freed her from wallowing in depression. Rather than becoming a nun, she became a poet, and when Leonel told her that an American poet was needed to witness the truth of the American supported atrocities in El Salvador, she trusted the spirit to lead her on, not knowing why this might be so. What use are poets, she wondered, in the U.S. where poetry "doesn't matter." She would soon help to change that.

There is an old Catholic prayer that goes like this: "Come Holy Spirit, fill the hearts of your faithful and kindle in them the fire of your love. Send forth your Spirit and they shall be created. And You shall renew the face of the earth."

Might such words have bubbled up from her unconscious? I have long felt it was a prayer for poets as well as the religiously faithful—are not all inspired together? Is there a difference? "I believe in the magic and authority of words," said Char, the French resistance fighter. Witness and resistance. Words. Poetry. Prayers.

It is best that I not tell you too much about Leonel. You will wonder about him, and you will wonder with Carolyn what her relationship with him is all about. You will discover his essence in the reading. You will learn that he once said to Carolyn that "it isn't the risk of death and fear of danger that prevent people from rising up, it is numbness, acquiescence, and the defeat of the mind. Resistance to oppression begins when people realize deeply within themselves that something better is possible." You might, like me, question whether this is true only for the most oppressed, or whether it applies to Americans whose lives depend on the subjugation of others in foreign lands.

You will be terrified to learn of the death squads, the brutality and cold-bloodedness of their murders, and Forché's close escapes as they hunted her. You will feel her fear.

You will learn of the courageous women who befriend her, her meeting with Monseñor Oscar Romero the week before he is assassinated while saying Mass and Carolyn has left the country at his urging, and you too will be lost in reveries as you travel between worlds of night and day, wealth and poverty, life and death, now and then.

If you are like me, you will be inspired by what the poet Char called "wisdom with tear-filled eyes."

This book is just that. It is a call to Americans to face the truth and resist.

A Conspiracy Theorist Confesses to His Petty Crimes

"Our research has shown for the first time the role that conspiracy theories can play in determining an individual's attitude to everyday crime. It demonstrates that people subscribing to the view that others have conspired might be more inclined toward unethical actions."

—**Professor Karen Douglas, University of Kent press release for the research entitled, "Belief in Conspiracy Theories and Intentions to Engage in Everyday Crime," in the** *British Journal of Social Psychology*

Let me be perfectly clear from the outset.

I am not referring to the conspiracy theories of George W. Bush, Colin Powell, Barack Obama, Hilary Clinton, Donald Trump and other such luminaries concerning events such as the attack of September 11, 2011, weapons of mass destruction in Iraq, the ongoing war on terror, Julian Assange's alleged ties to Russia, etc. These people's conspiracy theories have nothing to do with petty crime, for their handiwork is grand indeed. They are big people. In any case, I don't know what small stuff they might be up to when not killing so many people all around the world.

I got to thinking about my petty crimes after reading a profound article in *The New York Post* about how the aforementioned Professor Douglas and her comrades at two English research universities have proven—"backed up by science" as the *Post's* Rob Bailey-Milado says—that little people like me who have concluded that the U.S. national security state conspired to kill President

Kennedy, to take one example, are inclined to take to the dark side and pilfer M&Ms from the candy counter and stuff like that.

"Sure," Bailey-Milado writes in his elegant style, "we've been saying this about our wack-job uncle for years." Such a nut case might be a "9/11 denier" or believe "the ancient pyramids were built by aliens" or believe "myths surrounding the Mueller report to the chilling 'secret' behind Disney's *Frozen*."

As we all know, all these nutty beliefs are of equal value and validity, and to even harbor the thought that Bailey-Milado might have the CIA's 1967 secret Dispatch—Doc 135-960, showing how to counter and discredit the claims of conspiracy theorists pinned over his desk or in his mind—is to risk further accusations of being wacked-out and in need of examining one's proclivity toward everyday crimes. So I won't go there. I'm guilty enough.

So bless me, folks, for I have sinned. Let me confess.

Last week, after reading the *Post* article and the study itself, I found myself in my local co-op market. You might wonder where I had been looking for myself when I found myself there, staring into bins of dried fruit, but let's just say I had been around. When you're lost and wacked-out, you never know where you are or why you believe what you believe.

I was trying to decide whether to get the dried pineapple, mango, or figs. It was a tough choice, sort of like staring at forty different tubes of toothpaste on the store shelf and wondering which to buy or if the one advertised as specially for women would work for a man since men must have different teeth. The comparison is not exactly apt, I guess, for you can't test the toothpastes there, but the fruit looked so edible. So, when no one was looking, I first tried the pineapple, then the mango, and finally the figs. I thought I saw the store manager see me when I took the fig because I was so enjoying the fruits of my crime that I let my guard down.

When I was leaving the store, I had the odd thought that the cop car in the parking lot was there for me, so I turned and went out via the sidewalk, sighing in relief as I did. As I was walking home, I thought of my narrow escape and the brilliance of the study that connected my conspiratorial thinking to my criminal activity with the fruit. I also couldn't help thinking how the figs had reminded me of my latest conspiracy theory, but one supported by sources as confidential as those referenced by *The New York Times* or *The Washington Post*. In addition, like those devotees of truth and confidentiality, I will never reveal my sources.

Legend has it that Isaac Newton discovered the law of gravity while sitting in a garden, watching apples fall perpendicularly to the ground. However, this is not true. I have learned from my confidential sources that his nickname was Isaac "Fig" Newton and that those who claim the Fig Newton cookie was named after Newton, Massachusetts are involved in a great cover-up.

My sources tell me that when Isaac was a child, he was so fond of figs that his mother had to warn him against eating too many, for as you probably know, figs, like prunes, are filled with fiber and possess a laxative quality. Isaac was defecating so much and so often that his mother was alarmed. But a mother's panic at a child's toilet habits can be a source of insight years later.

So it was that years later it was Isaac's experience on the potty that gave him his great insight into gravity. Reflecting back on his childhood, he realized that shit always went down, never up (there were no electric fans in those days, so no one would say that it went up when "shit hit the fan"). He remembered his mother's loving words when as a boy he would tell his mom he had to "take a shit," she would always remind him that it was always better to give than take, so he should "give a shit."

Also, it was Isaac's chore to take the family potty out behind the house where it was emptied down into a deep hole about six feet under. Thus, the adult Isaac came to call his discovery gravity, after the grave. He scientifically proved what everyone already knew: that everything and everyone goes down, eventually. Not the most uplifting news, I grant you, but I have sources for that also.

So I readily admit I am guilty of this inclination toward low-level "crime," as Douglas and her colleagues explicate so brilliantly. No doubt, it is connected to my conspiratorial mindset. I hope that much is clear. Sometimes I just can't resist the forbidden fruit. Although not an apple, it seems to give me insight into the knowledge of good and evil.

For some reason, I suspect Douglas will not be studying the elite criminals who conspire to invade countries, kill millions, and blame it on others. Those are crimes against humanity, and are beyond the purview of research aimed at showing how sick everyday people are who suspect that their leaders are big-time criminals.

Painting a True Christ

There is an early scene in Terrence Malick's masterful new film, *A Hidden Life*—what I would call a moving painting—where the central character Franz Jägerstätter, an Austrian peasant farmer from an isolated small mountainous village who refuses to take an oath to Hitler and fight in the German army, is talking to an older man who is restoring paintings in the local Catholic church.

Franz, a devout Roman Catholic, is deeply disturbed by the rise of Hitler and the thought of participating in his immoral killing machine.

The older man tells Franz—who has already been admonished that he has a duty to defend the fatherland (homeland)—that he makes his living painting pretty holy pictures for the culturally conditioned parishioners for whom God and country are synonymous. He says:

> I paint their comfortable Christ with a halo over his head. We love him, that's enough. Someday I'll paint a true Christ.

Malick's "someday" has arrived with *A Hidden Life*, where the older Malick shows the younger Malick—and us—a moving picture of what experience has taught him is the complex essence of a true and simple Christ: out of love of God and all human beings to refuse to kill.

To watch this film is to undergo a profound experience, an experiment with truth and non-violence, a three-hour trial (Latin: *experimentum*—trial).

While Franz is eventually put on trial by the German government, it is we as viewers who must judge ourselves and ask how guilty or innocent are we for supporting or resisting the immoral killing machine of our own country now. Hitler and his Nazis were then, but we are faced with what Martin Luther King called "the fierce urgency of now." Many Americans surely ask with Franz, "What has happened to the country that we love?" But how many look in the mirror and ask, "Am I a guilty bystander or an active supporter of the United States' immoral and illegal wars all around the world that have been going on for so many years under presidents of both parties and have no end? Do I support the new cold war with its push for nuclear war with its first strike policy? Do I support, by my silence, a nuclear holocaust?"

I say that *A Hidden Life* is a moving painting because its form and content cannot be separated. A true artist, Malick realizes that what non-artists call form or style is the content; they are one. The essence of the story is in the telling; in a film in the showing.

The cinematography by Jörg Widmer, a longtime Malick collaborator, is therefore key. It is exquisitely beautiful as he paints with swiftly moving light the mountains and streams of the Austrian countryside, even as the storm clouds with their thunder and lightning roll in across the mountains. The ever-recurring dramatic scenes of numinous nature and the focus on the sustaining earth from which our food comes and to which we all return and in which Franz, his wife Fani, and their young daughters romp and roll and plant and harvest and dirty their hands is the ground beneath our feet, and when we look, we see its marriage to the sky, the clouds, the light, the shadows, which in their iridescent interplay of light and darkness beseech us to interrogate our existence and ask with Franz what is right and what is wrong and what is our purpose on this beautiful earth.

That question is especially focused when between the beauty comes the terror in the form of interspersed documentary footage of Hitler, his fanatical followers, and horrifying scenes of war and violence.

Like the movie, I think you would agree that we are always moving, asking, wondering, if we are not the living dead. All is now, and now is nevermore, as it disappears into the darkness behind us. The light is always pointing into the future, so we can see where we are going. We don't look at the light but by the light, as the great South African preacher, Alan Storey, puts it. But what is our light?

Where, asked Nietzsche, was the lightning before it flashed? To which the answer comes: it wasn't. It is its flashing. Only a doing, an act, just like love, not a thing but action. Just like the word God, *theós* in Greek, which has no vocative sense, as Roberto Calasso has pointed out in *Literature and the Gods*. "*Theós* has a predictive function: it describes *something that happens*." God is a verb; God is happening. God is happening when humans are happening, acting. Only then. "What you do (or don't) speaks so loudly that I cannot hear what you say," was the way Emerson phrased it.

The filmic interplay between Franz's agonized moral dilemma, his action, and the embodiment of Christ in the natural world, the body of Christ (*Corpus Christi*, not the erstwhile American nuclear submarine by that name), is its genius, one that might be lost on one impatient for action and garrulous dialogue.

"A Hidden Life" is far from Hollywood. Silence and natural beauty permeate it, as if to say the only way to grasp the mechanized and conscienceless brutality of Hitler or today's killers and grasp why some resist it, is to enter a contemplative space where the love of the incarnated world awakens our consciences to our responsibility to our sisters and brothers everywhere.

For in the silences one can also hear the screams of the millions of innocent victims beseeching us to heed their cries and intercede.

Malick shows us that the "true Christ" must be experienced as all of creation. No divisions. We must feel this in our flesh and blood, as does the rather inarticulate Franz, who speaks very little. His silence, however, and the marvelous acting of August Diehl, speak volumes. Valerie Pachner, as his supportive wife Fani, is gripping in every sense of the word, as Franz and Fani grip and grasp and hold each other in a fierce struggle to stay united in the face of the evil forces that threaten to separate them.

It tore me apart to watch their struggle, and I left the theater shaking.

In one of his insightful essays, "A Kind of Sharing," John Berger, writing about painting, said:

> The act of faith consisted of believing that the visible contained hidden secrets, that to study the visible was to learn something more than could be seen in a glance. Thus paintings were there to reveal a presence behind an appearance.

This could be Malick's motto, his faith. Or perhaps "to reveal a presence that is the appearance." The body is the soul. We are the world.

When I was young and in the U.S. Marines, seeking release as a conscientious objector, I read a book by Gordon Zahn, a sociologist and Catholic peace activist, called *In Solitary Witness*. It was the book that first brought Franz Jägerstätter to the world's attention. I found it deeply inspiring to learn about someone else who felt alone in his spiritual decision to refuse to fight in war.

Unlike Franz, who had been a wild motorcycle-riding young man prone to fighting, I had tried to be an upstanding, Jesuit-educated, patriotic, Irish-Catholic boy. Tried but didn't completely succeed. I prided myself on my toughness and sensitivity. Don't laugh. It's not that uncommon. We are often strangers to ourselves, complicated creatures, even the worst among us open to redemptive change.

But as I said then and say now, war is another matter. I felt it in my soul, as Franz clearly did, even if all he could say was, "I have this feeling inside me that I can't do what I believe is wrong."

War is a racket, as Marine Major General Smedley Butler put it. It is waged for the tyrannical oligarchs and always kills mostly civilians. Over ninety percent now, probably more. Innocent people. War is immoral. It is not complex. It is simple. Like the gospel message. Jägerstätter grasped that long ago and paid the price.

I paid no price since I was released from the Marines to "take final vows in a religious order," which was a complete lie, something I had never mentioned or considered but which allowed them to get rid of me. But I vividly remember the spiritual sustenance I got from Franz's witness as I awaited the ruling, for I was unequivocally determined to go to prison before ever donning the uniform again. I got off easy and still feel guilty that I pocketed their lie and went my merry way. Watching "A Hidden Life" reminded me of my cowardice.

Despite feeling "he had no one to turn to," despite being urged "to say the oath and think what you want," despite the advice of family and Bishop to compromise, despite the animosity of the villagers toward him and his family, despite being alone with his conscience, Franz remained faithful to his soul's promptings. He lived forward by the light.

Malick shows us the anguish that was involved in his decision, the agony for him and his wife, who, ironically, seems to have been instrumental when they married in his spiritual awakening and whose suffering is palpable as she supports his decision to the end. It is not easy to watch. Aside from Franz, who remains steadfast throughout all the abuse and suffering that he undergoes when jailed by the Nazis, the viewer is not fed a simple story of good against evil but instead is invited to examine one's own life, to ask what would one have done, to wonder whether Franz was right or wrong to subject his family to such suffering.

Even the humanity of the Nazi judge is shown when he privately tries to dissuade Franz from not signing the oath, telling him that no one will ever know of his sacrifice, that "the world will go on as before" and "someone else will take your place." We see the torment on this man's face and in his harrowed hands when he is left alone after Franz tells him simply that "I don't know everything" but "I can't do what I believe is wrong," despite knowing the consequences, and Franz is taken off to his solitary witness and his death.

The viewer is left to interpret the meaning of it all. Afterwards, we hear Fani says that "the time will come when we'll know what all this means."

Has that time come?

In 2007 the Catholic Church declared Jägerstätter a martyr and beatified him. The irony of making a saint out of a man whose spiritual witness was opposed by the institutional church authorities cannot be lost on a thinking person. Long dead, safely in his grave, a monument can be erected to his memory.

Or is it a monument erected to the church itself, the church whose silence was in those days deafening?

When I was leaving the theater with the seven other attendees, a man engaged me in conversation. I asked him what he thought of the movie. He said only that "it was beautiful." I was startled and had no response, but I thought of Rilke's words about beauty from the *Duino Elegies:*

> For beauty is nothing but the beginning of terror, which
> we still are just able to endure, and we are so awed because it serenely disdains to annihilate us.

A Hidden Life is like that.

Near the end we see Franz and a group of prisoners sitting on a bench awaiting their turns to be beheaded by the executioner in a black coat and bowler hat. A man just doing his job, a bored look on his face, loping off heads one by one, anxious to get the mornings work done and get to lunch. The terror on the victims' faces is palpable. I felt sick. While some prisoners struggled as they were led into the shed that housed the guillotine, Franz walked calmly in. Malik spares the viewer the details. All we are shown is the aftermath—a floor awash in blood. And as I recall, the light streaming in a high-up window.

Always the light to show us the way.

The Government that Killed Him Honors MLK Jr. with a National Holiday

As Martin Luther King's birthday is celebrated with a national holiday, his death day disappears down the memory hole. Across the country—in response to the King Holiday and Service Act passed by Congress and signed by Bill Clinton in 1994—people will be encouraged to make the day one of service. Etymological irony aside (Latin, *servus,* slave), such service does not include celebrating King's commitment to protesting a decadent system of racial and economic injustice or to non-violently resisting the warfare state that is the United States. Government sponsored service is cultural neo-liberalism at its finest.

"Nothing in all the world is more dangerous than sincere ignorance and conscientious stupidity," warned Dr. King.

The word "service" is a loaded word. It connotes many things, such as military service ("Were you ever in the service?"), community service ("She was sentenced to 30 days of community service."), being of service to others, etc. It has also become a vogue word over the past 35 years. Its popularity and use arose and expanded in tandem with the privatization of social life, social services, and the expansion of work for free, such as unpaid internships, etc. It is part of the privatization and unpaid volunteer movement engineered by the elites in recent decades. This cult of the service volunteer is a form of social control and exploitation aimed at inducing passivity in an individualized and divided population to prevent radical social change.

Its use for MLK Day is clear: individuals are encouraged to volunteer for activities such as tutoring children, painting senior centers, or delivering meals to the elderly. Clearly these are wonderful deeds when done on individual initiative and not through government, corporate, and institutional public relations that result in the concealment of an American prophet's radical message and his brutal assassination. Such service is a far cry from King's campaign to transform the institutional structures of American society.

But a day of such individual volunteer service once a year does make people feel good about themselves. Thus the government, corporate, and educational institutions strongly encourage it, as if Martin Luther King were born volunteering at the local food pantry and Oprah Winfrey were cheering him on.

Obviously, there is nothing wrong with feeling good when helping others, nor with serving others in need, but when it is divorced from public education about MLK's true mission and why he was killed, something is amiss.

The Assassination

After all, King was not assassinated because he had spent his heroic life promoting individual volunteerism. To understand his life and death—to celebrate the man—"it is essential to realize although he is popularly depicted and perceived as a civil rights leader, he was much more than that. A non-violent revolutionary, he personified the most powerful force for a long overdue social, political, and economic reconstruction of the nation." Those are the words of William Pepper, the King family lawyer, from his comprehensive and definitive study of the King assassination, *The Plot to Kill King*, a book that should be read by anyone concerned with truth and justice.

In other words, Martin Luther King was a transmitter of a radical non-violent spiritual and political energy so plenipotent that his very existence was a threat to an established order based on institutionalized violence, racism, and economic exploitation. He was a very dangerous man to the U.S. government and all the institutional and deep state forces armed against him. That is why they spied on him (and his father and grandfather going back to 1917) and used dirty tricks to try to destroy him. When he denounced the Vietnam War and announced his Poor People's Campaign and intent to lead a massive peaceful encampment of hundreds of thousands in Washington, D.C., he set off panic in the bowels of government spies and their masters. As Stokely Carmichael, co-chairman of the Student Non-Violent Coordinating Committee, said to King in a conversation secretly recorded by Army Intelligence, "The man don't care you call ghettos concentration camps, but when you tell him his war machine is nothing but hired killers, you got trouble."

Revolutionaries are, of course, anathema to the power elites who, with all their might, resist such rebels' efforts to transform society. If they can't buy them off, they knock them off. Fifty years after King's assassination, the causes he fought for—civil rights, the end to U.S. wars of aggression, and economic justice for all—remain not only unachieved, but have worsened in so many respects. And King's message has been enervated by the sly trick of giving him a national holiday and then urging Americans to make it "a day of service." The vast majority of those who innocently participate in these activities have no idea who killed King, or why. If they did, they might pause in their tracks, and combine their "service" activities with a teach-in on the truth of these matters.

Because MLK repeatedly called the United States the "greatest purveyor of violence on earth," he was universally condemned by the mass media and government that later—once he was long and safely dead and no longer a threat—praised him to the heavens. This has continued to the present day of historical amnesia.

For the government that honors Dr. King with a national holiday killed him. This is the suppressed truth behind the highly promoted day of service. It is what you are not supposed to know.

However, William Pepper's decades-long investigation not only refutes the flimsy case against the alleged assassin James Earl Ray, but definitively proves that King was killed by a government conspiracy led by J. Edgar Hoover, the FBI, Army Intelligence, and Memphis Police, assisted by southern Mafia figures.

The Trial

This shocking truth is accentuated when one is reminded (or told for the first time) that in 1999 a Memphis jury, after a thirty-day civil trial with over seventy witnesses, found the U.S. government guilty in the killing of MLK. The King family had brought the suit and Pepper represented them. They were grateful that the truth was confirmed, but saddened by the way the findings were buried by the media in cahoots with the government.

Pepper not only demolishes the government's self-serving case with a plethora of evidence, but shows how the mainstream media, academia, and government flacks have spent years covering up the truth of MLK's murder through lies and disinformation. Another way they have accomplished this is by convincing a gullible public that "service" is a substitute for truth.

But service without truth is slavery. It is propaganda aimed at convincing decent people into thinking that they are serving the essence of MLK's message even as they are obeying their masters, the very government that murdered this great American hero.

It is time for a slaves' revolt against the mind manipulation served by the MLK Day of Service. Let us offer service, but let us also tell the truth.

We need a Martin Luther King Day of Truth.

Between Heaven and Earth on a Spring Morning

> *"To give up beauty and the sensual happiness that comes with it and devote one's self exclusively to unhappiness requires a nobility I lack. However, after all, nothing is true that compels us to make it exclusive. Isolated beauty ends in grimaces, solitary justice in oppression. Anyone who seeks to serve the one to the exclusion of the other serves no one, not even himself, and in the end is doubly the servant of injustice. A day comes when, because we have been inflexible, nothing amazes us anymore, everything is known, and our life is spent in starting again. It is a time of exile, dry lives, dead souls. To come back to life, we need grace, a homeland, or to forget ourselves. On certain mornings, as we turn a corner, an exquisite dew falls on our heart and then vanishes. But the freshness lingers, and this, always, is what the heart needs. I had to come back once again."*
>
> —**Albert Camus, "Return to Tipasa"**

For a writer to fight injustice to the exclusion of creating beauty and living passionately contradicts the deepest desires of the human heart. Albert Camus taught us this. The love of life must inform the rebel's resistance to injustice. "It seems to me that the writer must be fully aware of the dramas of his time," he writes, "and that he must take sides every time he can and knows how to do so." But his refusal, his no, does not imply a renunciation but an affirmation, a yes, to the joy and grandeur of life that is everyone's birthright.

This is the difficult way of true art—the rebel writer's way—the tension that the writer must live with as he shuttles back and forth between his heart's desires and his commitment to resist evil. What is the point of fighting for a better world if one does not live as if that world were on the doorstep, and one's living and writing were the revelation of that reality. Camus somewhere said something to the effect that it is not your writings that I like, it is your writing. He knew that we are always on the way, and our wayfaring should prefigure the enigma of our arrivals.

It is spring as I write and I am thinking of Camus when that exquisite dew fell on his heart that early morning. No doubt Albert felt a bit of heaven. I'm feeling it now. Spring, the time of the resurrection of the living dead. All around new life bursts and blooms in wild array. A mountain stream races down the hillside, shouting its joy that the earth's new warmth has freed it at last from its frozen sleep. In the trees all around the birds have returned and sing exultantly of their homecoming. Almost before our eyes the flowers push their way up to the light. They have had enough of the underground, hungrily seeking the sun. It is a beautiful dawn, and I can smell it. I feel as though I have awoken from a long and deep sleep. The morning star welcomed me. The sun rose majestically. And across my window three early flies jitterbug in the first light. The whole earth is conspiring to explode with life and it is asking for our assent.

But dare the living-dead awaken? Shall we say yes to this paradise?

"This day you will be with me in paradise." That's what a man, convicted of crimes against the state and dying fast, once said. Like most memorable statements, it is open to various interpretations. But suppose, instead of offering one, we assume the existence of paradise, and ask a question that lurks unspoken and forbidden in every heart.

For there are some questions so obvious that we refuse to ask them for fear of having to answer. To be asked such questions seems an impertinence, an insult to our intelligence, and an assault on our integrity. Don't be ridiculous, we think, though we don't laugh. Isn't it obvious, we vaguely mutter, secretly knowing it is nothing of the sort. We are caught off-guard, something we don't do to ourselves. Even our dreams escape us. We prefer to live in the clouds.

But let's be daring for once. Let's put aside all our usual lies and evasions and not be afraid of the truth. Let's ask ourselves a few very simple and annoying questions, the kind children ask their tongue-tied parents, and let's not squirm away from answering.

What images of death do we live with?

Or, to put it another way, if you believe in life after death, what image of heaven do you entertain? Not what do you think heaven is, but what do you desire it to be? If you object and say you don't believe in life after death, the question is still interesting. For we are, of course, here playing a game of the imagination. You need only make believe, for the hell of it, that there is life after death. Or life before.

What would you like it to be? Imagine. What would you like this life to be? Maybe that's the real question.

The trouble with being born, of course, is that we are guaranteed to die and be aware of it most of our lives. When it comes to dying, we have no choice; death is our fate and against it freedom is a meaningless word. Living is another matter, though it is not something to which we generally give much thought, for we can choose not to live when breath is still ours. We are free to wait lovingly for annihilation by patiently enduring our lives, or we can commit quick suicide.

We don't have to live, but we must die. In our bitterness we may curse the fact that we find ourselves alive in the world; we didn't ask for it. This is obviously true and equally meaningless. Once we find ourselves alive, death is our destiny, like it or not. Whether life is a living hell for us or just a dull plod through the years—a "hanging in there," in those unconsciously evocative words—we hold in our hearts, however buried, images of what we would like life to be like if it were eternal.

That is, we all live with imbedded images of paradise, no matter how beclouded or unarticulated they may be.

Now, as I wander out in the early morning lulled by birdsong, I wonder what these images consist of. What, in our hearts' desires, do we yearn for? What heavens do we wish to inhabit?

For we are now in the school of imagination, what John Keats called the vale of soul-making, and must, like children everywhere, answer the following: Imagine paradise, on earth or in heaven, and describe it in as few or as many words as you wish. For future reference, learn your answer by heart.

Yes, to open our hearts. It is naïve, but not stupid. It is disturbing. It is surely easy to hide behind the word mystery, or cynically to reply that the world is what it is, a far cry from paradise, nor will it ever be, here or in some supposed hereafter, any different. The former is the believer's dodge, the latter the skeptical "realist's" way of begging the question. Both are phony.

Only as we become as little children can we enter into the kingdom of heavenly imagination, and it is the fear of ridicule, our own and others', that bars the gate. It is obvious that what happens after death is a mystery. Why we come and why we go is something that we'll never know, all beliefs to the contrary. We live by pure faith, though, as Thoreau noted, we are determined not to live by faith if we can avoid it. Which we can't, ultimately. Knowledge fails. And anyway, what we know and what we want are not the same thing. The images of paradise we hold don't illuminate death in the slightest; they do, however, enlighten our lives. After all, it is living that is within our power. We live in possibility. If we wish to pursue the ideal images of our heart's desires, we must first make manifest what they are.

What do you want? I know it is not easy living with a deep but dark longing. Perhaps it is the fear of disappointment that keeps us in the dark. Why, when the whole earth rises toward the light, do we shrink back in fear? Does beauty crush us?

I remember leaving my mother's house to go to the hospital where my dear father had just died. It was 5:30 AM on the first of May. Stepping outside, the birdsong and flowering bushes illuminated by the rising sun staggered me. How could this be: life and death in one hour, one moment. Where now was my father as his son walked through a garden of delight? Where was that man whom I had kissed a few hours before?

What do I want?

Camus, you wondered that too when you created your alter-ego Jacques Cormery in your novel, *The First Man*, and placed him at his father's gravesite. It was just a novel, as they say, but you were there and said:

> All that was left was this anguished heart, eager to live, rebelling against the deadly order of the world that had been with him for forty years, and still struggling against the wall that separated him from the secret of all life, wanting to go farther, to go beyond, and to discover, discover before dying, discover at last in order to be, just once to be, for a single second, but forever.

Just once and one time only. Isn't that it? No reruns. No playbacks. One life. Eternal.

Then what?

Perhaps our greatest fear is to passionately want something from life and death, "to go beyond" with Albert, to ask for something independent of society and others' wishes, and to dare intuit it into existence. Society drones: Don't dare feel it, don't dare say it, don't ask for too much. Narrow it all down, life is much too much, narrow it all down.

Sometimes I think, that, because so many people have meekly accepted this dictum, they are unconsciously in love with death, assuming that all their problems and the anguish of being placed between yes and no, heaven and earth, will then cease. I often think that we are living in the age of nihilism that Nietzsche predicted long ago, a time in which the will to nothingness is most clearly expressed in the sterile pursuit and embrace of things, a "paradise" of consumer goods at the expense of livingness.

"I cling like a miser to the freedom that disappears as soon as there is an excess of things," writes Camus, grasping in a few words a key link between a just and unjust world where most people are subjected to violence and degradation at the hands of the wealthy and powerful who seek to devour the earth.

Ah, but here we are walking in the spring sunshine, the time for resurrection and for truth. The whole earth is rising beneath our feet. We can feel it. The trees are budding forth and leaving toward the stars. We can see them. We can smell the earth warming in the rising sun. Perhaps like Camus, the spring smells seize us by the throat, and we find ourselves delirious with love and desire as "the gods speak in the sun and the scent of absinthe leaves," as we wander through a reborn world.

So why don't we say what we truly want? Can we even imagine it? Or is what we want so pathetic—more things, more money, anything to boost our egos and impress others, improve our appearances, elevate our social standing—that to admit it reveals the hollowness of our lives? Are our desires so vague and culturally constricted that they must be repressed lest they make us realize how spiritually dead we are when the resurrection all around us calls us to awaken to new life?

Suppose, rather than hiding behind the lies and evasions that we use to divorce ourselves from the tree of life, we dare to speak from the indivisible root of truth and desire, or true desire, the eternal tree. For to live truly and to die is to create out of that planting a full flowering, an exposed existence rooted in the earth and reaching to the stars. Then, heaven will be our immediate destiny, for it will proceed from our passions and usher in a glorious spring.

And yet, as Camus knew, our little imaginary heavens can lull us to sleep when world events call us to rise up and say no. Yes, but no, too. Desire needs will to renew the world. The lover who luxuriates in the spring sap rising must be a rebel. "But the true life is present in the heart of this dichotomy. . . . Life is this dichotomy itself," he tells us.

To live authentically is to live between yes and no.

Dostoevsky, who shared with Camus the belief that we must rebel to save the world, had Karamazov rightly say that if all are not saved, what good is the salvation of only one?

To which he added: "Life is a paradise and we are all in paradise, but we refuse to see it."

So it seems on this morning in spring as resurrection fills the air. And even though this feeling will fade, Camus is right that its freshness will linger, an exquisite reminder of why we must rebel joyously.

You are right, Albert, "We must simultaneously serve suffering and beauty."

Try Learning How
Not to Ride a Bicycle
So We Can Save the World

"Who would study and describe the living, starts / By driving the spirits out of the parts: /In the palm of his hand he holds all the sections, /Lacks nothing, except the spirit's connections."

—**Mephistopheles warning to the student in Goethe's *Faust***

"And how far would you like to go in?" he asked and the three kings all looked at each other. "Not too far but just far enough so's we can say that we've been there."

—**Liner notes to Bob Dylan's *John Wesley Harding* album**

"The shadow is what I am but will not admit I am. For the shadow of the psyche involves me in a deepening self-recognition which is more humiliating and emptying than the normal limits of endurance. In the end, acknowledging the shadow means acknowledging a bottomless void within me. The initial question of truth-force is: How deeply will I acknowledge my own emptiness?"

—**James W. Douglass, *Lightning East to West: Jesus, Gandhi, and the Nuclear Age***

We are haunted by a specter. Strange as it may sound, I was reminded of this when I saw a photograph of the quarterback of the Super Bowl-winning Philadelphia Eagles, Nick Foles, looking up and pointing to the heavens. Or to be more precise, the roof of the aptly named U.S. Bank Stadium, a fitting venue for this national celebration of violence and the warfare state. But if we can assume Foles' gesture was meant to penetrate the roof and travel up to heaven, then you too may find it a bit odd, if touching. Most people, as the poet Czeslaw Milosz has said, are ashamed to ask themselves a question about the implication of such a gesture. "They have experienced the collapse of hierarchical space," he writes, "and when they fold their hands and lift up their eyes, 'up' no longer exists. Let no one say that religion can manage without such primitive directions to orient people."

Modern science has brought this about. And together with its models of reality, it has given us its technological child: nuclear weapons. So now we live haunted by the shadowy thought that human beings, having assumed God's mantle, can bring this world to an end in a flash. As William Butler Yeats said in another context: "All changed; changed utterly." But while we live in these end-times, in a new symbolic universe, our sense of spiritual power to stop the nuclear madness has been sapped by our refusal to venture deep into the interior of this enigma and change our minds and spirits enough to change the world. We seem stuck riding our bikes when we need to stop the world we think we know and experiment with truth at the deepest level. We need a revolutionary spiritual transformation to give us faith and courage to counter the nihilists who wage endless wars for the American empire and threaten nuclear destruction at every turn. Where can we find this inconceivable spiritual energy?

∼•∼•∼•∼

I was thinking of this not long ago when something very strange happened to me. Six days previously I had written an article subtitled, "In Light and Shadows." On this particular morning I was sitting at the kitchen table contemplating that piece of writing and whether or not readers had grasped what I was trying to say by linking three very short stories that undulated like the flow of consciousness in waves of light and darkness. The phone rang, and as I answered I stood up and looked out the window at a flaming red bush, it being the height of fall's display of colors. I heard my wife sobbing on the other end. "My mother's dying," she cried. "Oh no," I replied, as I had an immediate flashback to my own mother dying five years earlier, and an inexplicably dark foreboding gripped me. For some reason I looked at my watch; it was 10:58 on Thursday morning. In that instant, as I raised my eyes back to the blazing bush, I saw a sliver of a crescent dark shadow creep into the inner corner of my right eye as I listened to my wife tell me through her tears how her mother, who shared the name Rita with my mother, had turned a corner toward her death. When she was done, I told her something strange had happened to my eye.

I had suffered a detached retina.

While I was fortunate to have excellent doctors for whom I'm very grateful, they were not very interested in my story of when the detachment occurred. Their job, as they rightly saw it, was to repair my eye and the rest was speculation since they operate within a materialistic paradigm. But as I recuperated, lying face down with my eyes closed for a few weeks, I had a lot of time to speculate (Latin, *specere,* to look at, view; pursuit of the truth by means of thinking).

As I lay there hour after hour, day after day, eyes closed, I found that what began as thinking turned into contemplation. I had come to a dark place. I had been stopped in my tracks. The world I took for granted, my routine, my habitual way of seeing, my known world was stopped, and while shocked, I realized that I was being given the gift of a revelatory experience if only I would accept it. With my eyes down and closed, I had entered the temple of contemplation where images rose to my inner eye, and if I paid enough attention, they would lead me to a place of insight.

As a sociologist, I teach my students that sociology is the study of our social habits of thought, speech, and action. These habits or routines, which often become crystalized into myths and institutions, imprison us in ways we are loath to admit. Our collective mental habits are so powerful because they lie far deeper than mere thought can reach, and therefore to break them is as difficult as learning how *not* to ride a bicycle after years of knowing how. Where does one begin?

George Orwell once observed that "we have sunk to a depth at which re-statement of the obvious is the first duty of intelligent men." Today restating the obvious doesn't seem to make much difference. At the level of the habits of group think and political and cultural propaganda, many of us have been trying to do that to little avail as the lies and deceptions of the U.S. power elites seem to win, day after day. It is blatantly obvious that these people lie endlessly in their pursuit of an empire built on sand and saturated with the blood of innocent victims at home and abroad. Yet despite the obvious, and despite it being pointed out again and again, vast numbers of otherwise intelligent people continue to imbibe the myth that the "other side" (now the Democrats, now the Republicans) will change the nihilistic trajectory of an evil capitalistic system leading to nuclear annihilation. The naiveté is frightening as these people calmly ride their bicycles down the primrose path of death denial.

~·~·~·~

As I lay contemplating the images that crossed my inner eye, I saw that we wear our mental social habits like shrouds that prevent us from seeing the truth of our lives and the power we possess to remake the world. But why? Sure, the political propagandists are skilled at their work, having learned from and greatly superseded their mentor, Edward Bernays, in the tricks of the trade. And the technology has made their job much easier, and the CIA and other intelligence services have their people throughout the mass media and whatever collective might be struggling to resist. Yet something was missing in this explanation, a deeper explanation.

It was then I again realized that there are different paradigms or experiences of reality operating in the world. The prevailing one today sees only a world of things, a material world that includes people and animals, a billiard ball world where surfaces without centers careen around in physical, cause-and-effect–determined movements. In this world the story of how my retina became detached is perhaps somewhat weirdly interesting but "just coincidental." I suspected that my good doctors, if we met for a drink, would still hold firm to their habitual paradigms of physical cause and effect. They would have a very difficult time trying not to ride their bikes and not try to persuade me to hop back on mine.

∼•∼•∼•∼

Another way of seeing is provided by Owen Barfield, English philosopher and poet, one of the most neglected and original thinkers of the twentieth century, who countered the superficiality of our materialistic collective thinking with these words:

> The real world, the whole world, does not consist only of the things of which we are conscious; it consists also of the consciousness and subconsciousness that are correlative to them. They are the immaterial component of the world. But today the only immaterial element our mental habit acknowledges is our own little spark of self-consciousness. That is why we feel detached, isolated, cut off not only from the world as it really is, but also from those other little sparks of detached self-consciousness we acknowledge in our fellow human beings.

Imprisoned in our isolated minds and failing to grasp the interpenetration of mind and matter, thought and feeling, a sequence of forms and patterns changing into other forms, Barfield argues that we end up treating not only other people and ourselves as things, but all of nature, including animals, as inanimate objects to be used. The world becomes a place for necrophiliacs, not the home of living interconnected spirits. In such a world schizoid experience becomes commonplace. In such a crazy world, "what the self of each of us feels isolated from, cut off from, by its encapsulation in the naked physical reality presented to it by contemporary culture, is precisely its own existential source." Such a physically encapsulated self is a false self without reality. It is no wonder that the use of drugs of every kind has risen exponentially, the earth despoiled, wars waged constantly, and ultimate weapons prepared to blow the planet to smithereens.

 I had been thrown off my bicycle and then my doctors got me up again. Of course I was so thankful for their medical expertise, but I needed to try to not ride the same old bike. How could I break the habit, and of what did the habit consist. I didn't want to say that I had gone not too far in but just far enough to say I'd been there. In where? During the days when I strictly, almost obsessively, followed my doctor's advice and, despite the great discomfort, lay immobile, face down, eyes closed, I found myself deep in a prison that seemed to open out into a place of fear and freedom simultaneously. Although I wasn't looking around and needed help with simple things, which my wife so kindly provided me, I experienced a weird sense of concentrated power from within the terrible vulnerability I felt. I am trying not to exaggerate, but this sense of power in vulnerability was very real. I had no interest in listening to the two books on tape I had; Tolstoy and James Baldwin seemed like intruders. They would distort the vision of what I was sensing. I think at its heart was a core of emptiness and powerlessness, which in the oddest of ways made me feel very powerful, as though all my teaching and writing and efforts to help others and make the world a better place and give advice and try to change people were useless and arrogant, but that their uselessness was their usefulness, and in accepting that I was embracing an essential truth.

 Earlier in my life I had numerous very profound experiences with synchronicity that had convinced me that our consensual reality conceals a level of truth rarely felt because of the power of habit. But these experiences had been all positive and had left me feeling amazed but powerful. One even involved the power of a look I gave another. The power of my eyes. This latest one was different since it frightened me and made me vulnerable. Telling you all this makes me feel doubly vulnerable, but now I don't care. I now know why I have long wanted to make a certain word my own but never could. The word is insouciant. Somehow it has become me more since this latest experience.

~·~·~·~

We are ruled by people who think they have everything under their control, including the nuclear weapons that are the ultimate expression of the hubris emanating from Einstein's equation of E = mc², the unimaginable amount of energy contained in a particle of matter. Those who brandish nuclear weapons operate within their consensual reality that is a form of madness, and these madmen will incinerate us all unless they are opposed by a force equal to that they brandish. How can we stop them?

In his extraordinary book, *Lightning East to West, Jesus, Gandhi, and the Nuclear Age*, James. W. Douglass suggests that there is such a force and a way to stop this holocaust. It lies within you and me. He says:

> Is there a spiritual reality, inconceivable to us today, which corresponds in history to the physical reality which Einstein discovered and which led to the atomic bomb? Einstein discovered a law of physical change: the way to convert a single particle of matter into enormous physical energy. Might there not also be, as Gandhi suggested, an equally incredible and undiscovered law of spiritual change, whereby a single person or small community of persons could be converted into an enormous spiritual energy capable of transforming a society and a world? I believe that there is, that there must be, a spiritual reality corresponding to $E = mc^2$ because, from the standpoint of creative harmony, the universe is incomplete without it, and because, from the standpoint of moral freedom, humankind is sentenced to extinction without it.

I believe it too. It arises in the hearts and minds of those totally committed to the truth no matter where it leads, and the passion to suffer it, even when it makes them look foolish. "A man needs a little madness, or else. . . . he never dares cut the rope and be free," Zorba tells the boss in Nikos Kazantzakis's *Zorba the Greek*.

So let's try to learn not to ride our bicycles, so we can save ourselves and the world.

SPEEDING INTO THE VOID OF CYBERSPACE AS DESIGNED

> *"The internet was hardwired to be a surveillance tool from the start. No matter what we use the network for today—dating, directions, encrypted chat, email, or just reading the news—it always had a dual-use nature rooted in intelligence gathering and war . . . . [Surveillance Valley shows] the ongoing overlap between the Internet and the military-industrial complex that spawned it a half century ago, and the close ties that exist between the U.S. intelligence agencies and the antigovernment privacy movement that has sprung up in the wake of Edward Snowden's leaks."*
>
> —**Yasha Levine,** *Surveillance Valley: The Secret Military History of the Internet*

> *"My Dear, here we must run as fast as we can, just to stay in place. If you wish to go anywhere, you must run twice as fast as that."*
>
> —**Lewis Carroll,** *Alice in Wonderland*

Speed and panic go hand-in-hand in today's fabricated world of engineered emergencies and digital alerts. "We have no time" is today's mantra—"We are running out of time"—and while this mood of urgency has come to grip most people's minds, deep thinking about why this is so and who benefits is in short supply. I believe most people sense this to be true but don't know how to extract themselves from the addictive nature of speed long enough to grasp how deeply they have been propagandized, and why.

This sense of ongoing urgency and dread accelerated by the Twin Towers bombing to facilitate the global war on terror was joined to the fast growing (and getting faster by the day) internet and cell phone world that has come to dominate contemporary life. We have entered a high-tech trap. Permanent busyness and speed—a state of on-edge nervousness and panic with digital alerts—are today's norms. The majority of people live "on" their phones with their constant beeps, and the digital media have fragmented our sense of time into perpetual presents that create historical amnesia and digital dementia. In a so-called progressive world of consumer capitalism, the era of what the astute sociologist Zygmunt Bauman has called "liquid modernity," time itself has become an online transaction, a liquid commodity that flows away faster than a scrolling screen.

We live in a use-by-date digital world in a state of suspended animation where "time is short" and we must hustle before our own use-by date is past. The pace of private and public life has outrun most people's ability to slow down long enough to realize a hidden hustler has taken them for a ride to Wonderland where the only wonder is that more people have not gone insane as they slip and slide away on the superhighway to nowhere.

John Berger, as only a sage artist would, noted this essential truth in his 1972 novel *G.*:

> Every ruling minority needs to numb and, if possible, to kill the time sense of those whom it exploits. This is the authoritarian secret of all methods of imprisonment.

Today the vast majority of people, trapped by the manufactured illusion of speed, are in and on their cells, quickly texting and calling and checking to see if they've missed anything as time flies by.

Much is said about various types of environmental pollution, but the pollution of speed and its effects on mind and body are rarely mentioned, except to express gladness for more speed. The rollout of 5G technology is a case in point, mental and physical health concerns be damned. Back in the 19th century, when space and time were being first "conquered" by the camera, telegraph, and telephone, these inventions were described as flying machines. Time flew, voices flew, images flew. Soon the phonograph and film would capture and preserve the "living" voices and the moving images of the living and the dead. It was scientific spiritualism at its birth. Today's comical research into downloading "consciousness" to conquer death by becoming machines is its latest manifestation.

That the clowns behind this speed culture are growing rich on this research at our elite universities that are funded by the Pentagon and the intelligence agencies doesn't make people howl with sardonic laughter puzzles me. Laughter's good; it slows you down. I just had a good laugh reading an article about scientists wondering why new research "suggests" that the universe may be a billion years younger than they thought. I love their precision, don't you?

My students, in their learned helplessness and desire to be told what to do, have often asked me how long their term papers should be, and when I tell them probably 37 1/2 words, they look at me with mouths agape. What do you mean? one finally asks. I tell them that writing 37 1/2 words is much faster than having to think slowly as you write, and when you have nothing left to say, to just stop. A fast 37 1/2 words solves the thinking problem. Maybe you can text me your paper, I often add, even though I don't do texting.

On a more serious note, a lifelong student of speed (dromology), the brilliant French thinker Paul Virilio, has shown how speed and war have developed together and how totalitarianism is latent in technology. Few listen, just as they did not listen to Jacques Ellul, Lewis Mumford, Neil Postman, and others who warned of the direction technology was taking us. Nuclear weapons are the supreme technological "achievement," of course, devices that can eliminate all space and time in a flash. They work fast. Virilio says:

> The speed of the new optoelectronic and electroacoustic milieu becomes the final *void* (the void of the quick), a

vacuum that no longer depends on the interval between places or things and so on the world's very extension, but on the interface of an instantaneous transmission of remote appearances, on a geographic and geometric retention in which all volume, all relief vanish.

As I write, I look down at my wristwatch lying on the desk and laugh. My sister gave it to me after her husband died. He had won it as a member of the Villanova track team that won the four-man, two-mile relay at the famous Coliseum Relays in Los Angeles in near world record time. Young men whose bodies were in motion to move across terra firma as fast as possible. No drugs produced in a technological chemical factory to aid them. No gimmicks. Just bodies in motion, unlike today. It is an analog watch that must be wound every day when the sun rises. But my brother-in-law never wound it because he never used it. He was saving it as a stashed-away memento in some sort of suspended time. I like it because it always runs a bit slow, unlike the Villanova flashes. I like slow.

In a brilliant book written in 1999 before the hyper-speed era was fully underway—*Speaking Into The Air: A History of the Idea of Communication*—John Durham Peters, while not especially focusing on the issue of speed and technology as does Virilio, indirectly explores the fundamental issue that underlies technology and its control by the elites. The problem with technology is that it is the use of a technique applied to physical things to control those who don't control the machines. Today that is the Internet and digital technology, controlled by those Virilio calls "the global kinetic elites." Many readers might remember the iconic line from the film *Cool Hand Luke* with Paul Newman: "What we have here is failure to communicate." That is our issue. How to communicate, and to whom, and who controls our means and speed of communication. Speed kills genuine communication, which may be its point.

Here's what Peters has to say about the new media of the 19th century:

Media of transmission allow crosscuts through space, but recording media allow jump cuts through time. The sentence of death for sound, image, and experience had been commuted. Speech and action could live beyond their human origins. In short, recording media made the afterlife of the dead possible in a new way. As *Scientific American* put it of the phonograph in 1877: "Speech has become, as it were, immortal." That "as it were" is the dwelling place of ghosts.

Despite our advanced technology today, we still die, but we live faster, which is not to say better. We live faster until modern medicine makes our dying slower. Speed grants us the illusion of control, an illusionary sense of stop-time in the midst of techno-time, digital time, pointillistic time where so much is happening simultaneously across the internet and we "have" it at our fingertips. Awash in cultural nostalgia that gives us a frisson of false comfort, we scroll the past as fast as we can. In the small town where I live, urbanites come in droves for nostalgia and create hyper-gentrification. I see them rapidly walking the country roads talking from their cells as bird song, rustling leaves, and lapping water passes them by, the technology serving as a shield from reality itself.

To realize that the Internet was developed as a weapon and has killed our sense of flesh and blood natural time to exploit us through speed should be obvious, though I suspect it isn't. The invention and control of the Internet by the Pentagon, the intelligence agencies, and their allies in Silicon Valley, as Yasha Levine chronicles in *Surveillance Valley,* is a fundamental problem that deserves focused attention. However, who can slow down enough to focus? As he says, "American military interests continue to dominate all parts of the network, even those that supposedly stand in opposition." This includes Tor and Signal, two encrypted mobile phone and internet services highly touted by journalists, political activists, and dissidents for their ability to make it impossible for governments to monitor communication. Levine writes:

While Internet billionaires like Larry Page, Sergey Brin, and Mark Zuckerberg slam government surveillance, talk up freedom, and embrace Snowden and crypto privacy culture, their companies still cut deals with the Pentagon, work with the NSA and CIA, and continue to track and profile people for profit. It is the same old split-screen marketing trick: the public branding and the behind-the-scenes reality.

The Internet is, as he argues, an "old cybernetic dream of a world where everyone is watched, predicted, and controlled." He claims that Tor is funded by the U.S. government and that Edward Snowden, most ironically or not, highly promoted it as a way to avoid government snooping. Very strange, this cyberworld.

We are homeless modern minds now, exiled from earth time, and if we don't rediscover our way back to a slow contemplation of our fate and the ontological reality of human being itself, I'm afraid we are speeding into the void.

The CIA Then and Now: Old Wine in New Bottles

> *"And as the flames climbed high into the night*
> *To light the sacrificial rite*
> *I saw Satan laughing with delight*
> *The day the music died"*
>
> —Don McLean, "American Pie"

The Nazis had a name for their propaganda and mind-control operations: *weltanschauungskrieg*—"world view warfare." As good students, they had learned many tricks of the trade from their American teachers, including Sigmund Freud's nephew, Edward Bernays, who had honed his propagandistic skills for the United States during World War I and had subsequently started the public relations industry in New York City, an industry whose raison d'être from the start was to serve the interests of the elites in manipulating the public mind.

In 1941, U.S. Intelligence translated *weltanschauungskrieg* as "psychological warfare," a phrase that fails to grasp the full dimensions of the growing power and penetration of U.S. propaganda, then and now. Of course, the American propaganda apparatus was just then getting started on an enterprise that has become the epitome of successful world view warfare programs, a colossal beast whose tentacles have spread to every corner of the globe and whose fabrications have nestled deep within the psyches of many hundreds of millions of Americans and people around the world. And true to form in this circle game of friends helping friends, this propaganda program was ably assisted after WW II by all the Nazis secreted into the U.S. ("Operation Paperclip") by Allen Dulles and his henchmen in the OSS and then the CIA to make sure the U.S. had operatives to carry on the Nazi legacy (see David Talbot's *The Devil's Chessboard: Allen Dulles, The CIA, and The Rise of America's Secret Government*, an extraordinary book that will make your skin crawl with disgust).

This went along quite smoothly until some people started to question the Warren Commission's JFK assassination story. The CIA then went on the offensive in 1967 and put out the word to all its people in the agency and throughout the media and academia to use the phrase "conspiracy theory" to ridicule these skeptics, which they have done up until the present day. This linguistic propaganda was successful for many decades, marginalizing those researchers and writers who were uncovering the truth about, not just President Kennedy's murder by the national security state, but those of Malcolm X, Martin Luther King, and Robert Kennedy. Today, the tide is turning on this score, as recently more and more Americans have become fed up with the manipulative use of this term.

The CIA Exposed—Partially

But back in the mid-1960s to the mid-1970s, some covert propaganda programs run by the CIA were "exposed." First, the Agency's sponsorship of the Congress of Cultural Freedom, through which it used magazines, prominent writers, academics, et al. to spread propaganda during the Cold War, was uncovered. This was an era when Americans read serious literary books, writers and intellectuals had a certain cachet, and popular culture had not yet stupefied them. The CIA therefore secretly worked to influence American and world opinion through the literary and intellectual elites. Frances Stonor Saunders comprehensively covers this in her 1999 book, *The Cultural Cold War: The CIA and the World of Arts and Letters*, and Joel Whitney followed this up in 2016 with *Finks: How the CIA Tricked the World's Best Writers*, with particular emphasis on the complicity of the CIA and the famous literary journal *The Paris Review*.

Then in 1975 the Church Committee hearings resulted in the exposure of abuses by the CIA, NSA, FBI, etc. In 1977 Carl Bernstein wrote a long piece for *Esquire*—"The CIA and the Media"—naming names of journalists and publications (*The New York Times, CBS*, etc.) that worked with and for the CIA in propagandizing the American people and the rest of the world. (Conveniently, this article can be read on the CIA'website (carl bernstein.com/magazine_cia) since presumably the agency has come clean, or, if you are the suspicious type, or maybe a conspiracy theorist, it is covering its deeper tracks with a "limited hangout," defined by former CIA agent Victor Marchetti, who went rogue, as "spy jargon for a favorite and frequently used gimmick of the clandestine professionals. When their veil of secrecy is shredded and they can no longer rely on a phony cover story to misinform the public, they resort to admitting—sometimes even volunteering—some of the truth while still managing to withhold the key and damaging facts in the case. The public, however, is usually so intrigued by the new information that it never thinks to pursue the matter further."

Confess and Move On

By the late 1970s, it seemed as if the CIA had been caught *in flagrante delicto* and disgraced, had confessed its sins, done penance, and resolved to go and sin no more. Seeming, however, is the nature of the CIA's game. Organized criminals learn to adapt to the changing times, and that is exactly what the intelligence operatives did. Since the major revelations of the late sixties and seventies—MKUltra, engineered coups all around the world, assassinations of foreign leaders, spying on Americans, etc.—no major program of propaganda has been exposed in the mainstream media. Revealing books about certain CIA programs have been written—e.g. Douglas Valentine's important *The Phoenix Program* being one—and dissenting writers, journalists, researchers, and whistleblowers (Robert Parry, Gary Webb, Julian Assange, James W. Douglass, David Ray Griffin, Edward Snowden, et al.) have connected the U.S. intelligence services to dirty deeds and specific actions, such as the American engineered coup d'état in Ukraine in 2013-14, electronic spying, and the attacks of September 11, 2001. But the propaganda has for the most part continued unabated at a powerful and esoteric cultural level, while illegal and criminal actions are carried out throughout the world in the most blatant manner imaginable, as if to say fuck you openly while insidiously infecting the general population through the mass electronic screen culture that has relegated intellectual and literary culture to a tiny minority.

Planning Ahead

Let me explain what I think has been happening.

Organizations like the CIA are obviously fallible and have made many mistakes and failed to anticipate world events. But they are also very powerful, having great financial backing, and do the bidding of their masters in banking, Wall St., finance, etc. They are the action arm of these financial elites, and are, as Douglass Valentine has written, organized criminals. They have their own military, are joined to all the armed forces, and are deeply involved in the drug trade. They control the politicians. They operate their own propaganda network in conjunction with the private mercenaries they hire for their operations. The corporate mass media take their orders, orders that need not be direct, but sometimes are, because these media are structured to do the bidding of the same elites that formed the CIA and own the media. And while their ostensible raison d'être is to provide intelligence to the nation's civilian leaders, this is essentially a cover story for their real work that is propaganda, killing, and conducting coups d'états at home and abroad.

Because they have deep pockets, they can afford to buy all sorts of people, people who pimp for the elites. Some of these people do work that is usually done by honest academics and independent intellectuals, a dying breed, once called free-floating intellectuals. These pimps analyze political, economic, technological, and cultural trends. They come from different fields: history, anthropology, psychology, sociology, political science, cultural studies, linguistics, etc. They populate the think tanks and universities. They are often intelligent but live in bad faith, knowing they are working for those who are doing the devil's work. But they collect their pay and go their way straight to the bank, the devil's bank. They often belong to the Council of Foreign Relations or the Heritage Foundation. They are esteemed and esteem themselves. But they are *pimps*.

El Diablo

Ah, the devil! He's their man. A man of many names, but always an impostor. These pimps know his story and how he works his magic, and this is what their paymasters want from them: ways to use the old bastard's bag of tricks to conjure confusion, and sow fear and paranoia. And to do this slow and easy in ways no one will recognize until it is too late.

For like culture, propaganda relies on myths, symbols, and stories. Some prefer to say narratives. And nothing is more powerful. Controlling the stories is the key to powerful propaganda. The pimps can spin many a tale.

Tell people endless tales of the good guys and the bad, of how the bad are out to get you and the good to save you. Think of the use of symbols in the telling of these stories. They are crucial. The word symbol comes from a Greek word to throw together. Symbols that represent the in-group or the "good guys" are used to create social solidarity within the in-group. Stories are told to accompany the symbols; stories, narratives, or myths tell of how the good guys are fighting to hold the group together and the bad guys are trying to rip the community apart. The symbolic and its opposite—the diabolic (to throw apart)—the angels against the devils—el diablo. Very simple, very old. The aliens are out to get us. And el diablo is always the ultimate other, the man in red, the reds, the commies, the Russians, the others, immigrants, the blacks who want to move next door, Muslims, gays—take your pick. Satanic rituals. Black magic. Witchcraft.

Methods of Propaganda

Infecting minds with such symbols and stories must be done directly and indirectly, as well as short-term and long-term. Long term propaganda is like a slowly leaking water pipe that you are vaguely aware of but that rots the metal from within until the pipe can no longer resist the pressure. Drip drop, drip drop, drip drop—and the inattentive recipients of the propaganda gradually lose their mettle to resist and don't know it, and then when an event bursts into the news—e.g. the attacks of September 11, 2001 or Russiagate—they have been so softened that their assent is automatically given. They know without hesitation who the devil is and that he must be fought.

The purpose of the long-term propaganda is to create certain predispositions and weaknesses that can be exploited when needed. Certain events can be the triggers to induce the victims to react to suggestions. When the time is ripe, all that is needed is a slight suggestion, like a touch on the shoulder, and the hypnotized one acts in a trance. The gun goes off, and the entranced one can't remember why (see: Sirhan Sirhan). This is the goal of mass hypnotization through long-term propaganda: confusion, memory loss, and automatic reaction to suggestion.

Intelligence Pimps and Liquid Screen Culture

When the CIA's dirty tricks were made public in the 1970s, it is not hard to imagine that the intellectual pimps who do their long-range thinking were asked to go back to the drawing board and paint a picture of the coming decades and how business as usual could be conducted without further embarrassment. By that time it had become clear that intellectual or high culture was being swallowed by mass culture and the future belonged to electronic screen culture and images, not words. What has come to be called "postmodernity" ensued, or what the sociologist Zygmunt Bauman calls "liquid modernity" and Guy Debord "the society of the spectacle." Such developments, rooted in what Frederic Jameson has termed "the cultural logic of late capitalism," have resulted in the fragmentation of social and personal life into pointillistic moving pictures whose dots form incoherent images that sow mass confusion and do not cohere. From the mid-1970s until today, this generalized disorientation with its flowing and eternal present of appearing and dissolving images has resulted in what is surely a transformed world, and with it, transformed worldviews. The foundations have collapsed. Meaning and coherence have become difficult to discern. Stable personality has been disassociated, memory downloaded, attention lost, the psyche materialized, sexual identity confused, the electronic mind-body interface established, and the electronic and pharmaceutical drugging of the population accomplished. Really? Yes.

Did not the intelligence agencies foresee all this? Did not they see it and plan accordingly? Did they not notice that about the time their old dirty deeds were being exposed, a movie burst onto the screen that introduced a theme familiar to them and their Nazi friends? I mean the 1973 hit, *The Exorcist,* wherein Satan struts his stuff, four years after Mick Jagger strut his across the stage at Altamont, singing "Sympathy for the Devil," while shortly after a killing took place down in front of him and the 1960s were laid to rest. But during the 1970s *The Exorcist* and its theme of the devil's hold on people came to life and was taken up with a religious fervor by the entertainment industry and promoted by Oprah Winfrey, Geraldo Rivera, and other media luminaries, who went about promoting el diablo's hold on so many helpless victims. Occult, magic, and satanic themes became pop staples and would remain so up until the present day. I would suggest that readers put aside their reservations at what may seem sensational and watch. Then ask yourself: what is going on here?

The CIA as Prophetic

But maybe a better question than did the CIA foresee these developments, would be to ask if it has been involved in the occult and satanic world itself, before and after the social developments of "liquid modernity." The answer is yes. Indeed, all the characteristics of the social and cultural developments I mentioned previously in reference to postmodernity have been a major part of its work *before* this new world emerged: "the disassociation of stable personalities, memory erasure and the implanting of false memories, materializing the psyche, confusing sexual identity, establishing the electronic mind-body interface, and electronic, hallucinogenic (the CIA introduced and spread LSD in the 1960s), and pharmaceutical drugging," to name but a few. In anticipating these developments the CIA was at the very least predictive. Disinformation, acts of terrorism, coup d'états, assassinations flow out of a marriage to the Nazis made in hell—Talbot's "devil's chessboard"—but they are linked to much more. Peter Levenda, in *Sinister Forces: A Grimoire of American Political Witchcraft*, a trilogy on sinister forces in American history, puts it this way:

> The CIA, satanic cults, and UFOs, the mythology of the late twentieth century is surprisingly coherent even though the masks change from case to case, from victim to alleged victim. The CIA, of course, does exist; their mind control programs from BLUEBIRD to ARTICHOKE to MK-ULTRA are a matter of public record. Their history of political assassinations and the overthrow of various foreign governments is also a matter of record. Satanic cults—or perhaps we should qualify that and say 'occult secret societies'—also exist and are a matter of public record; their attempts to contact alien forces by means of ceremonial magic and arcane ritual (including the use of some of the same drugs and other techniques as the CIA used in its mind control programs) are also well-known and documented. Some of these practitioners were—and are—well-known men and women who have not denied their involvement (such as rocket scientist Jack Parsons in the 1950s and Army Colonel and intelligence officer Michael Aquino in the 1990s). The CIA also aggressively researched American cults and secret societies in an effort to discover the source of paranormal abilities and ancient mind control mechanisms. And while the jury is still

out on the question of UFOs, there is no doubt that government agencies have attempted to track, to analyze them, and to explain them away. Again this is a matter of public record, including FBI and CIA documents in addition to military records.

Skeptical readers may find this strange to consider. That would be a mistake. The web of connections is there for anyone who cares to look. For more than fifty years occult themes and rituals have been part of worldview warfare. Drugs, shamanism, black magic, and the occult—staples of the CIA then and now. It is well known that Hollywood, television, and the media in general have been working closely with the intelligence agencies for a long time. Especially since 2001, films and television programs have glorified the CIA, our "good" spies, and the military. The mystification of reality has found its best friend in the electronic and internet revolution as strange and "subversive" beliefs are dangled like candy for little children. Good and evil move through the public consciousness like passing sun and shadows. Weird conspiracy theories "pop up" to titillate and obsess, and to drive out the serious findings of dedicated and disciplined writers and researchers who have discovered the truth about real government conspiracies. Sowing confusion is the name of this deadly game, and if you find yourself confused, you are in good company.

But many are catching on and realizing that what seems strange but innocent is part of a much larger effort to hypnotize the public to agree to their own destruction through the ingestion of what can only be called black magic.

The eloquent writer and brave American, Jim Garrison, the former District Attorney of New Orleans and the only person to bring a trial in the assassination of President Kennedy, put it this way in *On the Trail of The Assassins*, the story of his quest to solve the murder of JFK:

> I knew by now that when a group of individuals gravitated toward one another for no apparent reason, or a group of individuals inexplicitly headed in the same

directions as if drawn by a magnetic field, or coincidence piled upon coincidence too many times, as often as not the shadowy outlines of a covert intelligence operation were somehow becoming visible.

Rub Lucifer, the Prince of Darkness, the right way and the CIA emerges into the light. You can see its shadowy outline with your eyes wide shut. As it says on CIA headquarters: "You shall know the Truth, and the Truth will set you free."

The Canaries that Sang "Things Suck"

Don't get me wrong. I am not foul-mouthed or in any way vulgar, having been trained in the niceties of academic discretionary writing and research. I apologize for the title and even for using the personal pronoun "I." As "one" knows, to write as if you are a person with values and beliefs is very crude in the academy from which so many of our finest national priorities, like perpetual war-making and economic exploitation, emanate. In this case, however, I must use certain language that may be offensive to some sensitive folks in order to explain my thesis in the hope that it will encourage others to grasp why so many of our compatriots of every sex and gender dispensation imaginable have become such suckers. I hope you will grant the importance of such an endeavor and excuse the means used to achieve its ends.

Let me say this at the outset. To say something sucks has always confused me. I have asked many people how something—let's say a pizza—could suck, and they have just rolled their eyes. I know a vacuum cleaner can suck and a sump pump can suck or is it pump, but after that, I'm lost. How can a movie suck? Spaghetti? You can suck it but can it suck? You see my point?

Perhaps you have heard the saying that "there is a sucker born every minute." That seems to me to be so off, statistically. Do you agree? What's your estimate for the birth rate of suckers: a hundred, a thousand, ten thousand a minute? I don't know, but my theory or thesis, if you will, is not statistically based. And let's not get into that ridiculous debate about nature versus nurture. We both no doubt agree that suckers are both born and bred in the USA at a feverish rate.

I am a social theorist, not a statistician, so please just consider my theory. I can assure you that there is no conspiracy involved in it, since all the variables I note are well-known, if forgotten, by the general public. In this article I will touch on a few, for if I went on too long you might think this article sucked, despite the incongruity of your lingo. Indeed, there is an enormous amount of academic research to support my thesis, but this is not the place for footnotes or references. Trust me, as you do CNN or *The New York Times*.

It was in the early 1990s when I first noticed that many people were saying things "sucked" an awful lot. I would have thought that after the great American TV victory in the Gulf War and the election of the fresh-faced, forthright young governor from Arkansas to lead the ship of state, the sucking lingo would die down. No way! The pace picked up quite dramatically throughout the nineties. Movies sucked, the party sucked, the concert sucked—so much was starting to suck it frightened me, and I'm not easily frightened, having been toughened up in the academy with its fierce in-fighting over trivia and its short vacations.

There wasn't a "ton" of such sucking in those early days, but this way of talking struck me anyway. The word "ton" wasn't cool yet, as in "We had a ton of fun at the party," and so the heaviness of our new social reality hadn't fully sunk in yet; the massive growth in depression was just getting started. It was just "it sucks"/"that sucks" that was hot in those years. I started to wonder if this little phrase was a harbinger of things to come, the unconscious canary in the national mineshaft, the lack of breathable air shortening people's verbal responses to a growing unreality.

One day I was in the checkout line in a supermarket when a very elderly woman got into an argument with the checkout girl. The girl had charged the old woman twice for her *National Enquirer*, or so the old one said. The girl denied it and showed the old woman the receipt, which failed to mollify her. She stormed away, shouting, "That sucks. You suck." I couldn't help laughing, so incongruous was the scene. But I took note as a good academic should, and started to collect the variables that would eventually result in my present argument, one that has involved almost thirty years of diligent thinking and research, so I hope you will appreciate its significance. I would hate to think my years of toiling in the academy were for naught.

After the loud sound of all things sucking came the fear of being dehydrated, as if everyone, even people walking through Central Park in New York City, was lost in the Sahara Desert and was afraid they might collapse into a sere heap without constant water intake. I guess you can never be too careful. Everywhere you looked, there were people sucking on those plastic water bottles that sprang up like locusts. To be without one was then akin to being without one's cell phone today. Mr. Death seemed to be stalking the bottle-less ones, those not sucking. But to be more precise, people didn't exactly suck on the bottles until the sports tops were added. I heard there was a very creative entrepreneur who tried introducing water bottles with baby bottle rubber nipples, but that was too suggestive then, since adults were just starting to dress like kids and the kidification of adults had to be somewhat disguised in those early days.

Come on, can you imagine if you saw a forty-five-year-old man in a Yankee jersey and hat, walking around sucking on a plastic water bottle with a baby nipple. That would be too much, even if you were a Yankee fan. You could say the Red Sox sucked, but you couldn't be seen to be so obviously sucking, yourself.

Then there was that cool cat, Bill Clinton. Whenever you turned on the TV or glanced at a newspaper, there he was out jogging or walking with a huge soda or something, sucking away on the straw. Or blowing on that horn on Saturday Night Live. It almost seemed like the poor guy had an oral complex or something. On the golf course where he was often pictured, he and his pals had big cigars they sucked on, making cigar sucking very popular. The magazine, *Cigar Afionado*, born in the fall of 1992 when Bill and Hill so sincerely refuted those Paula Jones sexual allegations and won the White House, would soon publish covers with famous actresses fondling cigars in a not so subtle come-on. Stores everywhere had humidors hawking them. Sucking on quart-sized drinks and cigars took the country by storm, and please, I am not alluding to Stormy Daniels and her lurid tales, which come later.

I am just listing some of the many variables that I have spent my academic career gathering in preparation for the release of my upcoming book that I hope will be my crowning achievement: *Sucking and Suckers: A Qualitative Study.*

This cigar craze got so wild that one day I walked into my local liquor store and the owner showed me his new humidor. He said, "Eddie, you should try one on me." I said I didn't smoke, to which he replied, "But you really should just try one, they make you feel powerful, like a big man."

I told him I felt big, capacious, and enormous already, sort of like Walt Whitman, who said, "I am large, I contain multitudes." He just rolled his eyes and lit up.

I was reminded of a quote from Wilhelm Reich's book, *Listen, Little Man*, a long-forgotten book that is perfect for today:

> A great man knows when and in what way he is a little man. A little man does not know he is little and is afraid to know. He hides his pettiness and narrowness behind illusions of strength and greatness, someone else's strength and greatness.

And behind his cigar and bluster.

Then came Monica and Bill. I guess the cigars weren't enough, or the occupancy of the big White House, or eight years of continual bombing of Iraq and sanctions that killed well over 500,000 Iraqi children, or making all those sexed-up welfare queens with all their babies scream when he did away with welfare as we know it, or his sadistic bombing of Serbia and the El Shifa pharmaceutical factory in Sudan. It seems as though nothing is sufficient to make war criminals feel big enough.

Excuse the politics. I'm getting carried away from my theme, which sucks. Okay, there was Monica. But I will leave it to your imagination, if you dare. Sorry for being crude.

Variable number four or five are those pacifier necklaces, as if eight years of Bill hadn't been pacifier enough. Do you remember them? Did their wearers suck on them, or was a message being sent?

Then came the oral sex craze among the young, serendipitously connected to Bill and Monica. Stuff happens.

Perhaps for me, in my academic life, my eureka moment came one day in the early 2000s when I was teaching a class on the growing cleavage between the rich and the poor. Bush Jr. had the country pacified and simultaneously whipped into a war frenzy after the attacks of 9/11. He was lying his way to the invasion of Iraq after having been "accidentally" rescued from a disastrous economy by those nineteen Arab terrorists with boxcutters. I was explaining to the students, mostly college juniors and seniors, how the percentage of the very wealthy had been increasing for years and the poor and middle-class were suffering, when I looked down to see a pretty female student in the front row. Bingo! Instant insight, or was it outsight? I was about to say something wise about the economic gap but my voice cracked. Right at my feet was an example of a different form of cleavage that had my eyes quickly popping up to look straight ahead as if I didn't see what I saw. Right there was a culminating variable that I was able to notice for many years to come. Call it the cleavage phenomenon, but it was real, and it could be seen throughout the classrooms and byways of America ever since. I will let you take it from there.

Over the following years, I continued to collect my evidence for the phenomenon I call "suck." But I also noticed that under Bush Jr, as under Poppi Bush and Clinton, people were increasingly being taken for suckers by the authorities with their lies about Iraq, 9/11, the anthrax attacks, the economy, the weapons of mass destruction in Iraq, the war on terror, etc. It's true, I know, that the same happened under the presidency of Ronald Reagan, but he was generally considered an acting president and life in the 1980s a feel-good movie. Everyone was happy then, and suck was just a bad word that could spoil the fun of "Morning in America."

When in 2008 Bush Jr. returned to the ranch and full-time brush cutting, in rode Obama. Slicker than Slick Willy, he really sucker-punched liberals, who were desperate for some classy speech in the White House, someone who could correctly pronounce "nuclear" while promising to spend a trillion dollars on making a new generation of them. They got conned (I guess) when he immediately bailed out the banks and the Wall St. crooks, sent more troops to Afghanistan, cracked down on whistle-blowers, launched killer drones, increased surveillance, destroyed Libya and Syria, sent special forces throughout Africa, etc., smiling as he went marauding.

The power of the Obama propaganda was overwhelming, and so many were sucked in, as they still are. I started to wonder if my years of cultural research on the significance of suck, sucking, and suckers was a waste of my life. Maybe I had missed the bigger issues, having made diversity and sexuality my focus of teaching and research, since they had become the rage in academia.

Then Trump shocked the world with his election and Stormy Daniels burst forth and the rich got richer and the poor poorer and the wars continued and the little-big man tweeted out his foul rantings about immigrants and so many others while the country further descended into a cesspool of insanity as he threatened North Korea and Iran with nuclear annihilation and his buddy Robert Kraft got his quick suck and the fascist Israeli government got his approval to continue slaughtering Palestinians and the deluded citizenry fixated on the 2020 election and the next con-artist who will promise to make things suck no longer.

But I have seen the light. While my thesis still seems valid to me, and the variables I have mentioned here (a fraction of the whole) demonstrate that there's more to the seemingly trivial than meets the eye, I have concluded that the only thing I can conclude is that the American people are suckers and will continue to be so.

And I, too, have been a sucker for thinking that a simple, popular phrase wasn't profoundly true from the start. I began as a hopeful young professor, thinking that I would debunk the crassness of our society and make a name for myself. I thought I was so smart.

Now, however, I have to admit that I was wrong from the beginning: things do suck. The canaries were right. Or to be more precise: the political elites who run the country suck. And the presidents suck big time.

That's just the way it is.

THE ASSASSINATION OF RFK: A LIE TOO BIG TO FAIL

> *"'We're all puppets,' the suspect [Sirhan Sirhan] replied, with more truth than he could have understood at that moment."*
>
> —Lisa Pease, quoting from the LAPD questioning of Sirhan

In her book, *A Lie Too Big to Fail: The Real History of the Assassination of Robert F. Kennedy,* Lisa Pease correctly says that "the CIA takeover of America in the 1960s is the story of our times." That takeover culminated with the murder of Senator Robert Kennedy two months after that of Dr. Martin Luther King, Jr.

When RFK was assassinated on June 5, 1968, the American public fell into an hypnotic trance in which they have remained ever since. The overwhelming majority accepted what was presented by government authorities as an open-and-shut case—that a young Palestinian American, Sirhan Sirhan, had murdered RFK because of his support for Israel, a false accusation whose ramifications echo down the years. That this was patently untrue and was contradicted by overwhelming evidence made no difference.

Sirhan did not kill Robert Kennedy, yet he remains in jail to this very day. Robert Kennedy, Jr., who was 14 years old at the time of his father's death, has visited Sirhan in prison, claims he is innocent, and believes there was another gunman. Paul Schrade, an aide to the senator and the first person shot that night, also says Sirhan didn't do it. Both have plenty of evidence. And they are not alone.

There is a vast body of documented evidence to prove this, an indisputably logical case marshalled by serious writers and researchers. Lisa Pease is the latest. It is a reason why a group of 60 prominent Americans has recently called for a reopening of, not just this case, but those of JFK, MLK, and Malcom X. The blood of these men cries out for the revelation of the truth that the United States national security state and its media accomplices have fought so mightily to keep hidden for so many years.

That they have worked so hard at this reveals how dangerous the truth about these assassinations still is to this secret government that wages propaganda war against the American people and real wars around the world. It is a government of Democrats, Republicans, and their intelligence allies working together today to confuse the American people and provoke Russia in a most dangerous game that could lead to nuclear war, a possibility that so frightened JFK and RFK after the Cuban Missile Crisis that they devoted themselves to ending the Cold War, reconciling with the Soviet Union, abolishing nuclear weapons, reining in the power of the CIA, and withdrawing from Vietnam. That is why they were killed.

The web of deceit surrounding the now officially debunked Democrat-led Russiagate propaganda operation that has pressured Trump to double-down on his anti-Russia operations (a Democratic goal) is an example of the perfidious and sophisticated mutuality of this game of mass mind-control.

The killing of the Kennedys and today's new Cold War and war against terror are two ends of a linked intelligence operation.

Moreover, more than any other assassination of the 1960s, it is the killing of Bobby Kennedy that has remained shrouded in the most ignorance.

It is one of the greatest propaganda success stories of American history.

In her exhaustive new examination of the case, *A Lie Too Big to Fail*, Lisa Pease puts it succinctly at the conclusion of her unravelling of the official lies that have mesmerized the public:

The assassination of the top four leaders of the political left in the five-year period—President John Kennedy in 1963, Malcolm X in 1965, and Martin Luther King, Jr. and Senator Robert Kennedy in 1968—represented nothing less than a slow-motion coup on the political scene.

If anyone wishes to understand what has happened to the United States since this coup, and thus to its countless victims at home and throughout the world, one must understand these assassinations and how the alleged assassins were manipulated by the coup organizers and how the public was hoodwinked in a mind-control operation on a vast scale. It is not ancient history, for the forces that killed these leaders rule the U.S. today, and their ruthlessness has subsequently informed the actions of almost all political leaders in the years since. A bullet to the head when you seriously talk about peace and justice is a not-so-gentle reminder to toe the line or else.

"But the way the CIA took over America in the 1960s is *the* story of our time," writes Pease, "and too few recognize this. We can't fix a problem we can't even acknowledge exists." Nothing could be truer.

Lisa Pease has long recognized the problem, and for the past twenty-five years, she has devoted herself to shedding light on the CIA's culpability, particularly in the Robert Kennedy case. Few people possess the grit and grace to spend so much of their lives walking this path of truth. The extent of her research is dazzling, so dazzling in its voluminous detail that a reviewer can only touch on it here and there. She has written a book that is daunting in its comprehensiveness. It demands focused attention and perseverance, for it runs to over 500 pages with more than 800 footnotes. This book will remain a touchstone for future research on the RFK assassination, whether one agrees or disagrees with all of her detailed findings and speculations. For this book is so vast and meticulous in its examination of all aspects of the case that one can surely find areas that one might question or disagree with, as do I with some of her speculations at the end.

Nevertheless, Pease fundamentally proves that Sirhan did not shoot RFK and that there was a conspiracy organized and carried out by shadowy intelligence forces that did. These same forces worked with the Los Angeles Police Department, federal, state, and judicial elements to make sure Sirhan was quickly accused of being the lone assassin and dispatched to prison after a show trial. And the mass media carried out its assigned role of affirming the government's case to shield the real killers and to make sure the cover-up was successful.

No doubt others will investigate this case further. Yet I think no more research is really needed, for as with these other assassinations, additional analyses will only result in pseudo-debates about minutiae. Such debates will only serve to prolong the hallucinatory grip the perpetrators of these crimes have on a day of reckoning, suggesting as they would that we do not really know what happened. This is an old tactic meant to delay forevermore such a day of reckoning.

The facts are clear for all to see if they have the will to truth. All that is now needed is a public tribunal, which is planned for later this year, in which the fundamental, clear-cut facts of these cases are presented to the American public. In the case of Robert Kennedy's assassination as with the others, a little knowledge goes a long way, and only those who are closed to basic logic and evidence will refuse to see that government forces conspired to kill these men and did so because all were seeking peace and justice that was then, and is now, a threat to the war-making forces of wealth and power that control the American government.

Pease writes:

> Anyone who has looked closely and honestly at the evidence has realized that more than one person was involved in Robert Kennedy's death. So why can't reporters see this? Why can't the media explain this? Because the media and the government are two sides of the same coin, and those who challenge the government's version of history, as numerous reporters have found out, all too often lose status and sometimes whole

careers. Kristina Borjesson published an anthology of such stories in her book *Into the Buzzsaw*, in which journalists describe how they lost their careers when each of them expressed a truth that the government did not want exposed.

Lisa Pease discloses such truths. I am reporting on her work. Therefore, the mainstream media, except for an extraordinary reporter or two, such as Tom Jackman of *The Washington Post*, will likely ignore both of us, but the publication where you are reading this is on the side of truth, and in the disclosure of truth lies our hope.

Since more than one person was involved in the killing of RFK, there was—ipso facto—a conspiracy. This is not theory but fact. The fact of a conspiracy. For more than fifty years, mainstream reporters have been cowed by this word "conspiracy," thanks to the CIA. Many others have been intelligence assets posing as journalists, regurgitating the lies. This is a fact.

The official story is that after giving his victory speech for winning the 1968 Democratic California Primary, Kennedy, as he was walking through a crowded hotel pantry, was shot by Sirhan, who was standing to his left between 3–6 feet away. Sirhan's revolver held eight bullets, and as he was shooting, he was tackled by a group of large men who subdued him. All witnesses place Sirhan in front of Kennedy and all claim he was firing a gun.

Fact: As the autopsy definitively showed, RFK was shot from the rear at point blank range, three bullets entering his body, with the fatal headshot coming upward at a 45-degree angle from 1–3 inches behind his right ear. Not one bullet from Sirhan's gun hit the Senator. In addition, an audio recording shows that many more bullets than the eight in Sirhan's gun were fired in the hotel pantry that night. It was impossible for Sirhan to have killed RFK.

Let me repeat: More than one gunman, contrary to the government's claims, equals a conspiracy. So why lie about that?

What is amazing is that the obvious conclusion to such simple syllogistic logic (Sirhan in front, bullets in the back, therefore . . .) that a child could understand has been dismissed by the authorities for fifty-one years. The fact that the government authorities—the LAPD, the Sheriff's Office, the District Attorney, federal and state government officials, the FBI, the CIA—have from the start so assiduously done all in their power to pin the blame on "a lone assassin," Sirhan, proves they are part of a coordinated cover-up, which in turn suggests their involvement in the crime.

The fact that Robert Kennedy was shot from the back and not the front where Sirhan was standing immediately brings to mind the Zapruder film that shows that JFK was killed from the front right and not from the 6th floor rear where Oswald was allegedly shooting from. That unexpected film evidence was hidden from the public for many years, but when it was finally seen, the case for a government conspiracy was solidified.

While no such video evidence has surfaced in the RFK case, the LAPD made sure that no photographic evidence contradicting the official lies would be seen. As Lisa Pease writes:

> Less than two months after the assassination, the LAPD took the extraordinary step of burning some 2,400 photos from the case in Los Angeles County General's medical waste incinerator. Why destroy thousands of photos in an incinerator if there was nothing to hide? The LAPD kept *hundreds* of innocuous crowd scene photos that showed no girl in a polka dot dress or no suspicious activities or individuals. Why were *those* photos preserved? Perhaps because those photos had nothing in them that warranted their destruction.

While "perhaps" is a mild word, the cover-up of "the girl in the polka dot dress" needs no perhaps. Dozens of people reported seeing a suspicious, curvaceous girl in a white dress with black polka dots with Sirhan in the pantry and other places. She was seen with various other men as well. The evidence for her involvement in the assassination is overwhelming, and yet the LAPD did all in its power to deny this by browbeating witnesses and by allowing her to escape.

Sandra Serrano, a Kennedy campaign worker and a courageous witness, was bullied by the CIA-connected police interrogator Sergeant Enrique "Hank" Hernandez. She had been sitting outside on a metal fire escape getting some air when the polka dot dress girl, accompanied by a man, ran out and down the stairs, shouting, "We've shot him, we've shot him." When Serrano asked whom did they shoot, the girl replied, "We've shot Senator Kennedy." Then she and her companion, both of whom Serrano had earlier seen ascending the stairs with Sirhan, disappeared into the night. A little over an hour after the shooting Serrano was interviewed on live television by NBC's Sander Vanocur where she recounted this. And there were others who saw and heard this girl say the same thing as she and her companion fled the crime scene. Nevertheless, the LAPD, led by Lieutenant Manuel Pena, also CIA affiliated, who was brought out of retirement to run the investigation dubbed "Special Unit Senator," worked with Hernandez and others to dismiss the girl as of no consequence.

Lisa Pease covers all this and much more. She shows how Sirhan was obviously hypnotized, how the trial was a farce, how the police destroyed evidence from the door frames in the pantry that proved more than the eight bullets in Sirhan's gun were fired, how Officer DeWayne Wolfer manipulated the ballistic evidence, etc. Through years of digging into court records, archives, transcripts, the public library, and doing countless interviews, she proves without a doubt that Sirhan did not kill Kennedy and that the assassination and the cover-up were part of a very sophisticated intelligence operation involving many parts and players. She shows how no matter what route Kennedy took in the hotel that night, the killers had all exits covered and that he would not be allowed to leave alive.

While some of her more speculative points—e.g. that Robert Maheu (Howard Hughes/CIA) was "the most credible high-level suspect for the planner of Robert Kennedy's assassination," that Kennedy was shot twice in the head from behind rather than with only one fatal shot to the head as indicated by the autopsy—are open to serious debate, they do not detract from her fundamentally powerful case that RFK, like his brother John, was assassinated by a CIA-run operation intended to silence their voices of courageous resistance to an expanding secret government dedicated to war, murder, and human exploitation. The U.S. government of today.

But these speculations do open her to criticism from those who might want to use them to dismiss the factually based essence of her deeply researched case. They are unfortunate.

When Bobby Kennedy was entering the kitchen pantry, he was escorted by a security guard named Thane Eugene Cesar, a man long suspected of being the assassin. Robert Kennedy, Jr. believes Cesar was the killer. Cesar was carrying a gun that he drew but denied firing, despite witnesses' claims to the contrary. Conveniently, the police never examined the gun. He has long been suspected of being CIA affiliated, and now Pease says she has found evidence to confirm that. She writes, "It's hard to overstate the significance of finding a current or future CIA contract agent holding Kennedy's right arm at the moment of the shooting."

Yes, it is. As she rightly claims, the CIA takeover of America in the 1960s is the story of our time. And our time is now. None of this is ancient history. That is so crucial to grasp. For those who think that learning the truth about the 1960s assassinations is an exercise in futility reserved for those who are living in the past, they need to think again. Our descent into endless war and massive media propaganda to support it is part of a long-term project that began with the elimination of JFK, Malcom X, MLK, and Robert Kennedy. They were killed for reasons, and those reasons still exist. Their killers roam the land because they have become far more deeply part of the institutional structure of government and the media.

Pease says:

> It was horrible that Robert Kennedy was taken from us far too soon. It is horrible that one man has borne the guilt for an operation he neither planned nor willingly participated in. It's horrible the conspiracy was so obvious that bullets had to be lost and switched to hide it. And it's horrible that the mainstream media has never dared to tell the people of this country that

the government lied to us about what they really found when they looked into this case. Until the media can deal with the truth of the Robert Kennedy assassination, and until the people can be made aware of the CIA's role in slanting the truth on topics of great importance, America's very survival is in jeopardy. . . . We've come perilously close to losing democracy itself because of fake, CIA-sponsored stories about our history. Should America ever become a dictatorship, the epitaph of our democracy must include the role the mainstream media, by bowing to the National Security state, played in killing it.

By writing *A Lie Too Big to Fail*, Lisa Pease has done her valiant part in refuting the lie that is now failing. Now it is up to all of us to spread the word of truth by focusing on the fundamental facts so we can finally take back our country from the CIA.

Then we can say with RFK and his favorite poet Aeschylus:

And even in our sleep, pain which cannot forget falls drop by drop upon the heart, until in our own despair, against our will, comes wisdom through the awful grace of God.

Happenings in the Land of the Free and the Home of the Brave

> *"There's something happening here/*
> *What it is ain't exactly clear."*
> **—Buffalo Springfield, "For What It's Worth"**

The Sunday newspaper had been left on the park bench. Its book page had lists of best-sellers, as if numbers two through ten could be the "best" along with number one. Absurdities were everywhere for the taking. On the Non-Fiction Hardcover list, numbers 3, 5, and 10 each had the word fuck in the title. The books were published by two old and respected publishing houses: Harper and Little Brown. However, something was odd, for the word fuck was spelled f*ck. These books were about hope, acceptance, and living the good life, cliché topics in a feel-good culture: *The Subtle Art of Not Giving a F*ck, Everything is F*cked,* and *Calm the F*ck Down.* It seemed you had to be fucked first before you could accept the hope that the good life was coming your way. He wondered if these publishing houses thought that by eliminating the "u" they kept their hands clean and were not descending into the gutter with hoi polloi, while simultaneously titillating potential readers. Did they think readers would be offended by the word fuck, but would not be by f*ck? Then it occurred to him that he didn't know what the fuck non-fiction books were anyway. Maybe he had been wrong all his life and the opposite of up was non-up, not down.

~•~•~•~

On every table in the seaside resort's breakfast room there was a brightly colored flower in a clear watered vase. When he picked it up to smell the orange blossom, there was no smell and the water didn't move. He imagined an ersatz form of plastic happiness, a conjurer's delight, where everything was a trick, nothing moved, not even water.

~•~•~•~

Leaving the Marine Corps Base Camp Pendleton in southern California where white and black Marines were regularly fighting and there were even some killings never reported by the press, the two young Marines escaped the tense and claustrophobic atmosphere on a weekend pass. It was early February 1967, and they took an overnight bus up the coast to San Francisco where they wandered around and found a breakfast restaurant near Union Square. There they read in the newspaper that for the week of January 12-19 the U.S. military had suffered its highest casualty count so far in Vietnam: 144 killed, 1,044 wounded, and 6 missing-in-action. It jolted them awake more than the coffee. Later that afternoon, the two naïfs wandered into the Haight-Ashbury district where they were startled by the first waves of acid-dazed hippies, who would soon arrive in hoards for the "summer of love." In the evening when they visited a bar for some beers, the waitress who delivered their drinks was topless. While they regarded this slight anomaly with manly indifference, she must have noticed their military haircuts that stood out among the longhairs, and so she served them buttons with their beers. The buttons read: *Vietnam Love It Or Leave It.* Heading back to the base, they knew where they didn't want to go.

~•~•~•~

The young man was studying for a PhD. He was intent on learning what made the world and people tick. He was attending a small seminar at the home of his professor, a famous German emigre who had worked for the Rand Corporation and U.S. Intelligence. Each of the five students was to give a short presentation on the subject of propaganda and the issue of knowledge, since the course concerned the sociology of knowledge. The student began his presentation by quoting a famous philosopher's words:

> In formulating any philosophy, the first consideration must always be: What can we know? That is, what can we be sure we know, or sure that we know we knew it, if indeed it is all knowable. Or have we simply forgotten it and are too embarrassed to say anything? Descartes hinted at the problem when he wrote, "My mind can never know my body, although it has become quite friendly with my legs." By "knowable," incidentally, I do not mean that which can be known by perception of the senses, or that which can be grasped by the mind, but more that which can be said to be Known or to possess a Knownness or Knowability, or at least something you can mention to a friend.

The student paused and the eminent professor said, "So very interesting. Who is that philosopher?" The student replied, "Woody Allen." "He is very perceptive," said the professor, "and yet I have never heard of him. I will have to read his work." The student realized he was in good hands with such U.S. intelligence and Rand Corporation experts, so he asked the professor's wife for another glass of the German wine she was serving and toasted his good fortune with a wry grin. None of the other students got the joke either.

∼•∼•∼•∼

A young man was reading a book that he highly recommended to his uncle. Leafing through it, the older man came upon this passage: "the free individual is just a fictional tale concocted by an assembly of biochemical algorithms." So what was the point of reading such a book, he wondered, since doing so was an exercise in pre-programmed absurdity since there was no freedom.

~·~·~·~

You have probably seen the bumper sticker that says: "Shit Happens." Some people are just lucky, I suppose, and odd coincidences mark their lives. When he was just out of Columbia College and working for a reputed CIA front company, Business International Corporation, Barack Obama had a chance encounter with a young woman, Genevieve Cook, with whom he had a 1-2-year relationship. Like Obama and at about the same time, Cook just happened to have lived in Indonesia with her father, Michael Cook, who just happened to become Australia's top spook, the director-general of the Office of National Assessments, and also the Ambassador to Washington. Of course, Obama's mother, as is well-known, just happened to be living in Indonesia with Barack and Obama's step-father, Lolo Soetoro, an Indonesian military officer, who had been called back to Indonesia by the CIA-supported General Suharto three months before the CIA coup against President Sukarno. Suharto subsequently slaughtered between 500,000 and a million Indonesian Communists and Indonesian-Chinese. As is also well-known, it just so happened that Obama's mother, Ann Dunham, trained in the Russian language, after teaching English in the U.S. Embassy in Jakarta that housed one of the largest CIA stations in Asia, did her "anthropological" work in Indonesia and Southeast Asia financed by the well-known CIA conduits, USAID and the Ford Foundation. Then there is Cook's stepfather, Philip C. Jessup, who just happened to be in Indonesia at the same time, doing nickel-mining deals with the genocidal Suharto government. Anyway, "shit happens." You never know whom you might meet along the way of life.

~·~·~·~

The hostess at the seaside restaurant had an eastern European accent, so he asked her where she was from. She said, "Belgrade, Serbia." He told her he was sorry for what the U.S. government led by Bill Clinton had done to her country and that he considered

Clinton a war criminal. She said the bombing in 1999 was terrifying, and even though she was young at the time, she vividly remembered it. It traumatized her, her parents, and her family. Then she smiled and said that in the month she had been in the U.S. for her summer job, all the Americans she had met had been so friendly. He welcomed her to the U.S., and as he was walking away, he remembered that Clinton's savage bombing of Serbia that had killed so many Serbian children and other innocents had been code-named "Operation Noble Anvil." He wondered what kind of "noble" people would think of innocent children as anvils: "heavy usually steel-faced iron blocks on which metal is shaped," and did the friendly Americans accept Clinton's sick lies when he ended his March 24, 1999 war address to the American people with these words: "Our thoughts and prayers tonight must be with the men and women of our armed forces, who are undertaking this mission for the sake of our values and our children's future. May God bless them, and may God bless America."

The banal 1967 hit song, "San Francisco" (Be sure to wear flowers in your hair), which was influential in enticing young people to come to San Francisco for the Summer of Love, was written by "Papa" John Philips, who attended the US Naval Academy at Annapolis and whose father was a Marine Corps Captain. "Papa" John's wife had worked at the Pentagon and her father was involved in covert intelligence work in Vietnam. His neighbor and Laurel Canyon (Los Angeles) buddy was Jim Morrison of Doors fame, whose father U.S. Navy Admiral George Morrison commanded U.S. warships in Vietnam's Tonkin Gulf during the "Tonkin Gulf Incident." Frank Zappa, the father figure of Laurel Canyon's many musicians who just happened to converge in one place at the same time where a covert military film studio operated, had a father who was a chemical warfare specialist at Edgewood Arsenal. Stephen Stills, David Crosby and many other soon to be famous musicians all came from military and intelligence backgrounds and frolicked in Laurel Canyon. Although they were draft age, none of them was drafted as they played music, dropped acid, and created the folk-rock movement whose music was catchy but innocuous and posed no threat to the establishment. But then, "shit happens." In his disturbing book, *Weird Scenes Inside the Canyon,* David McGowan raises the question: "what if the musicians themselves (and various other leaders and founders of the 'movement') were every bit as much a part of the intelligence community as the people who were supposedly harassing them? What if, in other words, the entire youth culture of the 1960s was created not as a grass-roots challenge to the status quo, but as a cynical exercise in discrediting and marginalizing the budding anti-war movement and creating a fake opposition that could be easily controlled and led astray. . . . What if, in reality, they were pretty much all playing on the same team?"

∼•∼•∼•∼

The reporter was interviewing four of the Maharishi Mahesh Yogi's young "executive governors," who were all dressed in three-piece business suits. They were in the process of conducting Transcendental Meditation's weeklong course leading to supernormal abilities including flying, levitating, disappearing, x-ray vision, and other siddhis, or supernormal powers. Their recent press release had advertised the course as "a new breakthrough for human life on earth" for any person. The reporter was a bit skeptical that people could be taught—for a large fee—to fly or disappear. He asked one of the executive governors, "Can you literally rise into the air and move horizontally; can you see yourself and can others see you actually fly?" "Absolutely," Larry Johnson replied without hesitation, "absolutely. Once you eliminate all stress from your nervous system, you have unbounded, unlimited potential. A human can achieve any desire he wants, flying is only one of them." "People will be skeptical," the reporter continued, "How about a demonstration?" "A public demonstration would cause too much of a ruckus," said Johnson. "And we couldn't show you because we only do it for each other. Actually, we do our techniques with our eyes closed, but we do peek out once in a while and see each other flying around the room. You know, one of the siddhis is a technique for making yourself invisible, and the

Mararishi has said, 'Don't peek out to see if you've disappeared.'" Johnson giggled and added, "We can also teach people to x-ray their own bodies and see through walls. Absolutely, absolutely. It's all about infinite correlation. Absolutely." As the battered reporter left the interview, he wondered if the Maharishi was a creation of the CIA. He remembered John Lennon's song lines about the Maharishi's assistant: "But he often spread rumors through his right-hand man/Who used to be with the CIA."

What is "exactly clear" is that Buffalo Springfield (Stephen Stills, Neil Young et al.) toured with their Laurel Canyon buddies, the Beach Boys, in late 1967 (their other mutual bud, Charlie Manson, stayed out west presumably to work on his craft) and performed at a very odd venue for a "dissident" rock group, The U.S. Military Academy at West Point. At that time nearly 500,000 American troops were waging war on the Vietnamese. That concert was an odd happening, wouldn't you say?

If everyone actually looked, they'd see precisely what went down, "what's going down," and why we are going down. If you think many of these things "just happen" for no reason, then I guess you are just "f*cked." Excuse me, but it's true. Does the asterisk help?

When Time Stands Still

The intimate human experience of time standing still is universal, although rare. When we undergo it, we are stunned. Silence seems to enclose us. It is the correlative to the more common experience of time passing at different speeds, sometimes slowly, sometimes fast, despite clocks. These universal experiences do not accord with the teleology that underlies the modern world with its scientific principle that leads to entropic death triumphant. They are therefore, as John Berger, the English writer and art critic, writes, "dismissed as subjective, because time, according to the nineteenth-century view, is objective, incontestable and indifferent; to its indifference there are no limits."

As a result of living within this scientific and technical presupposition that the background ticking of the clock is the only truth and time is a one-way street, we are now living inside a hopeless mind-frame of a scientific theocracy that says all will end in entropy. This is nihilism; for at the end of this clock time is nothingness, the infinite void. This is the unstated "future," but a future that is also, now, a noxious injection that surreptitiously poisons people at the well of their lives where cracks in the consensual reality open and other truths fly in, or as Emily Dickinson said, "'Hope' is the thing with feathers/That perches in the soul/And sings the tune without the words/And never stops—at all."

The one-dimensional finality of the view of time as death triumphant is the nihilistic future Nietzsche said was coming, and now it is here. And being here, it tries to reduce any experience that transports us beyond time to personal lunacy and therefore worthy only of dismissal. It reduces human subjectivity and transcendent joy and despondent suffering to the ravings of a mad person. Facts are facts, says this unstated premise, and if you don't get that, you are a joker and will be rendered invisible.

In the movie *Joker*, the suffering Arthur Fleck, the eponymous Joker, is abandoned by a cruel American society whose capitalist order cares not a whit for its regular people, and in a penultimate scene when Arthur is appearing on a late-night television show where the snide and condescending host mocks him and his attempt at comedy, Joker says to the host:

> "Comedy is subjective, Murray. Isn't that what they say? All of you, the system that knows so much, you decide what's right or wrong. The same way that you decide what's funny or not."

In that quote lies our current fate, the dark night that has descended on our world. The system that knows and controls so much decides human truth and what is good and evil, always, of course, deciding in its own favor, even to suggest that all is woe and all hope is gone while heading to the bank with its ill-begotten lucre.

No wonder all the media, mainstream and alternative, are today filled with headlines and titles screaming about our impending extinction, doomsday, and the apocalypse. The end days are near. Just as our fictitious "telling of time" with advanced technology has sped up since the simplest clock and speed has devoured space, so too have all the admonitions to prepare for the end of the world, as if you could. Just pack your suitcase and you're off. These warnings are often accompanied by assertions that humans, having contaminated the planet, don't deserve to survive; that humans are vermin; and that, anyway, it's too little too late, we don't have time. Extinction will be arriving shortly, even if we protest its arrival. It's hopeless, so don't have children, or, if you have them already, teach them that "life is a tale told by an idiot signifying nothing." A one-way trip to dusty death where the trains run on time and the last stop is Nowhere.

Such political commentary, while often based on obvious problems caused by systemic structures of capitalist exploitation and technological hubris, implicitly rejects millennia of human experience and the testimony of the world's great art and spiritual experience. It rests upon a metaphysical assumption disguised as science that brackets out any word to the contrary. It is the triumph of technical reason over the revelation of hope that is rooted in love, sexuality, and the human body, not abstractions.

"Our totalitarianism begins with our teleology," writes Berger in his brilliant essay, "That Which Is Held."

He adds:

> What is ahistorical is the need to hope. And the act of hoping is inseparable from the energy of love, from that which "holds," from that which is art's constant example.

Such as the painting of a plaid suitcase by a little-known artist that hangs in my mental museum. My father once went on vacation, and when he arrived at his destination and opened this suitcase, he found that it is was empty. He had forgotten to pack and was overcome with joy at the realization. He wanted for nothing. This was his masterpiece, created when he wasn't looking.

Just yesterday, I was being visited by these thoughts as I took an early morning walk by the neighboring lake. A group of geese, like battleships on the sea, greeted me with their honking, and as I dawdled along, they dove to show me their white asses, as if they were college boys out on a drunken lark, mooning anyone who passed. It seemed as if I were being mocked for allowing these thoughts to drift into my mind, guests that I did not summon but came uninvited. Many days I feel as though I am visited by words and images that transport me into reveries of time lost and time found and time beyond time. Rilke captures a bit of this with these words:

> *O longing for places that were not*
> *Cherished enough in that fleeting hour*
> *How I long to make good from afar*
> *The forgotten gesture, the additional act.*

Who, among us, has not heard such words whispering into our silences?

Then I stopped by a swampy area at the end of the lake and took a look through the gently swaying bushes. A blue heron stood stock still on the far side, as if it were a statue or a silhouetted profile on an ancient Greek vase. I froze and watched intently, lost in the sight of the bird's eerie stillness. For an instant I was that blue heron. Its immobility and my stop-time staring seemed to fuse us in the way one is transported into a cataleptic state when watching dust motes in a flash of sunlight or unexpectedly seeing the full moon hanging on the world's edge when stepping outdoors with night coming on. It seems at these moments that a crack opens in the conventional reality machine that runs the world and one shivers with an erotic happiness that transcends description. Berger calls these "enclaves of the beyond."

When I finally shook myself loose from being the heron, I walked on by myself but with many voices whispering in my ears. Kris Kristofferson, whom I had recently seen in a documentary on country music, was singing "Me and Bobby McGee," which took me back to a night years ago when a woman I knew played the song over and over for me as she drank wine in her low-cut dress, coming on to me, even as my then wife sat with us.

There is an infinite sadness in this memory, the loneliness of her yearning, not just for sex but for love, for a relationship, for tenderness, for "that which is held," and while I remember the night vividly, I sadly can't remember her name and she slips into the penumbra of the dreamy past. But vividly alive, present. She walks with me as I head down the road, where the sign reads: Rough Road Ahead. The words live:

> *Then somewhere near Salinas, Lord, I let her slip away*
> *She was lookin' for the love I hope she'll find."*

Just a moment of time out of mind. A moment the timekeepers can't imagine.

We know it. We live it. We use and are used by our memories and forgetteries in equal measure, thinking we control the flow of life, which we don't.

There is an experience that lovers, writers, singers, and athletes have. Everyone has it at least once in a lifetime, or so I hope. It is called by some "being in the zone," by others "being unconscious," by others "ecstasy" and "inspiration"; in all cases it transcends clocks and the underlying bias of our age. It is hope incarnate. It is time out of mind. By discounting it, we embrace hopelessness, nihilism.

Living in the age of abstractions, we tend to abandon the body, the earth, and the chance that we might redeem this sordid era. By remembering that hope lies in the shadows, in the unexpected places and faces that flash through our times even when we are induced to believe we are only dreaming, we have a chance. But only if we reject the belief that entropy is time's arrow. Therein lies the real danger that will result in our forgetting how instantly time can stand still in the ultimate sense, as it did for the Japanese victims of America's murderous rage on August 6, 1945. Galway Kinnell, in his poem "The Fundamental Project of Technology" reminds us to remember:

> *The children go away. By nature they do. And by memory,*
> *in scorched uniforms, holding tiny crushed lunch tins.*
> ...
> *again and again, until the day flashes and no one lives*
> *to look back and say, a flash, a white flash sparkled.*

Where was the lightning before it flashed? To us it wasn't. Its flashing was it. It was its act. But the nuclear weapons that we once used and are now preparing to use already exist, and if they flash again, all time will be extinguished and we will be gone with it.

The road ahead is rough indeed. A despairing teleology will not save us. We need to see it for the trap that it is.

Rhythm, melody, and movement: from these life is born and sustained. They are also integral to art—music, writing, painting, sculpture, dance, etc.—even when they are apparently absent, as with my distorted perception of the seemingly immobile heron. They lie at the heart of spiritual experience, as breath is the inspiration that carries us along.

As I walk up the hill past the lake and my respiration increases, I see Alberto Giacometti's sculpture, "Tall Walking Figure" in my mind's eye. Its immobility implies movement, just as the ticking of the turning clock down through the ages has implied the earth's solid resistance to time's final victory, as the seasons turn and renew themselves timelessly. Movement and stasis, time and the timeless. Such paradoxical inclusiveness pertains to still-life painting as well. While seemingly immobile, and defined by some as dead life encompassed by the presence of the absence of movement and change, the essence of all living things, such paintings come to life in the encounter with the living. Relationship is all. To grasp the paradoxical nature of art—and life—one must approach them as an artist and see the wholeness in broken pieces. "Everything is broken," Bob Dylan sings, "take a deep breath, feel like you're choking."

It seems that way. But I am enjoying my walking reveries and so will let John Berger have the final word:

> There is no question of looking away from the modern world and its practices. There is no question of a Pre-Raphaelite flight back to the Middle Ages. It is rather that Dante advances toward us. And in the specific purgatory of the modern world, created and maintained by corporate capitalism, every injustice is grounded in that unilinear view of time, for which the only relation conceivable is that between cause and effect. In contrast to this, in defiance of this, the "single synchronic act" is that of loving.

Epilogue: The Messenger

Words are inadequate to describe certain experiences that happen outside the law of cause and effect. Although they are universal, they are often so weird that to recount them makes most people uncomfortable, unless they are New Agers, spiritualists, or mind-curers who believe in the great American tradition of the happiness machine, revelations on every bathroom wall, Jesus's face in cloud formations, or apparitions in every shadow. I am none of those.

But strange, real experiences do happen, however, usually very infrequently in one's life for those who are accessible but not looking for them. The Swiss psychoanalyst Carl Jung called them synchronicity, meaning meaningful coincidences in time without a causal relationship between psychic states and physical events, or dreams or thoughts, also without causal connections, that occur simultaneously across physical distances. Since a recounting of their outward manifestations is bizarre, and their meanings are personal, and since we live in the era of science as the dominant ideology, and a culture of pseudo-science, schlock weirdness, and "miracles," it is easy to skeptically mock, with a condescending grin, their reality.

Because American culture has always been replete with charlatans and scammers who have preyed on people's gullibility and ignorance, such experiences have gotten a bad name. To admit to experiencing such a meaningful coincidence is to open oneself to derision, despite the testimonies of such esteemed authorities as Jung and William James, to name but two.

But I think I'll take a chance.

I have been living in the rolling hills of western Massachusetts for forty years. It is beautiful country, known for its peaceful rural roads, lakes, streams, and vast tracts of mountain forests rife with wildlife. It is paradise for fishing and hunting, and the woods are filled with gorgeous hiking trails that attract urbanites in search of peace and quiet, those proverbial country escapes.

Ever since we moved here, I have made sure to get outdoors to run or walk in all kinds of weather, preferably alone and when few people were out. To be alone by a lake or stream in sun, rain, or a snowstorm is my idea of paradise. With my family I have hiked many of the mountain trails. And over the years I have seen many animals: bobcats, deer, foxes, bald eagles, herons—the list is very long.

But my great wish has never been granted: to see a bear and to see it up close. Friends and neighbors find this hard to believe; for anyone who has lived in this area for just a few years has usually seen one. Not me, for forty years.

When I was a boy, the only son with seven sisters, my father told me a story that has always stuck with me. In the early years of the twentieth century, his father, my grandfather, was picnicking with his family and a few other families at Bear Mountain in upstate New York along the Hudson River. As they were reclining on their blankets preparing to eat in a meadow below the mountain, a huge bear came ambling toward them out of the tree line. This was 1905. Seeing the bear approach, everyone except my grandfather got up screaming and ran downslope away from the bear. My grandfather stood his ground, as my grandmother and great-uncle told my father; he stood very tall and straight and started to play the penny whistle his father had brought with him from Ireland. What the tune was I never really knew. My father said my grandmother remembered strains of Amazing Grace but his uncle, Uncle Black Jack, a NYC Police Department blacksmith, remembered a lively jig. Who knows? The bear came walking toward him and the blankets spread with food, stopped just short, stood huge on its hind legs, let out a roar, then dropped down, turned, and loped back up toward the trees where he disappeared into the mountain forest.

My wish has never been to stand down a bear in such a manner. Just to see one up close would be enough. My grandfather had a fierceness that I lack, and anyway, I don't have a pennywhistle.

When I try to whistle with my mouth, little sound emerges, and what does isn't tuneful, and Pop was a master whistler as well. But bears have always been eluding me, as if the time was not ripe, or I was not prepared for their arrival.

Then just yesterday, Father's Day, I was sending an article of mine—"My Father's Voice"—to my only son and daughter. It begins like this:

> Although my father, whose namesake I am, died twenty-seven years ago, I just spent a hilarious and profound afternoon with him. For a few hours on a beautiful late spring afternoon, I sat out on the porch and listened to his inimitable voice beguile, instruct, and entertain me. He had me laughing out loud as I read through a large folder of letters he had sent me over the years. We were together again. It was his voice I heard, his voice speaking to me. It could be no other. In the beginning and end are the words. If we are lucky, we hear them.

I heard my wife scream from the kitchen for me to come fast. I ran to it and there, eight feet from the open window, was a bear facing us and almost swinging from the bird feeder and the branch above, its feet akimbo, an almost mischievous look on its face. It watched us as we watched it for 4-5 minutes. Then, afraid that it might break the open window that had another bird feeder stuck to it, I cranked the window in, the bear walked over, stood up and put its paws against the window, looked at us and the feeder that was too high for it, went down on all fours and started walking away as we rushed out to see it walk across the driveway and the neighbor's lawn. I feebly whistled after it; it stopped, turned and looked back, then continued on its merry way.

My wish had been granted, shortly after the summer solstice, the first day of summer, my wife's and my anniversary, and Father's Day. It immediately felt as if my father had sent me a gift. My wife quickly sent the photos of the bear she had taken to our son and daughter.

The night before, as a Father's Day gift, my son and girlfriend had taken us out to dinner. As we sat at an outdoor courtyard under the trees of an old inn, I was asked to speak of my father. Unusually for me, I was a bit lost for words, except to say he was a wonderful father, the best I could have hoped for and how close we were. At the back of my mind, I saw a photograph I love of him pushing in a stroller the son who sat to my left when he was very young. It was taken on the street outside the inn where we were dining, right behind my back.

Shortly after the bear had come to visit us, still amazed, we went for a long walk, and when we returned, there was a video on the computer from our son to whom I had earlier sent the article about his grandfather. In January, our son had moved back to town with his girlfriend after ten years living down south. They had bought a house about a mile away near the lake and woods where we had just walked. The same bear had walked through the woods adjacent to our walk, pushed over the fence around their large yard, and was in their yard eyeing their bird feeder. My son couldn't tell if the bear was whistling because his dogs were barking too loud.

But I heard my father laughing at the message he had sent.

I recalled how his letters that I had just read and written about were like mini-short stories, akin to a father sitting beside a child's bed and telling him a goodnight tale. They always ended on an up-note, no matter how serious what preceded. He was a storyteller talking to an adult son, just as in my childhood he would tell me bed-time improvisations on the Pinocchio story, tales of lies and deceptions and bad actors. Those stories had to have an edge to them, a bit of a question mark, just as his letters are peppered with the phrase *quien sabe* (who knows?)

Those letters came through the mail.

The latest message came by bear. That I know.

Quien sabe?
You?